Advertising

Advertising

Frank Jefkins

BSc (Econ), BA (Hons), MCAM, ABC,
FIPR, FAIE, FLCC, F InstSMM, MCIM

Second Edition

THE M & E HANDBOOK SERIES

Pitman Publishing
128 Long Acre, London WC2E 9AN

A Division of Longman Group UK Limited

First published 1985
Second edition 1991

British Library Cataloguing in Publication Data
Jefkins, Frank
 Advertising.—(The M & E Handbook series.)
 1. Advertising
 I. Title
 659.1 HF5821

ISBN 0-7121-0838-6

Founding Editor: P.W.D. Redmond

Printed and bound in Singapore

To my son John

Contents

Preface   xi

1 **Advertising and the marketing function**   1
   History of advertising; Definitions; Costs; Advertising
   and the marketing mix; Advertising as a communication
   process

2 **Types of advertising**   21
   Introduction; Consumer advertising; Industrial advertising;
   Trade advertising; Retail advertising; Financial advertising;
   Recruitment advertising

3 **The advertising agency**   38
   Introduction; Role of the advertising agency; Recognition
   and the commission system; Service agencies; Media
   independents; À la carte agencies; Agency personnel;
   Advertising agency jargon

4 **Advertising media: above-the-line**   63
   Introduction and definitions; The press; Radio;
   Television; Alternative television; Cinema; Outdoor and
   transportation

5 **Advertising media: below-the-line**   102
   Introduction; Types of media and their applications

6 **Sales promotion**   115
   Growing importance of sales promotion; Types of sales
   promotion scheme; Terminology; Problems and risks

7 **Sponsorship**   129
   Definition and examples; Objectives; Cost-effectiveness

8 **Direct mail and direct response**   142
   Introduction; Characteristics of direct mail; The sales

letter and enclosures; Mailing lists; Mail drops; Direct
response marketing; Consumer protection

9 **Exhibitions**   **168**
Importance of exhibitions; Types of exhibition;
Characteristics of exhibitions; Using exhibitions

10 **Copywriting**   **176**
Writing copy that sells; Copy devices; Copy elements

11 **Layout and typography**   **189**
Planning the advertisement; Design and layout;
Typography; Television commercials

12 **Printing processes**   **203**
The five main processes; Choice of process

13 **Public relations**   **210**
Differences between public relations and advertising;
Public relations consultancy services; In-house public
relations departments; Public relations and advertising;
Press relations; Case study: the Ever Ready Derby

14 **Corporate advertising**   **230**
Introduction; Prestige or institutional advertising;
Advocacy or issue advertising; Diversification and take-over;
Crisis advertising; Financial advertising

15 **Advertising research**   **238**
Value of research; Research in developing countries;
Research before, during and after the campaign; Media
research: sources of statistics; Tracking studies

16 **Law and ethics of advertising**   **257**
Legal and voluntary controls; Law of contract; Defamation;
Statute law; Voluntary controls

17 **Planning and executing an advertising campaign**   **289**
Introduction; Preliminary discussions; Development
of copy platform; Preparing the campaign;
The campaign and afterwards

Appendix 1 Addresses of societies and educational   **301**
              organisations

Appendix 2 Further reading   303
Appendix 3 Syllabi for the LCCI Third Level Certificate   305
           and CAM Certificate in Communications
           examinations in Advertising
Appendix 4 Specimen papers   312
Appendix 5 Examination technique   319

Index   323

Preface

Advertising is as old as civilisation and has long been used as the means of communicating the need to buy or sell goods, even for the sale of slaves in ancient times. In its style, it represents the society of the time. Consequently, it is an ever-changing process representing new products, services, supplies and demands, coupled with the new media and techniques for communicating the exchange situation. This book attempts to be as up to date as any textbook can be when the advertising scene is changing as never before.

Advertising tends to represent the economic progress of societies, and in this respect it ranges from the sophistication of the industrialised world to the new life-styles of developing nations. A nation's prosperity is reflected in the extent to which advertising is used.

This book has been specially written to cover the syllabus of the Advertising examination of the London Chamber of Commerce and Industry which attracts many hundreds of entries world-wide on an increasing scale every year. It is also a companion volume to the author's M & E Handbooks on *Marketing* and *Public Relations*. The trio provides an essential set of books for students preparing for the LCCI Group Diploma in Advertising, Marketing or Public Relations. A past exam paper is included in Appendix 4.

This book will also be useful for CAM Education Foundation and Chartered Institute of Marketing students in their study of advertising. A past CAM exam paper is included in Appendix 4. This revised edition has been expanded to meet the requirements of the CAM syllabus. In addition, advertising is a basic business subject, and its range of subject matter will enlighten both those seeking a career in business and those already engaged in a business career.

1991   F.J.

1
Advertising and the marketing function

History of Advertising

1. Introduction

Marketing is more than just distributing goods from the manufacturer to the final customer. It comprises all the stages between creation of the product and the after-market which follows the eventual sale. One of these stages is advertising. The stages are like links in a chain, and the chain will break if one of the links is weak. Advertising is therefore as important as every other stage or link, and each depends on the other for success.

The product or service itself, its naming, packaging, pricing and distribution, are all reflected in advertising, which has been called the lifeblood of an organisation. Without advertising, the products or services cannot flow to the distributors or sellers and on to the consumers or users.

2. Early forms

Advertising belongs to the modern industrial world, and to those countries which are developing and becoming industrialised. In the past when a shopkeeper or stall-holder had only to show and shout his goods to passers-by, advertising as we know it today hardly existed. Early forms of advertising were signs such as the inn sign, the red-and-white striped barber's pole, the apothecary's jar of coloured liquid and the wheelwright's wheel, some of which have survived until today.

3. Effect of urban growth

The need for advertising developed with the expansion of population and the growth of towns with their shops and large stores; mass production in factories; roads and railways to convey goods; and popular newspapers in which to advertise. The large quantities of goods being produced were made known by means of advertising to unknown customers who lived far from the place of manufacture.

Advertising grew with the development of media, such as the coffee-house newspapers of the seventeenth century, and the arrival of advertising agencies nearly 200 years ago, mainly to handle government advertising.

4. Advertising and the modern world

If one looks at old pictures of horse buses in, say, late nineteenth-century London one will see that they carry advertisements for products famous today, a proof of the effectiveness of advertising. Thus the modern world depends on advertising. Without it, producers and distributors would be unable to sell, buyers would not know about and continue to remember products or services, and the modern industrial world would collapse. If factory output is to be maintained profitably, advertising must be powerful and continuous. Mass production requires mass consumption which in turn requires advertising to the mass market through the mass media.

5. Advertising in the North and South

In the 'North' (i.e. the industrialised countries of the world) it is easy to take this process for granted. So used are people to buying well-known goods that they often criticise advertising. They sometimes complain that it is unnecessary, even a waste of money, and that prices could be cut if there was no advertising. This will be discussed later, but at this early point it is useful to remind the reader that the historical and economic process described in **3** is now taking place in the industrialising countries of the 'South'. The extent of advertising marks the development and prosperity of a country.

THE ILLUSTRATED LONDON NEWS, Nov. 18, 1899 — 731

STRENGTH, VIGOUR, AND PLUCK!

CADBURY'S COCOA is world-renowned for its absolute purity, and its strengthening and sustaining properties, the Medical Profession and all expert judges according it unstinted praise. The highest compliments have been paid to it; and NANSEN and JACKSON had Chocolate of CADBURY'S manufacture for their famous

Figure 1.1

Definitions

6.   Marketing

The (British) Chartered Institute of Marketing defines marketing as: 'the management process responsible for identifying, anticipating and satisfying customer requirements profitably'.

7.   Analysis

From this definition it is clear that modern marketing is based on the concept of producing and selling at a profit what people are likely to buy. Sometimes, as with new products like camcorders and home computers, it is necessary to anticipate what the market will accept. There is a difference, therefore, between a marketing-orientated company and a sales-orientated company. The latter seeks to sell what it has produced, without first identifying, anticipating and consequently satisfying customer requirements.

In developing countries the concept of 'marketing' is often misunderstood and wrongly applied to what is in fact 'selling'. In such countries there is a seller's market for imported, assembled or made-under-licence products which may have satisfied the original home markets but have not been designed for an identified buyer's market. Few foreign motor-cars, for instance, are specially designed to satisfy overseas markets, and they are advertised and sold, not marketed. Gradually, however, this situation is changing as marketing research is introduced and indigenous industry develops.

The Japanese were very clever marketers when they first introduced motor-cars like Datsuns to Britain. They exported motor-cars which were of a shape that was familiar to British motorists. The first Datsun to arrive in Britain in 1969 looked remarkably like the Ford Cortinas. That was good marketing.

8.   Advertising

The Institute of Practitioners in Advertising definition says: 'advertising presents the most persuasive possible selling message to the right prospects for the product or service at the lowest possible cost'.

9. Analysis

Here we have a combination of creativity, marketing research and economic media buying. Advertising may cost a lot of money but that cost is justified if it works effectively and economically. A good advertising campaign is one which is planned and conducted so that it achieves the desired results within an acceptable budget.

Costs

10. Who pays for advertising?

In **5** criticisms of advertising costs were mentioned and in **9** reference was made to economic advertising. Where does the money come from to pay for advertising, is its cost justified, and would prices fall if advertising ceased? These questions can be answered as follows.

(a) The cost of advertising is met in the price paid by the consumer, and is but one of the many costs, e.g. those arising from research and development, raw materials, manufacture and distribution, which have to be recovered before a profit can be made. It is therefore an investment. If the product fails, the manufacturer has to pay all the costs including advertising. Normally, however, it is the consumer who pays for advertising.

(b) The cost of advertising is therefore justified in two ways: it enables the consumer to enjoy the product (and, where there is competition between rival products, to have a choice), and it also enables the manufacturer or supplier to enjoy a profit.

(c) Generally, prices fall as advertising increases demand, and if advertising was stopped demand would also fall off and either the product would fail to sell, or the price would have to be increased as it would be more costly to produce and distribute a smaller quantity.

11. Advertising expenditure figures

The total annual expenditure on advertising in the UK is just under £7,000 million, representing less than 2 per cent of consumer expenditure or 1.71 per cent of the gross national product. The approximate totals spent on 'above-the-line' media (*see* **4:2**), including production costs, in 1988 were:

	£ million	%
Press	4,242	62.6
Television	2,127	31.4
Outdoor/transportation	244	3.6
Cinema	27	0.4
Radio	139	2.1
	£6,779	100

(*Source: Advertising Statistics Yearbook*, The Advertising Association 1989.)

To the above must be added further expenditure on 'below-the-line' media, i.e. direct mail, exhibitions, sales literature and other forms of advertising, plus sales promotion. Reliable figures for these items are not available and a realistic grand total is not possible, except that about £530 million is spent on direct mail and £700 million on exhibitions and shows.

The figures reveal the dominance of press advertising.

Advertising and the marketing mix

12. The marketing mix

To continue with the account of the relationship between advertising and the marketing function, the same approach to the marketing mix will be taken as in the author's companion HANDBOOK, *Modern Marketing*. This is not the conventional one, but is less academic and more in line with what actually happens in the marketing world. It is designed as a chronological sequence of actions.

13. Definition

The *marketing mix*, or the marketing strategy, is the combination of stages or elements necessary to the planning and execution of the total marketing operation. It should not be confused with the *product mix* which is the range of products or services a company may market, such as a range of cakes, biscuits and confectionery. Nor should it be confused with the *media mix* which is the range of advertising media that may be used in an advertising campaign, e.g. national newspapers, women's magazines, posters and commercial television.

14. Four Ps

The 'Four Ps' concept of the marketing mix, as introduced by E. Jerome McCarthy, developed by Philip Kotler, and widely adopted by marketing teachers, creates four divisions of the mix, namely, Product, Place, Price and Promotion. Advertising comes under Promotion, but so does Publicity which is the American authors' narrow interpretation of public relations. The fault with this oversimplification is that it destroys the sequential linking of the numerous elements of the mix. Advertising is divorced from a number of elements to which it is related, e.g. price and distribution which are put under different 'P' headings.

The 'Four Ps' concept is a handy, elementary version of the marketing mix, but its apparent simplicity is misleading and a more logical mix is given below in **15**.

15. A logical marketing mix

A more sensible presentation of the mix is to start at the beginning and finish at the end. In this way advertising can be associated with other elements. Although not every product or service will include every element, the following is an omnibus marketing mix of twenty elements.

(a) Conception, invention, innovation or modification of product or service. This includes research and development.

(b) The standard product life cycle and its variations, e.g. the continuous, recycled, leapfrog and staircase versions (*see* Figs. 1.2 – 1.6; these are discussed in detail in *Modern Marketing*).

(c) Marketing research.

(d) Naming and branding.

(e) Product image.

(f) Market segment.

(g) Pricing.

(h) Product mix, rationalisation and standardisation.

(i) Packaging.

(j) Distribution.

(k) Sales force.

(l) Market education.

(m) Corporate and financial public relations.

(n) Industrial relations.

(o) Test marketing.

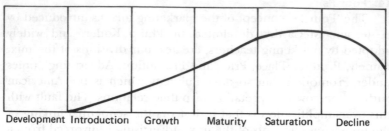

Figure 1.2 *Standard product life cycle.*

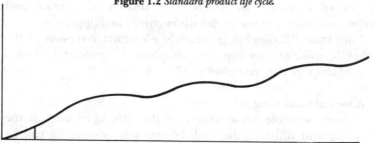

Figure 1.3 *Continuous product life cycle.*

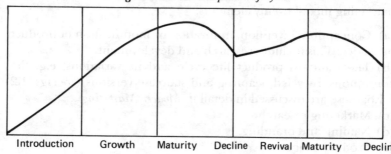

Figure 1.4 *Recycled product life cycle.*

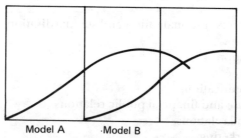

Figure 1.5 *Leapfrog effect product life cycle.*

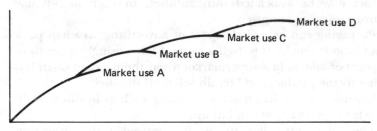

Figure 1.6 *Staircase effect product life cycle.*

(p) Advertising
(q) Advertising research.
(r) Sales promotion.
(s) The after-market.
(t) Maintaining customer interest and loyalty.

16. Advertising involvement

Although advertising is listed as a single element it is associated with almost every other element, borrowing from them or interpreting them.

(a) The volume, emphasis and timing of advertising will depend on the product life cycle situation. For instance, at the introductory or recycling stages, the weight of advertising will be heavier than at the maturity or decline stages.

(b) Marketing research will provide evidence of motives, preferences and attitudes which will influence not only the copy platform or advertising theme but the choice of media through which to express it.

(c) Naming and branding may be initiated by the advertising department or agency, and clearly plays an important role in advertisement design.

(d) The product image will be projected by advertising.

(e) The market segment will decide the tone or style of advertising, and the choice of media.

(f) Pricing can play an important part in the appeal of the copy. Is the product value for money, a bargain or a luxury? Pricing can be a very competitive sales argument. People are very price conscious.

(g) The product mix has many applications. In advertising, one product may be associated with another, or each brand may require a separate campaign.

(h) Packaging can be a vital aspect of advertising, as when pack recognition is sought. It is itself a form of advertising, especially at the point-of-sale, as in a supermarket when the package often has to identify the product and literally sell it off the shelf.

(i) Distribution involves trade advertising such as by direct mail, in the trade press and at exhibitions.

(j) The sales force has to be familiarised with advertising campaigns which will support their efforts in the field.

(k) Market education is a public relations activity aimed at creating a favourable market situation in which advertising will work.

(l) Corporate and financial public relations often uses institutional advertising in the business press.

(m) Test marketing requires a miniature advertising campaign simulating the future national campaign.

(n) Advertising research includes copy-testing, circulation and readership surveys and statistics, recall tests, tracking studies and cost-per-reply and cost-per-conversion-to-sales figures.

(o) Sales promotion can augment or even replace traditional advertising.

(p) The after-market calls for advertising to make customers aware of post-sales services.

(q) The maintenance of customer interest and loyalty may be achieved by advertising which promotes additional uses and accessories, or simply reminds.

The marketing mix described above is true of industrialised countries, but even then varies in application between North America and Europe because of geographic, social, political and ethnic considerations. There are also subtle differences between North American/European marketing situations and those of Japan. But the relevance of much of the marketing mix to developing countries is a matter of doubt since the conditions are so very different. This may not be obvious to readers who live in urban areas and see around them typical marketing mix elements which do not exist throughout their country as they do, for instance, throughout Britain. A supermarket may seem very sophisticated in Kuala Lumpur or Penang, but does not compare with the numerous supermarket chains in Britain which each own hundreds of huge stores. The exception may be the newly industrialised countries (NICs) such as Hong Kong, Taiwan, Singapore and South Korea.

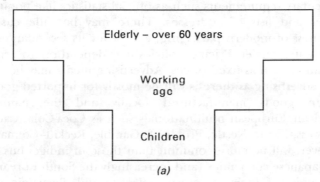

Figure 1.7 *(a) Population triangle of an industrialised country*

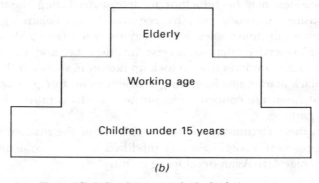

Figure 1.7 *(b) Population triangle of a developing country.*

A major problem is the nature of the population triangle (*see* Fig. 1.7) which may be the reverse of that in the North, with large populations of young people under 15 years of age who have no spending power. The number of people in the cash economy will be small, and even well-educated people (e.g. graduates in India) may be unemployed or too poor to even buy a newspaper.

In countries with large rural populations and with countries of large area (e.g. Nigeria, Zambia) there will be poverty, illiteracy and numerous ethnic groups speaking different languages, who are difficult to reach by marketing communication techniques.

Even in a country such as Indonesia where literacy is reasonably high, the country is so vast (equal to the width of the USA) that marketing is not easy outside cities like Jakarta.

Marketing research will be severely limited by the absence of elementary requirements such as official statistics like population figures and lists of addresses. There may be little customer awareness of modern packaging, except for its secondary use as, say, a water carrier. Pricing policies may depend on government legislation such as fixed prices. Advertising media may be scanty. Such advertising as there is will be mostly for imported goods or foreign goods manufactured locally and the names of American/European multinationals such as Coca-Cola, Cadbury, Guinness, Heinz, Nestlé, Procter & Gamble, Reckitt–Colman and Unilever, will be more common than those of indigenous firms. The Japanese companies (and increasingly the South Korean) will be promoting their motor-cars, electric and electronic goods. With a typical bazaar or market stall instant-sale philosophy, native businessmen may be reluctant to accept marketing theory and advertising methods which require forward-planning and investment in future sales which may seem unpredictable. As for after-sales service, that could be mythical because of lack of trained staff, unwillingness to lock up money in spares, or because of a black market not forgetting restrictions on foreign exchange so that funds are concentrated on new products rather than on spare parts.

In these circumstances, the likelihood of the marketing mix being relevant, except in a very modified form, is problematic in the average Afro-Asian developing country.

Advertising as a communication process

17. Marketing communication
Much of the marketing strategy is concerned with communication. Advertising is a specialised form of communication because in order to satisfy the marketing function it has to do more than inform. It has to *persuade* people to complete the marketing strategy which is designed to sell at a profit what the marketing department believes people are willing to buy. Advertising has to influence choice and buying decisions.

18. Another definition

This positive task is brought out in another definition which says that 'advertising is the means of making known in order to sell'. A name like Ford, Guinness or Texaco makes known—it identifies—but it does no more than, say, the name on a private house. The three examples above do not even explain what these companies make. In the case of brand names such as Stork, White Horse or Black Cat, they do not say that the product is a margarine, a whisky or a cigarette respectively. Therefore, advertising takes the communication process a step further and makes these three companies or three products known in ways which will sell them.

19. Effective communication

A graphic example of effective communication was the technique used by Thailand's Population and Community Development Association in 1984. The Association issued T-shirts bearing a picture of Winston Churchill giving his famous two-finger V-sign plus the words 'Stop at two'.

20. The VIPS formula

David Bernstein has explained the need for directness with his VIPS formula: Visibility, Identity, Promise, Singlemindedness. The advertisement must be visible, that is, easily noticed. The identity of the advertiser, or his product or service, must be obvious and not hidden by either too clever presentation or bad design. The offer (the promise) must be made clearly. To achieve all this the advertisement should concentrate on its purpose, and not be confusing by trying to say too many different things.

21. Value of simplicity

An advertisement can be so clever that all that is remembered is the gimmick or perhaps a very interesting picture, not the advertiser, the product or the offer. One of the most brilliant advertising campaigns was based on the simple saying 'Players Please' with its double meaning, the customer being encouraged to use those two words when buying cigarettes. Clever, but not noticeably so!

22. Changing attitudes

The object of advertising is usually to change or influence attitudes. It aims to persuade people to buy product A instead of product B, or to promote the habit of continuing to buy product A (they are unlikely to buy both product A and product B). For example in the case of a new ball-point pen, a simple selling *proposition* has to be converted into the idea that the pen makes an ideal gift or award. This principle can be seen in the advertising for Parker pens which contrasts with that for Tempo, including point-of-sale display advertising and the packing of the first in a presentation case and the second on a dispenser card.

Today, many products, services plus causes and social issues, are advertised which would not have been acceptable or even permissible not many years ago. The prime examples have been the official campaign to educate people about AIDS, and the commercial campaigns for condoms. There have also been environmental campaigns (often using direct mail) for Greenpeace and Friends of the Earth.

There is also a more intellectual attitude towards many products and some people are prepared to pay higher prices for purer, healthier or safer ones. With threats to the ozone layer and with fears about pollution, there has been the 'green' campaign, but sadly a number of manufacturers and retailers have exploited this issue. The Advertising Standards Authority has published warnings about this. *See* also 16:**36**, A Shade Less Green.

23. Inducing action

The example above shows that advertising is not just concerned with giving information. It must do so in such an interesting, original, characteristic and persuasive way that the consumer is urged to take action. This action may be to fill in a coupon, telephone an enquiry or order, go to a shop, or remember the product next time he needs to buy, say, a drink, a motor-car, a holiday or an insurance policy. In the case of the ball-point pen, advertising can help the buyer to make the appropriate purchase.

24. Communication barriers

If readers, listeners or viewers misunderstand the advertising message, the campaign is a waste of time and money. The ease with which people misunderstand has been discovered during marketing research surveys. People who were asked whether they owned a car said 'no' if they drove a company car. Similarly, when asked whether they owned a house they said 'no' if they were buying one with a building society or bank loan. In advertising, we have to be careful not to set up unintentional communication barriers. We may know what we mean—but do other people? We must never assume that people know what we are talking about, and this is where the market education work of public relations can help to make advertising effective.

25. Examples of misunderstanding
Here are some other examples.

(a) 'The Nigerian democratic system corresponded roughly with the American democratic system' could be misread to mean 'the Nigerian democratic system wrote rude letters to the American democratic system'.

(b) A communications problem in countries with cosmopolitan multi-racial societies—whether a large industrial city in the North or an Arab oil state—is that some words may either have different meanings or sounds or be pronounced differently. 'Lager' beer is often misspelt 'larger' beer, and 'poster' advertising is often called 'postal' advertising which is actually direct mail advertising

(c) The letters 'i' and 'e' may be pronounced differently or even confused, so that a foreigner visiting London might unwittingly post letters in a litter bin instead of a letter box, and be surprised that his friends at home never received them. Similarly, advertisements can be misread. Perhaps, because there is no 'z' sound in a local language, the word 'prize' is commonly written as 'price' by Africans. A prize competition becomes a price competition, a very different matter.

(d) In one LCCI Advertising examination candidates were asked to write and design an advertisement for a baby car. In Europe, a baby car is a small motor-car—a Mini or small Fiat, for example—but to most overseas candidates a baby car was taken to mean a toy model or a child's pedal car!

(e) In another LCCI examination, 'in the public interest' was frequently misread to mean 'interesting the public', which resulted in many wrong answers.

(f) Yet another misunderstanding arose with a question about armchair selling (i.e. mail order) which was misread as selling armchairs.

These examples emphasise that advertising is a communication process which must be free of misunderstanding. The message will be absorbed quickly as when people walk by a poster, listen to the radio, watch the television screen, or glance at a newspaper. This is very different from reading the instructions on a package, which is done more carefully and slowly, although clarity is still vital.

A lot of time may be spent on writing advertisement copy, but most readers are 'glancers' and get a quick impression from the large display lines. Only if these display lines interest them do they stop to read the more detailed copy in smaller type.

26. Words and pictures

One way to convey a message quickly is to use a jingle or slogan, e.g. 'British Airways Takes Good Care of You'. Another solution is a picture, e.g. the British Airways slogan is usually accompanied by a picture of a smiling BA air hostess.

Both forms of expression have been used in television advertisements which have established catch-phrases such as the Woolwich Equitable Building Society's 'I'm with the Woolwich', and the American Express saying, 'American Express? That'll do nicely, sir.' Another, which has survived for more than forty years, is 'Ah, Bisto!' with the two children sniffing the aroma of the gravy.

Thus, effective communication depends very often on a merging of words and pictures as indicated in Fig. 1.8.

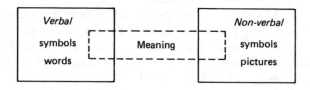

Figure 1.8 *Interaction of words and pictures to convey meaning.*

27. Problems of press advertising

Messages are said to be more readily seen than heard, and visual messages have greater impact than those which require the effort of reading. This tends to make written and read information the hardest to accept and recall. It implies that press advertising has to overcome many problems, especially in multi-ethnic societies or where there is a low level of literacy. Yet the press remains one of the best advertising media, there are multi-million circulation newspapers which are primary advertising media in the North, while the press expands in the South as literacy grows, Nigeria being an excellent example. The nature of press advertising is best understood when it is remembered that it is a static medium, lacking the benefits of sound and movement and often without the impact and realism of colour.

28. Advertising skills

How are these problems of press advertising overcome, and why does the press remain such a dominant means of communicating advertising messages? These questions form the themes of later chapters about copywriting, layout and press media, but in this introductory chapter here are two simple answers. First, creative skills are used to make press advertising larger than life, e.g. big type, slogans, size of space, dramatic pictures. Second, newspapers and magazines reach either mass or specialist readerships relatively cheaply and efficiently.

29. Heart of advertising

These two reasons provide an insight into the heart of advertising and the special skills involved. Creativity to attract and win the attention, the interest and eventually the action of consumers, and the most cost-effective choice and use of innumerable media, are the characteristics of successful advertising. All this calls for interaction between the three sides of advertising: the advertiser, the advertising agency and the media owner.

30. Importance of ideas

The skills necessary in press advertising also apply to other media such as radio, television, outdoor, direct mail, exhibitions, point-of-sale display, sales promotion and so on. Ideas are needed in order to communicate marketing messages, and buying and planning skills are required to exploit communication media effectively. Campaigns have to be planned and executed as sales battles. They are a blend of strategy and resources.

31. Reconsideration of definition

This brings us back to a reconsideration of the definition in **8**: 'advertising presents the most persuasive possible selling message to the right prospects for the product or service at the lowest possible cost'. These two requirements—creativity and the best use of media—should be remembered throughout the reading of this book, the study of this subject, and the practice of advertising itself.

32. Changes and developments

The 1980s and 1990s have seen more changes and developments in advertising than had occurred during the previous 200 years. Apart from the technological changes in newspaper production, and the transformation of British radio and television under the Broadcasting Act, the advent of the single European market has made London a more important advertising centre than New York. Berkeley Square has replaced Madison Avenue. This is because London has become the advertising springboard for continental Europe.

There are, of course, many European companies which use other advertising centres, to mention only BMW, Buitoni, Benetton and even Unilever. But for many pan-European advertising agencies—often those of American origin—London is the premier base.

According to Saatchi & Saatchi in 1990, advertising expenditure in Europe was as follows:

Britain	£11.7 billion
West Germany	£10.6 billion
France	£8.0 billion
Spain	£6.0 billion
Italy	£5.8 billion
Benelux	£3.3 billion

With the unification of Germany, Britain and Germany promise to vie for top place.

However, London's advantages are three-fold. (*a*) The English language is the language of marketing communication; (*b*) creative expertise, especially in the making of television commercials, which is the envy of Europe; and (*c*) Britain's initiative in defining advertising interests, conducting research, and training executives.

Meanwhile, on the other side of the world Japanese industry is served by Tokyo's advertising centre, with large agencies like Dentsu. There has also been a growth in public relations consultancy practice in a country which had been slow to adopt public relations techniques to match its marketing skills.

In the summer of 1990, the giant Japanese trading concern Mitsubishi, while retaining the Dentsu, Dai-Ichi Kikaku and Asatsu agencies for its motor and electric accounts, announced the setting up of an in-house agency to handle imports and international products.

Table 1.1 *Top ten British advertisers*

Rank	Advertiser	Spend (£m) Feb 89 – Jan 90
1	Procter & Gamble	61.54
2	Kellogg Company of Great Britain	50.20
3	Lever Brothers	45.17
4	British Telecom	44.87
5	Water Authorities Association	39.11
6	Ford	37.86
7	Nestlé	35.14
8	Rover Group	32.81
9	The Electricity Council	32.26
10	Halifax Building Society	30.22

Source: Campaign Report, 4 May 1990.

Progress test 1

1. Why does an industrial society require advertising? (**2, 3, 4, 5**)
2. What is the (British) Chartered Institute of Marketing definition of marketing? (**6**)

3. What is the difference between a marketing- and a sales-orientated company? **(7)**

4. How does the Institute of Practitioners in Advertising define advertising? **(8)**

5. Who pays for advertising? **(10)**

6. Approximately how much is spent on advertising in Britain each year? **(11)**

7. On which medium is most money spent—press or television? **(11)**

8. On which medium do advertisers of popular consumer goods spend most money? **(11)**

9. Explain the marketing mix. **(13)**

10. What are the Four Ps? **(14)**

11. List some of the principal items in a marketing mix which plot the sequence of actions from product design to the after-market. **(15)**

12. As a form of communication what is the chief task of advertising? **(17)**

13. What is the VIPS formula? **(20)**

14. Explain how advertising converts a proposition into an idea. **(22)**

15. Give an example of a communication barrier. **(25)**

16. How can words and pictures combine to give meaning? Give an example from recent advertising which you have seen. **(26)**

17. What are the two most important advertising skills? **(28, 31)**

18. Why has London become the European advertising centre? **(32)**

2
Types of advertising

Introduction

1. Scope of advertising

Advertising serves many purposes and many advertisers, from the individual who places a small classified advertisement in his local newspaper to the big spender who uses networked TV to sell popular brands to the nation's millions. Anyone can be an advertiser and advertising touches everyone. Even company newspapers contain sales and wants ads.

2. Types

It is possible to identify seven main categories of advertising, namely *consumer, industrial, trade, retail, financial, direct response* and *recruitment.* Each category is described in detail below (except direct response which is discussed separately in Chapter 8).

It will be seen that each requires its own treatment regarding creative presentation and use of media, i.e. the twin skills described as the 'heart of advertising' (*see* 1:**29**).

Consumer advertising

3. Different kinds

There are two kinds of goods bought by the general public, *consumer goods* and *consumer durables,* which together with *consumer services* are advertised through media addressed to the appropriate *social grades.* These four terms are best explained now as they will be used from time to time throughout this book.

4. Consumer goods

These are the numerous goods to be found in the shops, those which enjoy repeat sales like foods, drinks, confectionery and toiletries being called Fast Moving Consumer Goods (FMCGs). Pharmaceuticals which are packaged, branded and retailed are called Over The Counter (OTC) medicines to distinguish them from the ethical pharmaceuticals which are sold to pharmacists for fulfilling doctor's prescriptions.

5. Consumer durables

Usually more expensive and less frequently bought, consumer durables are of a more permanent nature than consumer goods and include clothes, furniture, domestic appliances, entertainment goods like radio, television and video, and mechanical equipment from lawn-mowers to motor-cars.

6. Consumer services

The service industries (including leisure industries) have shown remarkable growth in recent decades. They include services for security and well-being like banking, insurance, investment, repairs and maintenance, and those more to do with pleasure such as hotels, restaurants, travel and holidays.

7. Social grades

The IPA definition of advertising referred to the 'right prospects' and 'lowest possible cost'. The social grades system makes it possible to identify certain groups of people—prospective buyers—and then to pinpoint the media which will reach them most effectively. In developing countries where only a minority of people are literate, and they are mostly the ones reached by the media, the idea of selecting media to reach certain groups may seem strange. In such countries it may be more appropriate to talk about income or socio-economic groups.

However, in Britain the social grades, based on occupation and not income, are as shown in Table 2.1. In Table 2.2 the author has related social grades to British national morning newspapers, but this is a broad generalisation and some people will read a variety of newspapers.

Table 2.1 *Social grades in Britain*

Grade		Members	Percentage of population
A	Upper middle class	Top businessmen, other leaders	3
B	Middle class	Senior executives, managers	13
C^1	Lower middle class	White-collar, white-blouse office workers	22
C^2	Skilled working class	Blue-collar factory workers	32
D	Working class	Semi- and unskilled manual workers	20
E	Lowest level of subsistence	Poor pensioners, disabled, casual workers	9

Table 2.2 *Class readership of British press*

Social grade		Newspaper
A	Upper middle class	*The Times, Financial Times*
B	Middle class	*Daily Telegraph, Guardian, Independent*
C^1	Lower middle class	*Daily Express, Daily Mail, Today*
C^2, D, E	Working class	*Sun, Daily Mirror, Daily Star*

The class breakdown of British newspapers readership is shown in Table 2.2 because it is interesting to read the percentage of population figures in conjunction with the class readership placings. *The Times*, although world famous, has a very small circulation of about 400,000 while the *Sun* sells 4 million copies daily. Both happen to belong to the same company but each has a very different readership. The kinds of goods or services advertised in the one would not be advertised in the other.

In some countries, newspapers may not appeal to class differences so much as to different political, religious, language, nationality or ethnic groups of readers. For instance, there are English language newspapers in many parts of the world but also many others in local languages. In Hong Kong, for example, there are famous English language newspapers like the *South China Morning Post*, but also some hundred Chinese language newspapers.

The idea of social grades has to be regarded as something peculiar to British society where it is possible to have curious class distinctions as when the workers in the factory may be C^2 with typical trade unionist attitudes while the clerical and secretarial workers in the offices may be C^1 with more independent social attitudes. This has nothing to do with what they earn, and they may be neighbours in the same street, but it affects what they buy. For example, the former may tend to spend as they go, while the latter may prefer to save and invest. For advertisers they represent very different markets. The 'affluent worker' is not very socially mobile as a London University study conducted in Luton revealed. However, both social grades belong to the mass market which buys the majority of FMCGs and form the mass audience for popular TV, even if they may read different newspapers.

When planning an advertising campaign it is therefore necessary to define the social grade or grades of likely buyers, and to select the media which will reach them in the largest numbers at the lowest cost.

8. Media of consumer advertising

The media of consumer advertising will tend to be those with wide appeal, and even when more specialist journals such as women's magazines are used they will still have large circulations. In fact, the term 'consumer press' is applied to the publications which are displayed for sale in newsagents shops, on news-stands and on newspaper vendors' pitches.

Most of the trade, technical and professional journals have other forms of distribution such as special orders placed with newsagents, postal subscription or free postal controlled circulation. Controlled circulation (cc journals) are not to be confused with membership or subscription magazines. They are mailed (free of charge) to selected readers plus those who have requested copies.

In Britain there are also hundreds of 'free' local newspapers which are delivered door-to-door every week. With saturation coverage of urban areas they provide good advertising media for many local businesses.

The primary media of consumer advertising are the press, radio, television, outdoor and to a limited extent cinema, supported by sales literature, exhibitions and sales promotion. We should not forget sponsorship, especially the sponsorship of many popular sports which in turn can be supported by arena advertising at the sports venue.

NOTE: Primary media are first choice media and may be above-the-line or below-the-line according to the kind of advertiser. Traditionally, above-the-line media are press, radio, television, outdoor and cinema which pay commission on media purchases by advertising agencies.

Industrial advertising

9. Purpose
The purpose of industrial advertising is twofold:

(a) to promote sales of equipment and services used by industry—machinery, tools, vehicles, specialist consultancy, finance and insurance come within this category;
(b) to promote sales of raw materials, components and other items used in industrial production—under this heading come metals, timber, plastics, food ingredients, chemicals and parts for assembly into finished equipment from watches to aircraft.

Hardly any of these products and services will be bought by consumers, except as replacements as when a motor-car needs a new battery or tyres. Unless the formula or specification is stated, consumers will be unaware of most industrial products.

Many finished products are produced or assembled from materials, parts or components made by numerous suppliers. Few manufacturers are self-sufficient, supplying everything themselves. A building will consist of steelwork, cement, glass, timber, bricks, roofing materials and all the internal furnishings, together with special equipment such as escalators and services, e.g. water, gas and electrical systems. Secondary suppliers and subcontractors will be involved, together with consultants, although a main contractor or a consortium of contractors will be responsible for the final construction.

10. Media of industrial advertising

The suppliers of services, equipment, raw materials and components will usually advertise in media seldom seen by the general or consumer public. The media used will consist of trade and technical journals, technical literature and catalogues, trade exhibitions, direct mail, and technical demonstrations and seminars. Technical journals will have smaller circulations than the consumer press, and exhibitions will tend to have fewer exhibitors and smaller attendances than public exhibitions open to the general public; in fact, admission is usually by ticket or business card. The amount of money spent on advertising will be far less, and there may be more reliance on market education using public relations techniques such as video documentaries, external house journals and technical feature articles.

Industrial advertising media are very much a feature of the industrial North and are fairly rare in developing countries except large ones such as India which has a substantial industry ranking ninth in the world. The industrialising South depends very much on European and North American trade and technical journals which have international circulations. Some of these journals are so specialised that unless they did have international circulations they would not survive in their country of origin. Trade exhibitions, for the same reason, usually rely on international interest.

11. Special characteristics

Industrial advertising differs in yet another way. Whereas consumer advertising may be emotive, industrial advertising has to be more detailed and informative, although not unimaginative. Trade journals provide valuable international market-places for thousands of products and services, maintaining sales of long-established ones and introducing new ones.

Industrial advertising is mainly produced by advertising agencies which devote themselves to industrial clients so that agencies which handle clients or 'accounts' who market cranes, electronic equipment, chemicals or industrial insurance rarely handle accounts for mass consumer goods such as tea, petrol, beer or soap. The kind of creative staff are different, e.g. artists who can produce 'exploded' drawings which reveal the interior of an engine, or copywriters who can write meticulously in technical language.

The costs of such advertising are different, too, and the artwork may cost more than the space, while the space purchase will yield little commission and agency income may be derived from service fees charged to clients rather than from commission received from media owners.

There may be little advertising, or to be effective expenditure would be prohibitively expensive. Public relations activities, while not to be regarded as free advertising, may be more effective and economical, especially when the need is to educate the market and create knowledge and understanding. This is not to 'knock' advertising but to mention a more effective form of marketing communication.

Trade advertising

12. Definitions

Trade advertising is addressed to distributors, chiefly wholesalers, agents, importers/exporters, and numerous kinds of retailers, large and small. Goods are advertised for resale.

The term 'trade press' is sometimes used loosely and misleadingly to include all non-consumer publications. Strictly speaking, and the distinctions are sensible, the trade press is read by traders, the technical press by technicians (as described in the previous section on industrial advertising), and the professional press by professionals such as teachers, doctors, lawyers and architects. There are some journals which are difficult to define as sharply as that, and their readership may spread over more than one group. A building magazine, for instance, may be read in both the building industry and the architectural profession.

13. Purpose

The purpose of trade press advertising is to inform merchants and traders about goods available for resale, whether it reminds them about well-established brands, introduces new lines or, as is often the case, announces special efforts to help retailers sell goods, e.g. price reductions, better trade terms, new packages, consumer advertising campaigns or sales promotion schemes. Such advertising invites enquiries and orders and also supports the advertiser's field salesmen when they call on stockists.

14. Media of trade advertising

The trade press may or may not be used for this kind of advertising. There could be a mix of two or three media addressed to the trade. Direct mail is often used, especially when it is necessary to provide a lot of information such as consumer advertising campaign schedules giving dates and times when and where advertising will be taking place in the press or on radio and/or television. Replicas of advertisements may be reproduced, perhaps full-size, e.g. a large 'broadsheet'—the size of a newspaper page—which folds down to a convenient envelope size for posting. This direct mail shot may also include pictures and details of display material which is available, together with an order form. It may also include the details of 'co-operative' advertising schemes in which the manufacturer contributes in some way (artwork, part payment) to the retailer's own advertising in local media.

Another useful medium is the trade exhibition, sponsored by a trade magazine or trade association, which will be attended by distributors. Some of the larger exhibitions may also be open, or open on certain days, to the general public as well, e.g. motor-car and furniture exhibitions.

Occasionally, commercial television time may be bought to tell retailers about new lines, or retailers may be mailed to tell them that consumer advertising campaigns are about to appear on TV. In the television regions, a number of joint schemes may be organised with the aid of television companies such as the provision of special sales teams to visit retailers, or studio visits when retailers in the region are invited to preview forthcoming commercials.

15. Special characteristics

Since the object of trade advertising is to encourage shopkeepers (whether large chains or one-man businesses) to stock up the product (especially to achieve *adequate distribution* in advance of a consumer advertising campaign), emphasis will be placed on the advantages of so doing. The advantages will be higher sales and more profits, and the appeal will be to the retailer's desire to make money. In so doing, trade advertising will also have to compete with the 'selling-in' activities of rival manufacturers.

Trade advertising will be seen as part of the total advertising campaign for the product and so will be produced by the same advertising agency that handles the consumer advertising. However, whereas consumer advertising aims to persuade the consumer about the benefits to be gained from buying the product, trade advertising aims to persuade the retailer about the benefits which will result from selling the product. Trade advertising supports distribution. It prepares the way. There is no point in advertising products and encouraging consumers to buy them if the goods are not in the shops. The demand created by consumer advertising must be satisfied by the availability of the goods in the shops. That is what is meant by 'adequate distribution'. If the advertised goods cannot be bought, customers will buy either nothing or, worse still, a rival product!

16. Selling-in and selling-out

It will be seen from **15** that trade advertising is part of the selling-in process while consumer advertising is part of the selling-out process. This is also known as the 'push-pull' (or sometimes 'pull-push') strategy meaning that efforts to urge the retailer to buy in stocks 'push' the product to the trade while efforts to urge the consumer to buy 'pull' the goods through the distribution system.

Retail advertising

17. Introduction

Here we have a form of advertising which lies between trade and consumer advertising. The most obvious examples are those for department stores and supermarkets, but it can include the advertising conducted by any supplier including a petrol station, restaurant or insurance broker.

This will be dealt with separately in Chapter 8, but a major form of retailing nowadays is direct response marketing or retailing without shops. This is the modern form of mail-order trading which has moved from the traditional club catalogues to sophisticated off-the-page and direct mail campaigns for products and services, of which financial houses and department stores have become leading participants.

18. Purpose

The purpose of retail advertising is threefold, as outlined below.

(a) To sell the establishment, attract customers to the premises and, in the case of a shop, increase what is known as 'store traffic', that is the number of people passing through the shop. If they can be encouraged to step inside they may possibly buy something which they would not otherwise be tempted to buy. This was the original philosophy of Gordon Selfridge who encouraged people to enjoy a visit to his London store, or Jesse Boot who laid out the goods for all to see on the counters of his chemist's shops. They were pioneers of modern shopping.

(b) To sell goods which are exclusive to the shop. Some distributors are appointed dealers for certain makes, e.g. the Ford dealer. Others, such as supermarkets, sell 'own label' goods, having goods packed by the manufacturer in the name of the retailer. All the goods in the shop may bear the same brand, or certain lines such as tea, coffee, biscuits or baked beans may bear the retailer's own label. They will be in competition with nationally advertised brands, and usually be cheaper in price. About 30 per cent of grocery products in Britain are 'own' or private label according to AGB/TCA. Many products have own labels, e.g. frozen foods, beers, wines and soft drinks, soaps and detergents, stationery goods and pet foods. These foods are often made to special specifications by the manufacturers of nationally advertised brands. There are also firms like jam manufacturers who simply put different shop labels on quantities of jam ordered by different shops. This is a very old system which dates back to 'family grocers' and the like long before the arrival of chain stores and supermarkets. The largest product category having own labels are dairy products (42.1 per cent) followed by frozen foods (38.6 per cent) and baking products (35.8 per cent), according to AGB/TCA.

(c) To sell the stock of the shop, perhaps promoting items which are seasonal, or presenting a representative selection, or making special offers. The latter could be regular policy, or could be organised as shopping events such as winter or summer sales.

19. Media of retail advertising

Except in the cases of big London stores which advertise in the national newspapers (and then mostly to sell by post), or chains which advertise in regional newspapers covering large areas or on regional television, most retail advertising is confined to local media. One other exception is when the shop is in a major city centre which attracts shoppers from a large area. Even then, a regional evening newspaper will serve both a city and its suburbs and outlying towns and villages. The principal media for retail advertising are:

(a) local weekly newspapers, including numerous free newspapers which gain saturation coverage of residential areas by being delivered from door to door;

(b) regional daily newspapers, of which most are 'evenings';

(c) public transport external posters and internal cards, and arena advertising at sports grounds;

(d) direct mail to regular or account customers, and door-to-door leaflet distribution;

(e) regional commercial television;

(f) independent local radio;

(g) window bills and point-of-sale displays within the shop;

(h) window and in-store displays;

(i) catalogues.

The shop itself is a considerable advertising medium, and it may well be a familiar landmark. Marks & Spencer rarely advertise, but their shops are so big they advertise themselves. With retail chains, the corporate identity scheme will quickly identify the location of a branch.

20. Special characteristics

Retail advertising is characterised by four main aspects: creating an image of the shop, establishing its location, variety of goods offered, and competitive price offers. Nearly always, the object of the advertising is to persuade people to visit the shop, although telephone ordering and the use of credit accounts and credit cards is a growing feature. Many stores have developed postal sales, but these really come under the heading of direct response marketing (*see* Chapter 8), the modern name for mail order advertising (whether 'off-the-page' with press advertising, or by direct mail).

21. Co-operative advertising

This was mentioned in **14** when discussing the media of trade advertising. Advertising support given by manufacturers to retailers is also known as 'vertical advertising'. Co-operative advertising is an important facet of retail advertising, and can take many forms, including the following.

(a) *The use of logotypes.* A logotype (or 'logo') is a specially designed distinctive symbol used to identify a company or a brand. It may be a sign, shape or trade character like those for Mercedes-Benz, Shell and White Horse whisky, or a name written in a certain way as used by Coca-Cola, Ford and Fokker. Retailers can identify themselves as stockists by using their suppliers' logos on letter-headings, in catalogues and in press and other visible advertising. Owners of logos supply retailers with the necessary artwork.

(b) *Shared costs.* The cost of buying advertisement space in the press or airtime may be shared by a supplier if his product is promoted by the retailer.

(c) *Supplied artwork.* Manufacturers may supply retailers with camera-ready artwork for press advertisements, to which the retailer has merely to add his name, address and telephone number. Camera-ready copy means that it is ready for photographing when plates are being made for offset-litho printing.

(d) *Suppliers share costs.* Large retail advertisers, such as big supermarket chains and variety chain stores like Woolworth, may take advertisement space in national, retail or local newspapers, the whole cost being shared by different suppliers whose goods are sold in the advertiser's branches.

(e) *Stockists lists.* These are another form of co-operative advertising, usually at no cost to the stockists who are listed in press advertisements or in cinema or TV commercials placed by the manufacturer. Thus, customers are directed to a source of supply.

Financial advertising

22. Introduction

It is probably difficult to put a limit on what can be contained under this heading, but broadly speaking financial advertising includes that for banks, savings, insurance and investments. In addition to advertising addressed to customers or clients it can also include company reports, prospectuses for new share issues, records of investments in securities and other financial announcements.

Some, like building society and National Savings advertisements, may be addressed to the general public while others will appear in the financial and business press only, e.g. the *Financial Times, The Economist* or the *Investors Chronicle.* It is interesting that while trade and technical magazines may be scarce in developing countries there is often a business or financial weekly, sometimes distinguished by pink paper for which the British *Financial Times* is famous.

23. Purpose

The object of financial advertising may be to borrow or lend money, conduct all kinds of insurance, sell shares, unit trusts, bonds and pension funds or report financial results.

24. Classes of financial advertising

The main categories in this field are as follows.

(a) Banks advertise their services which today are not confined to traditional bank accounts but include deposits, loans, insurance, house purchase, wills and executorship and advice on investment portfolios. Some banks specialise in certain areas of banking, and others concentrate on certain kinds of business. For instance, one may finance business loans or underwrite new share issues, while another may seek to attract university students or specialise in servicing the farming community. A number are associated with credit or charge cards.

(b) Friendly societies and private medical care organisations like BUPA offer schemes to provide insurance in time of illness.

(c) Building societies both borrow money from savers and lend money to house-buyers. Most of their advertising is directed at not only raising funds but keeping funds so that they have sufficient money to meet loan applications. Competitive interest rates are important sales points, and today in Britain there is rivalry between building societies, banks and insurance companies for the same kind of business.

(**d**) Insurance companies exist to insure against almost any risk from big commitments like ships and aircraft worth millions to covering the risk that rain may stop play. Some insurance not only covers risks but provides benefits to savers or pensions in old age. In the cases of fire and theft, insurance companies are also selling peace of mind should damage or loss be suffered.

(**e**) Investments are offered, not only in share issues but in unit trusts and other investments in which smaller investors can share in the proceeds of a managed portfolio of shares.

(**f**) Savings and banking facilities are offered through post offices which sell National Savings certificates and various bonds and operate the Giro and Post Office banks.

(**g**) Brokers offer insurance, pension and investment schemes and advise their clients on how to manage such financial commitments. The Automobile Association acts as a broker for motor insurance.

(**h**) Credit and charge card companies, such as Access, and Barclaycard, American Express and Diners' Club, promote plastic money facilities, often on an international scale.

(**i**) Local authorities borrow money from the public, usually on short-term loans which are advertised.

(**j**) Companies announce their intentions and final dividends, giving summaries of annual reports, and often offering copies of annual reports and accounts.

25. Media of financial advertising

Choice of media will depend on the target audience. Building societies appeal to small savers and therefore use the mass media of the popular press and television. The big national banks with branches everywhere also use the national press and television. Investment advertising will appear in the middle-class and business press. Prospectuses for share issues, which usually occupy two or more pages, appear in newspapers like *The Times* and *Financial Times*. Banks may take stands at exhibitions. They also produce sales literature about their services, as do insurance companies especially in the way of proposal forms.

Financial houses have adopted database marketing, and have become one of the biggest users of direct mail and 'off the page' direct response techniques. The availability of huge share registers of investors in privatised industries (e.g. British Gas), plus the services of list brokers who rent mailing lists, and sociographic systems of social grading the postcoded population, have made potential investors accessible to promoters of financial services.

26. Special characteristics
Financial advertising in the press, and especially the business press, tends to occupy large spaces and contain detailed information necessary to explain schemes and achieve confidence. The emphasis is generally on benefits which are usually represented by figures such as interest rates and returns on investments. Profit, benefits, security, confidence, credibility and reputation are the keynotes of the copy appeals.

Recruitment advertising

27. Introduction
This form of advertising aims to recruit staff (including personnel for the police, armed forces and other services) and may consist of run-on classified advertisements or displayed classified, although other media such as radio and television are sometimes used. Before recession and mass unemployment occurred, recruitment advertising had become an important source of revenue for the media and there were many specialist recruitment advertising agencies or divisions of advertising agencies devoted to handling this kind of advertising. Famous ones like Austin Knight Advertising have survived.

Today, recruitment advertising makes good use of smaller circulation newspapers with AB (middle and lower middle-class) readerships such as the *Guardian* and the *Independent* to recruit highly skilled, managerial or executive staff.

28. Different kinds
Recruitment advertising is mainly of two kinds, that inserted

by employers whether identified or using box numbers, and that placed by employment or recruitment agencies which have been commissioned to fill vacancies.

29. Media of recruitment advertising

Except for the occasional recruitment advertisement on radio and television, the media are mainly made up of the following categories of press.

(a) *National newspapers.* Different newspapers appeal to different target groups, e.g. the managerial advertisements in the *Daily Telegraph* and *Sunday Times* and the teacher advertisements in the weekly education feature in the *Guardian* and the *Independent.* Very few jobs are advertised in the popular tabloids.

(b) *Trade, technical and professional journals.* These are the more obvious market-places for recruitment advertising addressed to those with special skills, qualifications and experience. For example, jobs in advertising are advertised in *Campaign* and those in public relations in *PR Week.*

(c) *Regional press.* Local dailies and weeklies are used to advertise jobs offered by local employers.

> NOTE: Many of the publications listed in **(a)–(c)** are bought and read solely for the purpose of seeking work or changing jobs.

(d) *Free publications.* A number of freely distributed publications gain their revenue chiefly from recruitment advertising, e.g. those which are distributed in the street to office workers such as secretaries. Recruitment advertising is also featured in the free newspapers delivered weekly to homes.

30. Special characteristics

The art of recruitment advertising is to attract the largest number of worthwhile applications at the lowest possible cost. The advantage of using a recruitment or selection agency is that applications can be obtained discreetly and they can be screened to provide employers with a short list of the best candidates. Two skills have to be applied. The advertisements must be so worded that they both sell the job and attract the best applicants, while correct choice of media will bring the vacancy to the notice of the largest number of good applicants as economically as possible. The readership as well as the rates call for media planning and buying skills which is why this is a specialist agency service. Regular users of recruitment advertising usually have a standard style of advertisement complete with company logo.

Progress test 2

1. What are consumer goods? Explain FMCG and OTC. (4)
2. What are consumer durables? (5)
3. What are consumer services? (6)
4. What are the six social grades, and what kind of people does each grade represent? (7)
5. How do the media of consumer advertising differ from those for industrial advertising? (8, 10)
6. Why is trade advertising necessary? (13)
7. What is the purpose of retail advertising? (18)
8. How can co-operative advertising help both the manufacturer and the distributor? (21)
9. What kind of advertisers are included under financial advertising? (24)
10. What are the special characteristics of recruitment advertising? (30)

3

The advertising agency

Introduction

1. Servicing the client

An advertising agency is a team of experts which services clients who are known as 'accounts'. This use of the word 'accounts' has nothing to do with accountancy. An account is simply an advertiser who uses the agency's services. In the trinity that forms the advertising business—the advertiser, the advertising agency and the media owner—the agency occupies the middle position between those who wish to advertise and those who provide the means of doing so.

2. History

The first advertising agencies were set up at the beginning of the nineteenth century and Britain's first agency, White's, was founded in London about 1800. It began by producing advertising for government lotteries, and then went on as advertising agent for the War Office, Admiralty, HM Commissioner for Prisons, the Colonial Office and later the Crown Agents. Mostly, it handled recruitment advertising.

The first agencies were no more than space brokers, selling press advertising space on a freelance basis for newspapers. As newspaper production improved with greater variety in the sizes and designs of type and the introduction of illustrations, the space brokers began to compete by offering copywriting and design services. In this way, the creative advertising agency was born. Advertisers bought advertising space through the agencies which offered them the best ideas. After the Second World War the modern service agency developed with additional services such as marketing, marketing research and media planning as media statistics became available. With the advent of commercial television in 1955, another agency service was added so that the biggest advertising agencies, the ones handling mass market goods, became those which bought airtime and produced TV commercials.

3. Agencies today

In Britain there are now some 750 advertising agencies ranging from studios which specialise in industrial advertising to large and often international full service agencies.

Table 3.1 *Top twenty advertising agencies 1989*

Rank 1989	Rank 1988	Agency	Billings in £m 1989	Billings in £m 1988	Staff 1989	Staff 1988
1	1	Saatchi & Saatchi	373.00	324.00	855	832
2	2	J. Walter Thompson	308.00	264.00	512	520
3	3	BSB Dorland	285.02	261.47	400	535
4	4	Young and Rubicam	238.00	181.00	325	352
5	7	BMP DDB Needham	216.00	191.10	365	465
6	6	D'Arcy Masius Benton and Bowles	208.00	170.00	379	385
7	5	Ogilvy and Mather	206.00	175.00	388	355
8	8	Lowe Howard- Spink	173.80	153.10	267	274
9	10	Collett Dickenson Pearce	161.00	122.00	248	245
10	32	Still Price: Lintas	160.55	128.90	228	296
11	9	Grey	159.00	136.76	247	227
12	11	WCRS Mathews Marcantonio	152.70	121.30	208	208
13	15	Leo Burnett	120.00	90.30	246	241
14=	16	Publicis	117.50	86.10	250	220
14=	12	McCann-Erickson Advertising	117.50	115.00	254	273
16	13	Abbott Mead Vickers SMS	116.10	100.25	210	180
17	14	KHBB	110.70	95.60	185	187
18	19	Gold Greenlees Trott	98.20	80.50	150	138
19	17	Allen Brady and Marsh	95.68	84.60	128	142
20	22	Bartle Bogle Hegarty	95.10	71.50	169	166

(*Source: Campaign Report*, 23 February 1990.)

Many of the latter, like J. Walter Thompson, are American in origin. More than 260 agencies representing 50 per cent of agency business are members of their trade association, the Institute of Practitioners in Advertising.

The main types of agency are discussed in **11–25** below.

The agencies listed in Table 3.1 are the first 20 of *Campaign*'s top 300 advertising agencies. To compile the table agencies were asked to provide billings which included (*a*) Spending by clients who have moved account/s from the agency during the period up to the time the account/s departed and the agency ceased to handle the advertising; (*b*) Spending on advertising for which the agency was responsible, but which was placed through a media shop; (*c*) Fees paid by clients on top of commission received from media; (*d*) Fees earned from any other activity on behalf of clients, e.g. new product development work, public relations work, research; (*e*) Mergers/takeovers: agencies so affected were requested to provide a combined billings figure, including the billings figure since 1 January 1989 and up to the time of the merger/takeover. Agencies were asked to exclude annualised amounts or budgets nominated or unspent. Included were spending on press, television, radio, direct mail and below-the-line.

4.   Location

While the majority of agencies are located in capital cities such as London or New York, they are also to be found in most industrial cities, especially if such cities are media centres with publishing houses and radio and television stations. Large agencies often have their head office in the capital and branches in the regions. In Britain, there are important agencies in major cities such as Birmingham, Edinburgh, Bristol, Glasgow, Leeds, Liverpool, Manchester and Newcastle.

5.   Public relations

In this chapter public relations is not included as an advertising agency service or department, although it is true that in small agencies (especially in developing countries) public relations services are often provided (probably limited to press relations in association with advertising campaigns), while a number of large advertising agencies do have subsidiary public relations consultancies. Because advertising and public relations are two different forms of communication with different purposes, and public relations is actually a far bigger subject than advertising, it is discussed separately in Chapter 13. For a fuller study of the subject the reader is referred to the author's companion HANDBOOK, *Public Relations.*

Role of the advertising agency

6. Agent acts as principal

The role of the advertising agency is to plan, create and execute advertising campaigns for clients. However, the extent to which it does so varies today according to the kind of agency it is. There are agencies which offer every kind of service, those which only buy media, those which only create, and others which offer special services.

Generally, however, the old idea holds that the advertising agency is strictly speaking the agent of the media (like the original space broker), if only to the extent that the agent's legal status remains that 'the agent acts as principal' and is responsible in law for payments. This legal precedent or 'custom of the trade' means that, if an advertiser defaults, the agency is responsible for paying debts incurred on the client's behalf. Agencies can be financially vulnerable and some have gone bankrupt when their clients have failed.

7. Middle position

Operating in this middle position—almost like a wholesaler—between advertiser and media owners, the role of the advertising agency can be summarised in two ways.

(a) It offers the client a team of highly skilled experts which can be shared with other clients. It would not be economic for the majority of clients to employ such a team full-time. The agency is also skilled at buying ancillary services such as film and video production, artwork, photography, print, typesetting, market research and so on.

(b) It offers the media an economic way of buying and selling space and airtime since the media owners have to deal with a relatively small number of agencies compared with thousands of individual advertisers. The quality of advertising production will be high and will match the standards and requirements of the media, and the advertisements will comply with the law and the British Code of Advertising Practice and the Independent Television Commission (ITC) and Radio Authority (RA) Codes in respect of television and radio commercials.

Recognition and the commission system

8. Recognition

Recognition does not mean that the agency is approved or has special qualities, nor is recognition granted by the professional bodies such as the Advertising Association or the Institute of Practitioners in Advertising. Recognition is granted by the bodies representing the media owners. These are the Newspaper Publishers Association (NPA), the Newspaper Society (NS), the Periodical Publishers Association (PPA), the Independent Television Association (ITVA) and the Association of Independent Radio Contractors (AIRC).

9. Office of Fair Trading ruling

Before April 1979 only a 'recognised' agency could claim commission on its purchases of advertisement space in the press or of airtime on commercial television or independent local radio. Standard rates of commission were agreed for different kinds of media.

However, in 1979 a ruling of the Office of Fair Trading under the Restrictive Trade Practices Act 1976 held this to be an illegal, restrictive and monopolistic practice in that it did not permit agencies and media owners to negotiate competitive commission rates. Moreover, since a new agency could be set up only if it was recognised and so able to get commission, and to do so it had to have clients worth a certain volume of business, another monopolistic situation existed. Prior to the OFT ruling it was extremely difficult for a new agency to operate, unless perhaps directors broke away from an existing agency and took clients with them. (*See* also 16:**21**)

10. Effect of ruling

The current system of recognition establishes the creditworthiness of agencies so that they are entitled to buy space and airtime on credit, provided that they adhere to the British Code of Advertising Practice. A direct result of this has been the setting up of 'à la carte' agencies which are creative only, and do no media buying (*see* **19–25**). They do not require 'recognition', and are not hampered by the requirement to have a certain volume of business.

Commission is still important to the larger agencies which handle the bigger campaigns. It is their main source of income. Because of this income, the client enjoys many services free-of-charge (e.g. the advice of the account executive and agency marketing manager, campaign planning, and all the expertise and clerical work involved in media, print and other buying). The client pays for all space, air-time, artwork and production costs, on which the agency earns commission or charges a percentage. When the volume of billings provides inadequate commission income, as occurs with small and especially industrial accounts or in overseas countries where the scale of advertising is smaller, a service fee based on time is charged. However, there are some large agencies which prefer to rebate commissions and charge fees for their time and expertise.

Service agencies

11. Full service agencies

These are large or medium-size agencies capable of conducting a complete advertising campaign. They may have subsidiary companies or have associations with other companies dealing with marketing research, public relations, recruitment advertising, or sales promotion. A number of these big agencies, e.g. Saatchi & Saatchi, Abbott Mead and Lopex are public companies with shares quoted on the Stock Exchange. They handle the campaigns for top advertisers such as Procter & Gamble, John Player, Mars, Cadbury-Schweppes, Brooke Bond Oxo, Rowntree Mackintosh, Ford, Boots and Van den Berghs each of whom annually spend between £20 and £60 million. Of the top 100 British advertisers, those at the bottom of the list spend about

£8 million each. The big agencies are therefore responsible for a vast proportion of the total annual expenditure (over £6,000 million) on British advertising.

12. Medium-size agencies

There are many other medium-size service agencies which are responsible for more modest accounts, augmenting their regular staff with freelance and specialist services as and when required. There are, for instance, many first-class freelance copywriters and visualisers who prefer to work independently. The future is likely to see an expansion of home-based creative staff who can draw layouts on computers, write copy on word processors, and transmit their work to terminals in agency offices.

13. Industrial agencies

As the name implies, these agencies specialise in advertising industrial and technical goods, mainly in the trade and technical press, at trade exhibitions, and by means of printed materials such as catalogues and technical data sheets. Payment is usually on a fee basis. Often, the principals of the agency will have worked in industry, perhaps as advertising managers. The creative staff will be familiar with industrial jargon, and capable of writing and designing authentically. Industrial advertising calls for meticulous attention to detail. Although the accounts are smaller in value, they tend to be more stable compared with big consumer accounts where clients change agencies more frequently in search of fresh ideas.

Media independents

14. Development of media independents

During the 1970s agencies which concentrated on buying media—and did so very competitively—became a new feature of the agency world and in 1981 the Association of Media Independents was formed. The existence of these agencies emphasises the second of the two aspects of advertising described in **1:29**. In the ten years 1974–1983 their billings (*see* **53**) increased nearly six times. (*See* also Table 3.2.) They are usually 'recognised' by the ITVA, NPA and PPA.

Of these 'indies' or media shops, by far the largest is Zenith. Some advertisers divide their campaigns between media independents and 'à la carte' creative agencies in order to get the best of both worlds, while some of the large service agencies use media independents.

Table 3.2 *Top twenty media independents of 1989*

Rank	Agency	Own billings (£m)
1	Zenith	593.10
2	TMD Advertising Ltd	142.70
3	CIA Billett & Company	95.80
4	The Media Business Group	87.20
5	Media Buying Services	68.20
6	John Ayling & Associates	60.38
7	IDK Media	56.32
8	Phillips Russell Plc	43.50
9	Media Advertising	38.00
10	Yershon Media	32.10
11	Michael Jarvis & Partners	30.00
12	TCS Media	28.90
13	Media Solutions	26.24
14	Bygraves Bushell Valladares & Sheldon	25.20
15	The Media Shop	24.50
16	AMS Advertising	21.53
17	Tony Rowse Media	21.49
18	BBJ Media Services	19.40
19	Squires Robertson Gill	17.51
20	Paul Gage Media	17.00

(*Source: Campaign Report*, 23 February 1990.)

15. Reasons for success of media independents
The reasons for their success are threefold as follows.

(a) The breakdown of the former fixed commission system.
(b) The media explosion, including new publishing techniques and alternative television (*see* 4:**22–33**).
(c) The inflated cost of media. Media buying had become more critical regarding cost-effectiveness, and wider knowledge was required of new or changing media. The influence of free newspapers, colour supplements, new specialist international

journals, independent local radio, teledata and Viewdata, Channel 4 TV and breakfast TV had revolutionised media planning and buying. Now there are other media fields such as satellite television and the effects of the Broadcasting Act 1990.

16. Media breakdowns

The breakdown of media buying by media independents is roughly:

Cinema	2%
Outdoors	2%
Radio	2%
Newspapers	21%
Magazines	20%
Television	53%
	100%

17. Remuneration

The method of charging varies according to the size of client and the kind of media used. Media independents buy media as keenly as possible and negotiate the best rates of commission they can get, whereas under the old system recognised agencies were either assured of or limited to standard rates of commission paid by all the members of the recognising media body. The media independents may be remunerated by commission from the media, or by a mixture of commission received and additional fees charged to clients, or commission may be rebated (clients being charged net instead of gross media rates) and then charged a fee according to the workload.

This is a realistic way of charging (or paying for media), with clients benefiting from buying skills and paying for them accordingly. No longer do the media subsidise the advertiser by allowing agencies commission with which to give clients free services. It also maintains the usefulness of agencies to the media since fewer accounts are involved and prompt payment is assured.

18. Relationship to creative agencies

Media independents also place much of the advertising produced by 'à la carte' agencies (*see* **19–25**) which, since they are purely creative, do not buy media directly, do not need to be 'recognised' nor are they handicapped in setting up business because of recognition requirements about minimum number of clients and volume of billings or media turnover.

À la carte agencies

19. Development
À la carte agencies, often working on *ad hoc* assignments, have developed from what used to be (and may still be referred to) as 'hot shops'. They are wholly creative agencies which undertake a variety of work such as new product launches, rejuvenated products, packaging ideas, corporate identity schemes, sales conferences, exhibition stands or the creative aspects of a total advertising campaign. Some of them are so individual in the services they offer that they are considered under separate identifying headings in **20–25** below.

20. Creative agencies
These produce copy platforms or themes and create campaigns for different media, perhaps inventing characters and writing jingles and music for TV commercials. They complement the media independents who are then responsible for placing advertisements. We are back to our two basic skills of creativity and media buying. The client has to consider whether the larger full service agency can satisfactorily provide both skills, or whether it is better to use the buying and creative expertise of two separate agencies. It may seem more complicated to do this, but the highly competitive recession situation has made client requirements more demanding.

It is claimed that the newer agencies are a response to the inadequacy of the traditional full service agencies. The answer may be in the size of the campaign and the predominance of TV usage. It is significant that agencies associated with some of our major advertisers in the multi-million expenditure bracket are handled by agencies like Saatchi & Saatchi and Allen Brady and Marsh which have grown into very big agencies. Others, e.g. Ogilvy and Mather, have themselves set up specialist subsidiaries in fields like direct response. It will be seen that the agency world has been adjusting itself rapidly to the demands of the times.

21. New product development agencies

These agencies claim superiority over the traditional agencies because they get involved very early on in the various stages of the marketing mix (*see* **1:12–15**). They may influence the original concept of the product, and certainly participate in naming products, packaging designs, pricing and market segmentation, distribution, test-marketing, and selling-in to the trade operations as well as the main consumer advertising campaign.

Since the majority of new products fail, and probably some 50 per cent fail even after apparently successful test-marketing, clients will take up the advantages of using new product development agencies which have a keener approach to everything likely to influence a successful launch. These agencies have a substantial record of success, and they offer proof of this in their advertisements in *Campaign, Marketing* and *Marketing Week*.

22. Direct response agencies

Campaigns for mail order traders, including the promotion of magazine subscriptions, business travel, package tours, credit cards, savings and investments, and other services sold by mail, as well as the off-the-page offers frequently seen in the weekend colour magazines, are handled by direct response agencies. Many campaigns are conducted entirely by direct mail, using sales letters, sales literature and catalogues. Again, these agencies have responded to demand, and direct response in all its forms, including the use of commercial television as a medium, has become a very skilled and powerful marketing operation. Among the biggest users of direct response are financial houses and department stores, eclipsing the mail-order catalogue clubs which used to dominate mail order.

The technique is to sell direct, by post or telephone, and devices such as Freephone and Freepost, plus invitations to give credit or charge card details on coupons or order forms, are all part of the effort to attract direct sales. Sometimes there may be addresses where goods can be inspected and bought, but usually direct response means retailing without stores. (*See* also Chapter 8.)

23. Incentive scheme agencies and premium houses

Two kinds of agencies have been put together here because they have similarities. Both buy and supply goods and services which are offered as gifts or premiums to customers or as incentive awards to employees. Incentive scheme agencies offer packaged schemes which can be awarded to the staff whose ideas improve productivity or who are top salespeople. The schemes may range from weekend holidays to the award of points which can be accumulated in order to claim items from a catalogue. (Some of the direct response catalogues normally used by mail-order clubs are adapted for this latter purpose.)

Premium houses buy and supply the numerous items which are used for sales promotion purposes such as self-liquidating premium offers when customers send in so many tokens from packages together with cash to purchase goods at less than normal shop price. Most of these goods, both incentive and premium, are standard lines, but some are purpose-made. The reader of trade press advertisements for incentives and premiums, will find many familiar products on offer. The manufacturers employ special sales executives to promote this class of business which can produce considerable volume sales.

In the case of premium offers to consumers, and mail-ins which are free offers, another side of the business is the redemption of tokens and payments. This requires warehouse and packing facilities, and it is important that goods are despatched promptly even though offers usually stipulate that delivery may take twenty-one days. The premium house may handle everything, but a *fulfilment house* may be employed to deal with the response only. Fulfilment houses also service the sales promotion agencies which are described in **24**.

24. Sales promotion agencies

Some of these are subsidiaries of full service agencies, others are independent. Sales promotion (which has largely replaced the former expression 'merchandising') consists of marketing activities, mostly at the point-of-sale, which lie between consumer advertising and retail selling. This will be discussed more fully in Chapter 6. Here, we are concerned with agencies with the expertise to organise such activities. Unlike the offer of well-known goods as incentives or premiums, a modern sales promotion scheme is very often an original exercise created for short-term operation.

Typical examples are big prize competitions, in-store demonstrations, various collecting schemes based on the trading stamp idea, money-off flash packs, cross-couponing schemes whereby a token on a pack can be used as a price-cut on another product, high street redemption schemes allowing discounts on purchases at certain stores, charity promotions and promotional games.

To some extent the more sophisticated promotions, requiring considerable originality, planning and execution, have come about because of economic changes during the early 1980s. The new demands have justified the existence of the sales promotion agency or, when it already existed, its greater value to the marketing strategy. The subject now occupies many pages in magazines such as *Marketing* and there is also the specialist magazine *Sales Promotion.*

There are two reasons for this: the inadequacy of traditional consumer advertising media (including television), and the inadequacy of traditional sales promotion such as self-liquidating premium offers and mail-ins for free offers. Dissatisfaction with media is partly to do with its demassification and disproportionate or increased cost, while disenchantment with schemes requiring customer effort stems from the price competition which now exists in the shops for similar goods. It is no longer an advantage to send away for a set of premium offer saucepans when they can be bought as cheaply in a local shop. As a result, the sales promotion schemes have had to be more ingenious.

25. Sponsorship agencies

Sponsorship may be for marketing, advertising or public relations purposes, and quite often may embrace all three (*see* also Chapter 7). Sponsorship is big business and vital to the marketing of some companies. It is not the pretence at public relations which one finds in developing countries where steel bands, basketball teams and football teams are sponsored as if that was all public relations was about. There are two sides to sponsorship: people, activities and events which need financial support, and companies which are prepared to invest money in whatever will aid the marketing strategy. Sponsorship agencies bring the two together.

One of the most costly sponsorships is motor racing which requires the means of maintaining teams of men and machines at international grand prix, which is why the cars may bear evidence of co-sponsorship. Motor racing enjoys hours of TV coverage. The trend is towards sponsorship of big events, including ones such as football and cricket which are so long established that their adoption by sponsors has caused astonishment (*see* 7:2, 4).

A sponsorship agency not only brings sponsor and sponsored together, and does so in ways which are mutually satisfactory, but is responsible for all the associated activities such as arena advertising, media coverage and its monitoring, sale of concessions (e.g. T-shirts), hospitality for journalists (e.g. lunch boxes for cricket commentators) and for the sponsor's guests who are invited to attend events. It will also be involved in organising prizes and prize presentations.

Agency personnel

26. Diversity of agency personnel

In this section a wide division of labour, and a number of specialist jobs, will be described. All of these will be found in the largest full service advertising agencies (*see* also Fig. 3.1). However, in the smaller agencies to be found in the regions and especially in smaller or developing countries, many of these jobs will be carried out by the same person. (For a fuller discussion of the role of agency personnel in planning and executing an advertising campaign, *see* Chapter 17.)

27. Role of the advertising manager

A common mistake is to assume that the advertising manager works in the agency. He or she is in fact in charge of the client's advertising department. The agency–client relations and negotiations will be conducted between the agency account executive and the company advertising manager (or whoever is in charge of advertising on the client's behalf which could be the marketing manager, sales manager, product or brand manager or even the proprietor).

28. Account director

Usually one of the partners or directors of the agency, the account director (and there may be several in a large agency) will be responsible for a group of accounts (or clients). Working under the account director will be account executives who handle one or more accounts. The account director will be responsible to the board of directors, is concerned with profitability, will lead negotiations for new and renewal business, and will direct policy matters such as whether or not to accept certain accounts especially if there is any risk that they may conflict with existing accounts.

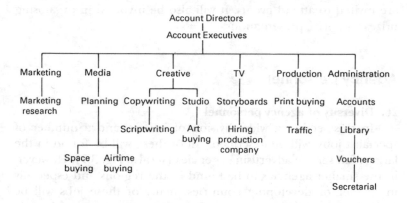

Figure 3.1 *Departments and functions of a large full service advertising agency.*

29. Competing accounts

It is not unethical for an agency to handle competing accounts, and there may be some advantage if the agency has experience in a certain field, e.g. banking, provided the rival firms do not object. They may, on security grounds, object and it might, for instance, be undesirable for an advertising agency to handle the accounts for two rival motor-cars in view of the intensity of this rivalry.

30. Account executive

In the days of the early agencies which emerged from the space brokers, and right into the 1930s, the person seeking business was called the 'contact man' who was little more than a salesman, and it has become a derogatory term today. Even the title of account executive has been dropped by some agencies in favour of representative, just as advertising managers are more often known as brand or product managers. However, account executive remains in general use.

He or she maintains the liaison between the agency and the client, and that does not mean being merely a go-between. The account executive has to understand the client's needs, and the business and industry, and interpret these needs to the agency. Conversely, the account executive has to present the agency's proposals, ideas and work to the client. It is a delicate, diplomatic job and with responsibility to keep the account. The account executive should have a broad knowledge of advertising and be able to work with everyone in the agency, directing their efforts in the interest of the client. He or she may be a graduate who entered the agency as a trainee, and whose future lies in agency directorship, a better job with another agency, partnership in or ownership of his or her own agency, or advertising management with a company. The recognised professional qualification in Britain is the CAM Diploma.

31. Contact report

Essential to good management of an account is the contact or call report. After every client meeting the account executive quickly submits to the client a special form of minute. At the top is stated when and where the meeting was held, who was present, and to whom in the client's organisation and the agency the report is being distributed. The report will give a brief statement of items discussed and decisions taken. A vertical rule is printed on the right-hand side, and in the margin are annotated instructions and the initials of those who are to carry them out. It should be distributed immediately after the meeting so that there is opportunity to make any necessary revisions, and misunderstandings are avoided in the future. The reports are filed in a facts book which becomes a concise record for constant reference and also the basis of the agency's annual report to the client.

32. Marketing manager

The modern agency is marketing conscious, and the agency marketing manager fulfils several functions. Marketing advice is offered to clients who do not have marketing managers, or it complements company marketing managers who are given more confidence if the agency is marketing-orientated. Unless there is a separate executive responsible for marketing research, this executive will also advise on the use of marketing research and commission surveys by independent research units. Advice will be given, for instance, on aspects of the marketing mix such as product development, naming and branding, packaging, market segment, test-marketing and distribution.

33. Contribution to campaign

The marketing manager's contribution may well affect the success of the advertising campaign, and the importance of adequate distribution is worth emphasising here. Distribution to meet demand provoked by advertising could depend on lead times determined by such factors as the length of journey cycle of the company's sales representatives, that is the time gap between their visits to retailers. Similarly, it is important that everyone is clear about the market segment which could affect brand name, packaging, price, kind of stockist, choice of advertising theme and choice of advertising media. The entire sequence of elements is of marketing significance, and an advertising campaign could be a disastrous waste of money if all these elements were not harmonised.

34. Limitations of 4Ps

This is also a practical example of the limitations of the 4Ps concept of marketing (*see* 1:**14**) because the marketing manager of an advertising agency is not only concerned with the fourth P, Promotion. Advertising has to be related to the *sequence* or chronological order of marketing considerations. This, of course, is what the new product development agencies are all about. They discount the idea of planning an advertising campaign for a given product: they want to be involved in the whole marketing mix. Under the old 4Ps principle so familiar to American marketing (or to those whose training is based on the American 4Ps marketing concept) advertising is brought in rather late in the marketing strategy. But if we dispense with the 4Ps, and start at the beginning, the eventual advertising campaign evolves throughout the stages of the marketing mix. This could mean that the account executive and the agency marketing manager should sit in on the advertiser's decision-making conferences from the earliest possible moment (*see* also 17:4).

35. Marketing aspects

To take the definition of marketing again, it becomes possible—indeed necessary—to consider how advertising will be able to contribute to selling at a profit what people will buy. This brings the agency marketing manager in at the threshold of product design.

It has been known for a product to be killed at birth, or redesigned, or sent to an independent test house, because the advertising agency has been able to express opinions or doubts at a very early stage. This could also apply to such stages as:

(a) *naming* — does the name lend itself to good promotion;
(b) *packaging* — would it be easier to promote the product if it were packed differently;
(c) *distribution* — would it be more economical to sell direct to retailers rather than through wholesalers?

Like other members of the agency team, the marketing manager, without divulging any trade secrets, will be able to advise clients on the basis of wide experience. For example, something which helped in the successful marketing of a sewing machine might also be applicable to a vacuum cleaner. Or a problem which occurred in the distribution of a soft drink to supermarket chains (e.g. lead time between obtaining orders and delivery) could apply equally to a new cheese spread, and so would affect the timing of the appearance of advertisements. Failure to reckon with such a lead time resulted in a disastrous marketing operation when an expensive television advertising campaign occurred *before* the product had reached the shops, and the advertising expenditure was a total waste of money.

36. Media planner

In large agencies there will be a division between media planning and media buying, but in a smaller agency one person will handle both. Media planning calls for an intimate knowledge of the range and values of available media. In Britain, as in most industrial countries, media are extensive. There are thousands of national and regional newspapers and magazines; numerous television and radio stations; thousands of outdoor and transportation sites (including the London Underground railway); and many other advertising media. The media mix is usually carefully selected on the basis of a *minimum* use of media of *maximum* advertising value, and there will be primary spearhead media and secondary support media. A modern agency will use a computer to assess and select media.

37. Media statistics

The media planner is assisted by statistics both from independent sources, and from the media themselves as part of their sales campaigns (*see* also Chapter 15). Figures on circulation are provided by the Audit Bureau of Circulations (ABC). Figures on readership, and profiles of readers, are provided by the Joint Industry Committee for National Readership Surveys (JICNARS). Television audience figures are supplied by the Broadcasters' Audience Research Board (BARB) and radio audience figures are supplied by the Joint Industry Committee for Radio Audience Research (JICRAR). There are many surveys covering other media, while individual publishers, TV companies and other media owners conduct their own special surveys and supply agencies and advertisers with their figures.

38. Media rates

The media planner now has to marry statistics to costs. These are expressed as cost-per-thousand sales, readers, viewers, listeners, passengers, passers-by, households and so on.

The rate for a whole page in Journal A may be £1,000, but only £800 for Journal B. Which is really the best buy? We have to look at more critical figures such as circulation (those who buy) and readership (those who read). Then we can calculate the cost-per-thousand buyers or readers. Suppose Journal A has a circulation of 10,000 copies per issue. The cost-per-thousand is £1,000 ÷ 10 which is £100. However, if Journal B has a circulation of only 5,000, its cost-per-thousand is an uneconomical £160 (£800 ÷ 5).

It is a case of getting what you pay for. Although it is often suggested that television advertising is very expensive, it could be very cheap if the rate is divided by millions of viewers. It is only expensive if it is wasteful to convey the sales message to so many people.

There is another way of looking at this issue. What is the *quality* of the readership? While Journal *A* in the above example may seem a bargain, it could be a waste of money if the journal was read by the wrong social grade(s). Here, it is useful to refer back to Tables 2.1 and 2.2 in Chapter 2. For example, a supermarket chain needing to sell to many thousands of customers will find it economic to pay a high rate to reach the millions of readers of the *Sun*, but the maker of a main-frame computer would find the *Sun* completely useless and would find it more economic to spend far less to reach the more specialised readership of *The Economist*.

39. Media schedule

Having completed his media study and calculations, the media planner then draws up a *media schedule* which is a plan or diary of the proposed insertions in the press, or appearances on radio or television, or use of other media, over the period of the advertising campaign, with their costs. This schedule will be included in the presentation made to the client of the whole campaign, or directly to the client if there is no major presentation as can happen if various programmes are being drawn up during the course of a year. When the media schedule has been approved, or amended, it becomes the media buyer's task to make the bookings.

40. Media buyer

The media buyer (or space buyer as he used to be called before the arrival of commercial broadcasting, and still is called in some agencies) negotiates with the media for purchase of space and airtime. His skill lies in getting the best positions and times at the best rates. Some media may have to be booked months in advance and so tentative bookings may have to be made before the media schedule is presented for client approval. He will have good relations with the sales representatives of the media who will be contacting him from time to time with offers and proposals which may or may not fit in with the allocations of the media schedule. It should not be thought that space and airtime is simply placed and accepted. The media are eagerly trying to induce the media buyer to use their media. Like any other buyer, the media buyer is constantly being approached by hard-selling sales representatives.

41. Copywriter

The copywriter is responsible for writing the wording of advertisements (*see* also Chapter 10). He or she has to have the ability to convert sales propositions into selling ideas, creating themes or copy platforms for campaigns and distilling sales arguments into the fewest number of necessary words. His or her writing style is unlike any other. Complete grammatical sentences are not always written, but words and punctuation and their typographical presentation are written like a painter uses colours and shapes. The copywriter can write a one-word one-sentence paragraph that grips the reader's interest and desire. The English language can be virtually used for effect. A thousand words may be written but every word will count. He or she can sell. (The copywriter may also write scripts for television and radio commercials, or there may be a *scriptwriter.*)

Agencies employ copywriters in different ways. There may be a copy department headed by a copy chief, or there may be creative groups headed by copywriters or, again, a creative director may use freelance copywriters. Many of the best and most highly paid copywriters work freelance.

42. Art director

Head of the studio, the art director in a large agency will have a team of visualisers, layout artists and typographers (*see* also Chapter 10). In a small agency the art director will perform all these creative tasks. If there is no separate art buyer, artwork will be bought through artists' agents, or direct from artists. Photography will be commissioned and models engaged, usually through a model agency.

43. Visualiser

The visualiser is the creative counterpart of the copywriter, a first-class artist who is able to interpret in visual terms the copywriter's ideas. They usually work together as a team, as in the creative team which works on one or more accounts. The visualiser produces roughs or scamps, and may scribble many versions until the ideas are sufficiently well expressed for them to be finished up with dummy pictures and hand lettering. The client is usually shown visuals without final photography, drawings and typesetting, but they will be sufficient to give a good impression of the finished advertisement. When approved, the artwork is commissioned.

44. Layout artist
A layout is an exact plan of the advertisement, converting the visual into a measured representation of the advertisement which can be followed by the printer or made up as camera-ready copy. The layout will be marked up with instructions regarding typefaces and type sizes. For various space sizes, *adaptations* are made of the original layout. The layout artist draws the layout and adaptations of it.

45. Typographer
A typographer is a master of type, knowing the hundreds of display and text typefaces and how to use them both to create effect and to ensure legibility. The typographer will take the written copy and the drawn layout, and select and instruct the typesetter on the faces and sizes required. To do so, the typographer will also cast off the copy, that is calculate the number of words and size of type to fit spaces. (Sometimes the layout artist and typographer will be the same person.)

46. Television producer
In the large agencies which handle accounts requiring television campaigns, the producer creates ideas for commercials, and these are presented in the form of a storyboard which resembles a series of cartoons in shapes like television screens or rectangles (*see* Chapter 11, Fig. 11.4). The TV producer will also be responsible for casting the actors and presenter, hiring music, and appointing a director and film unit. The distinction should be made between the agency producer who creates and assembles the necessary resources, and the outside director and his production unit which actually shoots the film or video.

47. Production manager

The task here is to organise the production of advertising throughout the agency, according to a set timetable, so that advertisements are delivered to the media on time. The production manager acts as a progress chaser, is also responsible for ordering typesettings and supplying finished advertisements as they are required for flexography, photogravure or offset-litho printing (*see* Chapter 12). As offset-litho becomes increasingly used for printing newspapers and magazines, camera-ready copy has to be supplied. In large agencies, work flow will be maintained by the *traffic controller* who supplies duplicate copies of instructions to all departments which need to be aware of work in progress. As several separate campaigns are likely to be progressing simultaneously, progress has to be checked daily.

Advertising agency jargon

48. Special terms

A lot of advertising jargon has been used in this chapter. Most of these words with their special meanings have been explained, but a few need further clarification and some others are now introduced. Attention has already been drawn to expressions like recognition and the commission system (**8–10**), à la carte agencies (**19–25**), the advertising manager (**27**), account (**1**), account executive (**30**), circulation and readership (**37–8**), television producer and television director (**46**), and production manager (**47**), which may not be quite what they seem and are frequently misunderstood by examination students.

49. Plans board

In some agencies the plans board system is operated (*see* also Chapter 17). The plans board consists of the account executive and the heads of agency departments, generally the marketing manager, copy chief, art director and media planner. When the account executive introduces a new client or product, or an account is renewed, a report is submitted to these departmental heads and a meeting is called. The new proposition is discussed very frankly, and then the departmental heads disperse to consider ideas and prepare schemes. At the next meeting these ideas and schemes are discussed, and the campaign begins to take shape. After this the campaign is prepared for presentation to the client.

In some advertising agencies there is an overall *account planner* who integrates the work of departments and personnel. Working closely with the account executive, the account planner prepares the creative brief, and is associated with all the research, marketing, promotional strategy and day-to-day internal control of the campaign.

50. Review board
A refinement may be to have a review board comprising executives not involved in the campaign who review the proposed campaign critically before it is presented to the client.

51. Presentation
This word has two meanings:

(a) the presentation of the campaign to the client with copy and visual ideas and the recommended media schedule;
(b) the presentation or appearance of the advertisement itself.

52. Copy
There are four meanings to the word 'copy' which are relevant here:

(a) the wording of an advertisement;
(b) the whole advertisement or any material for printing, that is all the words and illustrations;
(c) a single copy of a newspaper or magazine;
(d) a duplicate, e.g. carbon copy.

53. Billings
Strictly speaking, this means the value of space and air-time bookings, but it is more often taken to mean the total financial turnover of an agency.

54. Voucher
A voucher copy is a copy of the journal in which the advertisement has appeared, and is supplied by the publisher as proof of appearance. The person in charge of vouchers is called

the voucher clerk. Sometimes only the advertisement and not the whole publication is sent to the client (or even by the publisher to the agency) and this is called a 'tear sheet'.

55. Media

It should be remembered that the word media is the plural of the word medium. The press is a medium, but radio and television are media. We refer to 'the media' and 'a medium'.

Progress test 3

1.   Explain the legal precedent that 'the agency acts as principal'. (6)

2.   What is the role of an advertising agency? (6–7)

3.   What does 'recognition' mean, and how has this changed since 1979? (8–10)

4.   Name the bodies representing different media owners which recognise advertising agencies. (8)

5.   What is a media independent? (14)

6.   How does an à la carte advertising agency differ from a full service agency? (19)

7.   Identify the different kinds of creative agencies. (20–25)

8.   What service does a sponsorship agency provide for the clients? (25)

9.   Describe the responsibilities of the account executive. (30)

10.   What is the importance of the contact report? (31)

11.   Distinguish between the duties of the media planner and the media buyer. (36, 40)

12.   What do the initials ABC, JICNARS, BARB and JICRAR stand for? (37)

13.   What information is contained in the media schedule? (39)

14.   How does the copywriter contribute to the creativity of an advertising campaign? (41)

15.   Describe the work of the visualiser. (43)

16.   Distinguish between the roles of the television producer and the television director. (46)

17.   Explain how the plans board operates. (49)

18.   Give the two meanings of 'presentation'. (51)

19.   Give the four meanings of 'copy'. (52)

20.   What is a voucher copy? (54)

4
Advertising media: above-the-line

Introduction and definitions

1. Variety of media
Advertising media consist of any means by which sales messages can be conveyed to potential buyers. The variety of media is immense in the 'North' (i.e. industrialised countries), but may be very limited in the 'South' (i.e. developing countries). In Britain, for instance, *Benn's Media Directory* lists over 14,000 publications. Almost anything can and has been used as an advertising medium—the sky, bus tickets, matchboxes, street litter bins, taxi cabs, parking meters, shopping bags and ball-point pens. Moreover, there are people who will try to exploit almost anything as an advertising medium, and it is necessary to consider the advertising value very carefully. All too easily, much money can be wasted on weak media, let alone rackets to do with spurious media of no advertising value. Media buying is therefore a skilled business, the object being to get the most effective advertising at the lowest cost.

2. Above-the-line and below-the-line
With the change in the recognition and commission system brought about by the Restrictive Trade Practices Act 1976 and the Office of Fair Trading ruling of 1979 (*see* 3:8–10) the terms 'above-the-line' and 'below-the-line' have lost much of their original significance. While the media independents continue to concentrate on above-the-line media, the creative agencies do not.

Moreover, the early 1990s saw a recession in the use of above-the-line media and a tremendous growth in the use of below-the-line media such as direct mail.

Originally, above-the-line meant the five media which paid commission to advertising agencies, namely *press, radio, television, outdoor* and *cinema*, and it is these which will be discussed in this chapter. The rest (which usually paid no commission and incurred on-cost percentages) were direct mail, exhibitions, point-of-sale display aids, print and sales literature and all kinds of miscellaneous media, referred to as below-the-line media (*see* Chapter 5). The bulk of service agency income is still derived from above-the-line media, and no doubt the two terms will remain a convenient means of distinguishing the different groups of media.

3. Primary and secondary media

Sometimes confused with above-the-line and below-the-line, primary media are those which spearhead a campaign, and secondary are those which provide support. The choice of these media will depend on what is being advertised. Television could be a primary medium for a food product, outdoor supersites for a cigarette, direct mail for magazine subscriptions, a catalogue for a direct response or mail order house and posters on the London Underground for a London shoe shop. Sometimes, a primary medium may be chosen because it is not being used by a rival. One brewer may advertise on television and another may use posters. Secondary media will be those which back up the main thrust of the campaign. The media mix combines the fewest number of media necessary to gain the greatest impact and response.

The press

4. Importance of the press

As shown in 1:11, the press takes up 62.6 per cent of the total expenditure on above-the-line advertising in Britain. The press predominates in literate, industrial countries. It may be arguable that television has greater impact and realism, and it is true that the biggest spenders on advertising spend most of their money on TV, but the number of TV advertisers is relatively small and the amount of time available for television advertising is limited. The number of advertisers in the press runs into millions and the number of publications exceeds 14,000. It is not really a matter of saying which is best since there is no comparison in their users, usage or volume.

5. Press outside Britain

This situation may differ outside Britain for the following reasons.

(a) *Size of country.* Local or regional papers based on cities (as in Australia, Canada, Germany and the USA) may replace the national newspapers of Britain, largely for geographical or historical reasons. Britain is a compact country with good road, rail and air communications, and London has always been the capital. For these reasons a London-based national press developed in the nineteenth century.

However, changes have been taking place in the USA with the failure of many famous city newspapers and bids for national circulation by the *Wall Street Journal* followed by the *New York Times* and the space-satellite-supported Garnett company with its new *USA Today.*

(b) *Extent of literacy.* The circulation figures of journals, and the number of titles, is related to educational and literacy standards. A further problem will be multi-ethnic and multi-language situations which require publications either addressed to different ethnic groups or in different languages. Vernacular newspapers, since they appeal to sections of the community, inevitably have smaller circulations than those addressed to a nation as a whole. In Nigeria, for instance, where English-language newspapers have predominated for decades, there are now newspapers in Hausa and Yoruba.

(c) *Purchasing power.* In poorer countries, not even the educated and literate may be able to afford to buy newspapers and magazines. The volume of advertising may be small, newsprint will be costly to import, and the cover price will be high.

NOTE: It is interesting that in countries where newspapers are not widely used, e.g. Arab countries, television is regarded as the superior medium. This is less so in the West Indies where English is standard, and even less so in Hong Kong where some 100 Chinese dailies are published.

6. Characteristics of the press

The power and dominance of the press is explained by some of the following special characteristics.

(a) *In-depth coverage and permanence.* Both radio and television are ephemeral and usually brief, but newspapers and magazines can provide detailed reports which can be read, re-read and retained if required. This is true even though the life of a city newspaper may be only a few hours, but many publications survive for some time, and items can be cut out and kept.

(b) *Variety of subjects covered.* Not only do newspapers represent class, political, religious, ethnic and language groups, but magazines represent every sort of special interest. This is perhaps where the press best demonstrates its strength because by selecting the right journals it is possible to reach particular and well-defined sections of the reading public. This cannot be done with mass media like radio, TV and posters.

(c) *Mobility.* Newspapers and magazines can be carried about and read almost anywhere, for example in the house, while travelling, at the place of work, in a waiting room or in a library.

(d) *Results assessable.* By using coupons, and by the additional use of 'keys' or codes which identify from which publication the coupon was clipped, it is possible to measure the pulling power and cost-effectiveness of different journals. Evaluation is possible by dividing the cost of space by the number of replies received. If a space cost £1,000 and produced 1,000 replies, each would cost £1. If the space cost only £500 but produced only 250 replies, the cost-per-reply would be £2 or double. Thus, the response or hit rate is most important. In the above example the lower cost is the more expensive, and the higher cost is the more economical.

(e) *Statistics available.* In industrial countries, and increasingly in other countries, net sales are audited and readerships are researched so that a wealth of statistical information exists about a large number of newspapers and magazines. The media planner can confront the media salesman with computer calculations to justify his media schedule of recommended space and airtime bookings. (*See* 3:**36–9**)

(f) *Improved printing.* The majority of newspapers and magazines are printed by offset-litho while some of the very big circulation magazines are printed by photogravure (*see* Chapter 12). Picture quality, even in black and white, is nowadays very good since the dot screen used for offset-litho is usually nearly twice as fine as that formerly used for letterpress printing. Magazines printed by offset-litho are usually better printed than those produced by photogravure, pictures being produced more sharply.

The flexography process was adopted in 1989 by the *Daily Mail* group at their new plant in South East London, this being superior to offset-litho.

7. Categories of press

There are so many different kinds of newspapers, magazines and other publications that a detailed analysis is necessary in order to appreciate their range and variety and to understand the different terms used.

(a) *National newspapers.* Published daily in the morning or on Sundays, these are nowadays published in a major city (e.g. London) and distributed throughout the country. However, they are no longer printed in Fleet Street. New plants have been built in the Docklands area of East and South East London, while some newspapers are printed at strategically located plants in, say, Portsmouth.

There are now more national newspapers in Britain than there were a few years ago, largely because modern newspapers printed by web offset-litho and using computerised editorial techniques have replaced the labour-intensive letterpress process, making smaller-circulation newspapers economically viable and even profitable. *Today*, the *Independent* and the *Independent on Sunday* have all joined the national titles. Greater competition, and higher cover prices, may be partly responsible, but the 1990s have seen dramatically falling circulations. In 1989 the total average daily sales of national dailies were about 15.5 million, but in 1990 they had fallen to about 14 million. The only papers to show an increase in circulation were the *Daily Star*, the *Independent* and the *Financial Times*, all others losing sales.

The Times may be Britain's best-known newspaper outside Britain, but its circulation is no greater than Nigeria's most popular daily, the *Daily Times* of Lagos, that is around 400,000.

The following are approximate circulations of Britain's 21

national dailies and Sundays, based on rounding off Audit Bureau
of Circulation figures:

Dailies		Sundays	
Sun	3,900,000	News of the World	5,000,000
Daily Mirror/Record	3,900,000	Sunday Mirror	3,000,000
Daily Mail	1,700,000	People	2,500,000
Daily Express	1,600,000	Mail on Sunday	1,900,000
Daily Telegraph	1,000,000	Sunday Express	1,700,000
Daily Star	900,000	Sunday Times	1,100,000
Today	600,000	Sunday Telegraph	570,000
The Times	430,000	Observer	540,000
Guardian	420,000	Sunday Sport	430,000
Independent	410,000	Independent on Sunday	330,000
Financial Times	290,000		

MEAL figures published in *Marketing Week* (30 March 1990),
give the top ten users of newspapers as:

MFI
Curry's
B & Q
Water Authority
Sky Channel
Texas Homecare
Dixon's Photo & Audio
Halifax Building Society
Tesco
Abbey National Building Society

Retailers, especially do-it-yourself suppliers, predominate in
the top ten users of newspapers.

A significant change in national newspapers from the point of
view of advertisers has been the availability of on-the-run (rather
than pre-printed) colour which has deprived the big popular
women's magazines (e.g. *Woman, Woman's Own, Woman's Weekly*
and *Woman's Realm*) of a third of their advertising revenue.

(b) *Regional newspapers.* Outside London, a hundred newspapers—mostly evenings—are published daily. In Northern

Ireland, Scotland and Wales such regional dailies are virtually the national press for those parts of the UK. There are also a few regional Sunday newspapers. In addition, there are weekly papers covering one or more counties and often published in series with localised titles (e.g. the *Kent Messenger* series with 17 localised titles, the *Surrey Advertiser* series with 19 titles, or the *Packet* newspapers of Cornwall with 10 titles); town weeklies; and—in parts of London, for instance—suburban weeklies.

Advertising expenditure in the regional press has been rising during the 1980s and 1990s, largely due to the free newspaper explosion. For many years it has been Britain's second largest medium after television. According to MEAL, the largest single advertising category using the regional press is retail and mail order, which is double that of motor-cars, the second largest category.

The regional (or provincial) press was nearly eclipsed after the Second World War by the cost of replacing its old letterpress printing machines. It had been built up by largely political newspapers of historical significance such as the famous Liberal *Mercuries* (e.g. *Leicester Mercury*) while the *Yorkshire Post*'s owners used to be called Yorkshire Conservative Newspapers. The arrival of television helped some of the regional evenings who began to publish features about television and other home interests so that these papers became family reading and were able to attract retail and other consumer advertising.

However, many regional weeklies were rescued by Woodrow Wyatt's initiative in introducing large American web-offset-litho presses which could be installed strategically to print a number of newspapers over a wide area. This led to colour printing a long time before Fleet Street succumbed to modern printing, followed by computerised photo-typesetting and the paperless newsroom.

In the late 1980s this was extended to the printing of some national newspapers at a number of outside London presses since newspapers such as the *Independent* had no presses of their own. For example, the News Centre at Portsmouth has three huge Metroliner presses which run for 22 hours a day, printing national daily and Sunday newspapers, regional weeklies, free newspapers, magazines and the six editions a day of its own *News* series with editions for different parts of southern England.

(c) *Free newspapers.* The number of local newspapers delivered free of charge door-to-door has increased in recent years, and most of them are members of the Association of Free Newspapers which has about 160 members representing some 560 titles with 27.5 million copies being printed weekly. As a result of the success of free newspapers, the circulations of paid-for regionals dropped by three million in 1989. Reed and Emap dominate the free titles. Free newspapers offer a cost-per-thousand rate which is half that of paid-for weeklies. This is a phenomenon of British publishing. Free newspapers succeed in selling advertisement space because of the guaranteed circulation saturation of urban areas. In some large towns two or three free newspapers are delivered to every house every week.

(d) *Consumer magazines.* This term is somewhat loosely applied to popular magazines sold by newsagents. Among them are the numerous women's magazines, many with multi-million circulations. Women's magazines range from long-established ones which have been published for up to 50 years and which loyal readers tend to read for a lifetime, to ones with more sophisticated or special age-group readerships. German and French publishers have entered the British market with English-language versions of continental women's magazines often referred to as 'clones'. Other consumer magazines include the very big circulation *Radio Times* and *TV Times*. With the deregulation of programme listings, the *Radio Times* and *TV Times* (while retaining copyright) lost their monopoly so that newspapers and other magazines are now permitted to publish programme information in advance.

Table 4.1 is an extract from the top 30 list of magazines produced by MEAL and published in *Marketing Week* (11 May 1990), which is interesting for a number of reasons. First, the table gives a good impression of the variety of magazines, but especially revealing is the volume of advertising attracted by the give-away weekend magazines or supplements. We will also look later at the strength of some of the new titles, often of continental Europe origin. Many of the older magazines lost colour advertising to newspapers.

Table 4.1 *Display expenditure and circulations, MEAL's top 30 magazines 1989*

Rank	Title	Display ad revenue (£000s)	ABC Circulation (June – Dec. 1989)
1	You Magazine	70,899	1,892,158
2	Sunday Express Magazine	70,062	1,854,492
3	Sunday Times Magazine	54,467	1,248,027
4	TV Times	49,023	2,944,737
5	Sunday Magazine	40,197	5,185,472
6	Radio Times	39,121	3,037,612
7	Sunday Mirror Magazine	30,545	2,925,540
8	Telegraph Weekend Magazine	28,379	1,102,609
9	Observer Magazine	22,766	639,294
10	Woman's Own	20,493	902,155
11	Country Life	16,063	53,932
12	The Economist (UK)	15,644	226,958
13	Vogue	14,495	172,387
14	Good Housekeeping	13,595	333,259
15	Plus Magazine	13,467	n/a
16	Woman	13,396	855,827
17	Cosmopolitan	12,220	400,135
18	Independent Magazine	10,763	411,953
19	Prima	10,034	844,512
20	People Magazine	9,434	2,641,973
21	Family Circle	8,993	476,668
22	Ideal Home	8,365	282,429
23	Best Magazine	8,317	832,208
24	Reader's Digest	8,303	1,527,560
25	Woman's Weekly	8,191	1,139,596
26	Sunday Telegraph 7 Days	7,929	632,923
27	Elle	7,467	220,236
28	Harpers & Queen	7,100	85,828
29	Smash Hits	6,904	691,198
30	Woman & Home	6,721	509,925

Women's magazines are numerous in Britain, they fall into the four categories of *home interest monthlies, general interest monthlies* and *young women's* and *general interest women's weeklies.* The leaders in each category are, respectively, *Good Housekeeping* (333,259), *Vogue* (172,387), *Just Seventeen* (282,016), and *Woman's Own* (931,295).

Titles come and go. Most of the leaders have existed for up to 50 years or so. Newer ones like *Elle, Marie Claire, Bella* and *Chat* are now well-established British versions of foreign magazines.

The one category of magazine which has never succeeded in Britain is the news magazine, unlike the American *Time.* The topic which has spawned the largest number of new magazines in recent years has been the computer, for which there are more than 200 titles, and these range over consumer special interest, trade, technical and professional journals.

The MEAL report in *Marketing Week* (30 March 1990) gave the following as the top ten users of magazines.

Benson & Hedges Special King Size
Benson & Hedges Silk Cut
Franklin Mint (collectables)
Player Special King Size
Britannia Music Club
Sainsbury
NatWest Bank—personal
C & A
Sky Channel
Peugeot 405

Here we see a greater mixture of advertisers among the leaders compared with newspaper and television, but cigarettes (banned on television) predominate.

(e) *Special interest magazines.* These journals are also to be seen in newsagents shops and on news-stands, but they cover special interests such as gardening, photography, philately, Hi-fi, computers, motoring, house-buying, health and beauty, and many sports, pastimes and hobbies.

(f) *Trade journals.* Mainly addressed to tradesmen such as butchers, bakers, chemists, and other retailers, they are also published for the larger retailers such as department stores, supermarkets and large mixed retailers.

(g) *Technical journals.* Sometimes confused with the 'trade press', technical journals are produced for the technicians in various industries.

(h) *Professional journals.* Here we have another group of journals specially edited for professionals such as doctors, teachers, lawyers or architects.

(i) *Directories and yearbooks.* These annual or periodical volumes can be valuable advertising media, and *Yellow Pages* business telephone directories are familiar world-wide. Some directories are indispensable and because constant reference is made to them they can be useful advertising media. A typical example is *Advertisers Annual.*

8. Methods of distribution

Newspapers and magazines reach their readers by different methods, and the value of a journal as an advertising medium may be influenced by the method of distribution and the effect this may have. The main methods are as follows.

(a) *Retail distribution* by home delivery, newsagents shop or street vendor, or in certain other shops, e.g. women's magazines on sale in supermarkets or philately magazines in stamp dealers. Vending machines are also used to sell newspapers.

(b) *Subscription,* the journal being subscribed to and delivered by post.

(c) *Controlled circulation.* Many trade and technical journals are mailed free of charge to a combination of selected readers and ones who have requested copies. By this method it is possible to obtain better penetration of a market than by journals which rely on subscriptions.

Sometimes a new trade or technical journal will be launched as a controlled circulation journal, but once established it may be sold on a subscription and retail basis with a limited number of free copies. This has happened with *Direct Response, Marketing Week* and *PR Week.*

(d) *Free circulation.* Whether distributed in the street like magazines addressed to office workers and carrying advertisements for office jobs, or newspapers of domestic interest delivered door-to-door, free magazines and newspapers have become numerous in Britain. One successful form of free newspaper is the kind which concentrates on property news and advertisements.

9. Advantages of the press

Certain advantages of the press as an advertising medium are evident from what has been discussed already and from other characteristics. They may be summarised as follows.

(a) The press is one of the cheapest means of reaching a large number of unknown or unidentified prospective buyers, whether they be in a town, region, county or even overseas.

(b) Advertisements can be inserted quickly compared with the time required for making commercials for television or designing and printing posters. An advertisement could be inserted in a newspaper virtually overnight. Classified (or small run-on advertisements) are often sold by telephone.

(c) Response can be achieved by means of coupons, or the giving of telephone numbers, and this can be further encouraged by Freepost and Freefone facilities.

(d) Press advertising can be targeted to certain people by using the newspapers or magazines read by them.

(e) Newspapers and magazines have the capacity to accept a large number of advertisements compared with the limited time on television.

(f) Press advertisements can be re-read and retained, and some publications such as magazines have very long lives, being kept, filed or passed on to other readers.

(g) A number of offset-litho printed nationals and regionals offer colour, and some of the nationals offer pre-printed colour pages, while the *Observer, Sunday Times, Sunday Telegraph, Mail on Sunday* and *News of the World* and other Saturday and Sunday newspapers have their colour supplements or magazines.

10. Disadvantages of the press

All media have their merits and demerits, and while the press dominates in literate countries, it does have its weaknesses, as summarised below.

(a) *Short life.* A daily or Sunday newspaper is unlikely to survive for more than a day, and in some cases the reading life of a newspaper may be exhausted in a few hours, as when newspapers are read on the way to and from work.

(b) *Poorly printed.* Web-offset and flexography printing have brought about better printing standards, especially of photographs because of the finer dot halftone screen used.

Nevertheless, two problems remain: the poor quality of newsprint, and the speed with which multi-million circulation newspapers have to be printed.

(c) *Passive medium.* An effort has to be made to read press advertisements, unlike cinema, radio and TV advertisements which have captive audiences. The advertisements in the press have to compete with the editorial for attention and interest, whereas cinema and broadcast advertising does not occur at the same time as the programme.

(d) *Static medium.* The press advertisement lacks the realism of sound, movement and often the colour of TV or cinema commercials, and even the sound of radio advertising.

(e) *Badly presented.* Advertisements may be massed together so that they may be overlooked, unless an effort is made to find them, whereas with most other media each advertisement is presented individually and can be absorbed one at a time.

Radio

11. Development of radio advertising in Britain

In many parts of the world radio advertising accompanied the introduction of radio, and has been a long-established medium, but this was not so in Britain where it is comparatively new. Before the Second World War, the only commercial radio listened to in Britain were English-language programmes transmitted from continental stations in France, Holland and Luxembourg, of which only Radio Luxembourg returned after the war. In the 1960s there were some off-shore pirate radio stations, but they were made illegal under the Marine Broadcasting Offences Act 1967. Their popularity, and the success of commercial television since the 1950s, encouraged the setting up of Independent Local Radio (ILR), and with the Sound Broadcasting Act 1972 the Independent Television Authority (the commercial counterpart to the BBC) became the Independent Broadcasting Authority (IBA). By the end of 1984, about 50 ILR stations were operating. Today there is a great variety of commercial and non-commercial radio stations, and there are ones aimed at special interest audiences. With the new Radio Authority, commercial radio promises considerable development in the future.

A feature of commercial radio in Britain has been the growth of *split frequency* broadcasting, where one station appeals to two types of audience on different frequencies. This has attracted larger radio audiences, and enabled advertisers to target audiences more precisely, both geographically and demographically.

12. Importance of radio advertising outside Britain

Not surprisingly, radio advertising had not until recently attained the importance it enjoys elsewhere in the world, one reason being its newness, and another its localised character. In addition, local commercial radio has to compete with national and local BBC stations which do not carry advertisements. The importance of radio as an advertising medium is best looked at from an international standpoint, where its impact is greatest, before returning to the British scene. In such world-wide terms, the nature and value of the medium can be summarised as follows.

(a) *Cheapness.* It costs little to own and run a radio set, especially with the introduction of the battery-operated transistorised portable radio, even if batteries are sometimes expensive in poorer developing countries. Radios are often placed in public places, and in some countries like Singapore rediffusion services at low rentals are popular. In addition, it is cheaper to produce a radio commercial than a TV commercial—in fact, the former can merely be read out as a spot announcement.

(b) *Penetration.* Provided the signal is sufficiently powerful, radio can reach large audiences over great distances, and is a means of reaching people who may have access to no other media. Moreover, where there are multi-language and multi-ethnic societies, radio messages can be broadcast in different languages. Radio can also reach illiterates who cannot read the newspapers, while battery-operated receivers and car radios overcome lack of electricity. These are all advantages which help to make radio popular in developing countries.

(c) *Transmission times.* Radio programmes are usually broadcast for many hours of the day.

(d) *Human voice and music.* The use of sound, whether vocal or musical, makes it a live medium compared with passive and static media such as the press, outdoor, print, direct mail and point-of-sale displays. Sound effects can also be used.

(e) *Does not require sole attention.* Unlike reading a newspaper or watching television, radio does not demand the listener's sole attention. He can do other things at the same time, from working to driving a motor-car, and radio can be listened to in numerous locations or situations.

(f) *Companionship.* Radio is often listened to as a form of companionship.

The above are general characteristics, but there are more specific ones which apply to radio advertising in Britain.

13. Characteristics of British radio

These relate to a situation where radio has to be compared with existing, and often much longer established, media, in a country where the conditions are usually the opposite to those in developing countries. People are literate, the press is widely read, and most people have electricity. In these very different circumstances, radio advertising has to be seen as an important medium for quite different reasons.

(a) *It is local.* Although there are large advertisers who place radio commercials on a large number of stations, networking as they do on television, it is also an excellent medium for local advertisers, competing with the regional press.

(b) *It can be addressed to different audiences.* People of different kinds listen to radio at different times of the day, and commercials can be broadcast accordingly. There are those who like to listen to radio at breakfast time for a time-check, others who listen to their car radios when driving to and from work, housewives who listen while doing their housework, factory workers who listen while they work, and young people who listen to pop music at night when their parents are watching television. The medium thus becomes attractive to advertisers who wish to reach certain audiences, and such audiences are more distinct than occurs with television.

(c) *In addition to television.* Moreover, for many people radio can be listened to when they cannot watch television. Its mobility, whether about the house, out-of-doors or in the car, makes radio more accessible than most other media. Radios go almost everywhere—on building sites, on the milk float, in the car park attendant's kiosk, on the beach, and on foot when people wear headphones and a Walkman set.

14. Resistance to radio advertising

There has been a certain amount of reluctance by some British advertisers to use radio largely because it cannot be seen and physically evaluated like other media. This could be a foolhardy prejudice because the versatility of radio is remarkable. It is perhaps less easy to measure than other media, but both Radio Luxembourg and the AIRC (Association of Independent Radio Contractors) have produced audience figures which are impressive. The AIRC represents all the Radio Authority-appointed ILR stations. Although radio advertising has been available in Britain for nearly 20 years it is probably Britain's most underrated medium.

15. ILR stations

The following are some of the stations which were operational at the time of writing. These include 'community' radio stations with small local reception areas.

Beacon Radio (Wolverhampton and Black Country)
BRMB Radio (Birmingham)
Capital Radio (London)
Cardiff Broadcasting Co. (Cardiff)
Chiltern Radio (Luton/ Bedford)
County Sound (Guildford)
CRMK (Milton Keynes)
DevonAir Radio (Exeter/ Torbay)
Downtown Radio (Belfast)
Essex Radio (Southend/ Chelmsford)
GCM AM (Derby)
GCM AM (Leicester)
GWR Radio (Swindon)
Hereward Radio (Peterborough)
Invicta Radio (Kent)
LBC (News Radio) (London)

Leicester Sound (Leicester)
Manx Radio (Isle of Man)
Marcher Sound/Sain-Y-Gororau (Wrexham and Deeside)
Mercia Sound (Coventry)
Metro Radio (Tyne and Wear)
Moray Forth Radio (Inverness)
Northants 96
Northsound (Aberdeen)
Pennine Radio (Bradford with Huddersfield and Halifax in 1984/5)
Piccadilly Radio (Manchester)
Plymouth Sound (Plymouth)
Radio Aire (Leeds)
Radio Broadland (Norwich)
Radio City (Liverpool)
Radio Clyde (Glasgow)
Radio Forth (Edinburgh)
Radio Hallam (Sheffield and

Rotherham with Barnsley in
1985)
Radio Mercury (Crawley)
Radio Orwell (Ipswich)
Radio Tay (Dundee/Perth)
Radio Tees (Teesside)
Radio Trent (Nottingham)
Radio 210 (Reading)
Radio Victory (Portsmouth)
Radio Wyvern (Hereford/
Worcester)
Red Dragon Radio (Cardiff)
Red Rose Radio (Preston and
Blackpool)

Saxon Radio (Bury St.
Edmunds)
Severn Sound (Gloucester and
Cheltenham)
Signal Radio (Stoke-on-Trent)
Sound FM 103.2
Southern Sound (Bristol)
Swansea Sound (Swansea)
TFM Radio (Stockton-on-Tees)
Trent FM 102.8 (Derby)
2CR (Two Counties Radio)
(Bournemouth)
Viking Radio (Humberside)
West Sound (Ayr)

16. Airtime buying
A number of specialist agencies buy airtime for clients, but so
do many media independents and general advertising agencies
which have AIRC recognition.

Television

17. Television advertising in Britain
Since the 1950s television has been a major advertising
medium in Britain, but from 1991 all forms of broadcasting were
revolutionised by the new Broadcasting Act 1990. This was not the
only change in broadcasting because cable television had been
gaining a foothold in previous years, Sky satellite television (both
by dish and cable) was stealing audiences from the BBC in 1990,
taking over the ill-fated British Satellite Broadcasting.

The Broadcasting Bill was debated in Parliament in 1990, and
was based on the White Paper, *Broadcasting in the 90s: Competition,
Choice and Quality*, published on 8 November 1988. Its
controversial proposals were the replacement of ITV (the
commercial stations) by regional Channel Three with reduced
public service obligations, no requirements to produce networked
programmes, and station contracts (subject to suitability tests) to
be auctioned instead of being appointed. A fifth channel was
proposed which would be funded by advertising, sponsorship and
subscription, and started in 1993. The BBC licence fee was to be
replaced by subscriptions. The IBA and the Cable Authority were
to be combined in a new Independent Television Commission

and regulated by 'light touch'. Commercial radio was to have its own Radio Authority. There were many other proposals which were debated before the bill received the Royal Assent at the end of 1990 with effect in 1991. However, the industry still refers to 'ITV'.

CAM and LCCI students are recommended to buy a copy of the Act from Her Majesty's Stationery Office, or through their local bookshop. Its new regulations need to be studied carefully as they revolutionise British broadcasting.

In addition there has been some relaxation of sponsorship rules. In the past commercial organisations were not permitted to sponsor whole programmes (in contrast to the practice in many overseas countries). Among the first sponsors were Powergen's sponsorship of the ITV weather forecasts, and Lloyds Bank's sponsorship of BBC 2's *Young Musician of the Year* competition.

Some interesting surveys revealed changing attitudes towards television. In a report published by the IBA on 7 February 1990, 80 per cent of viewers (in a sample of 1,170 adults) wanted to see more recently released films (which was shown by the popularity of Sky Movies in a later survey). Two-thirds of viewers wanted more nature and wildlife programmes, and half thought there should be more adult education, plays, drama and comedy. Only a third wanted more international news, only a quarter more national news. Half of those interviewed wanted fewer soap operas (in line with the diminished popularity of soaps like *Dynasty* and *Dallas* in the USA), while two-fifths were opposed to chat, game and quiz shows.

On the same day the Institute of Practitioners in Advertising reported in *Attitudes to Television in 1989* that viewing figures were decreasing, and that advertisers were alarmed because ITV attracted down-market and older viewers while BBC 1 attracted younger, more upmarket people. Significantly, a report on Sky satellite television showed that it attracted down-market viewers. Trends seem to suggest that television is mostly watched by those with the least spending power, which is bad news for advertisers, but also for commercial television companies which are funded by advertising revenue. Against this has been the complaint in recent years that the Government has bought so much air-time (e.g. to promote privatisation share issues) that commercial advertisers have been deprived of air-time.

The nature of advertisers has changed over the years. While

many FMCGs such as detergents, drinks, pet foods and confectionery are still advertised on television they no longer dominate as was the case, for instance, with the 'whiter than white' detergent wars. In spite of the reports mentioned above, a MEAL report in *Marketing Week* (30 March 1990) showed that the top ten users of television were:

Water Authority (privatisation)
McDonald's
British Telecom Call Simulation
Halifax Building Society
Abbey National Building Society
Barclays Bank—personal
Woolworth
Prudential Assurance
Midland Bank
Yellow Pages

It is noticeable that finance houses predominate among the top ten users of television.

For a national advertiser of a FMCG it is economic to pay the apparently high cost of television advertising, although increases in media rates are criticised as being far in excess of the rate of inflation.

18. What is advertised on television?

Few homes are without a television set, and some have more than one set, and for popular goods to be found in any High Street throughout the country, it is an impactive medium since it takes the advertisement right into the home where it will be seen by the prospective buyer including others in the household who influence purchase. Consequently, commercials generally advertise popular goods such as foods, drink, toiletries, confectionery, cosmetics, oil and petrol, pharmaceuticals, decorating materials, newspapers and magazines, gramophone records, chain stores and also consumer durables such as domestic appliances and lawnmowers. In recent years, more expensive products and services have appeared on television ranging from home computers to air travel. Banks, insurance companies and building societies also use television. Motor-cars are advertised and new models are launched on TV.

19. Advantages of television

These apply world-wide, although a few are specifically British.

(a) *Realism.* Because of the combination of colour, sound and action, television has assets no other medium can offer (with the exception of the cinema which no longer has the big audiences which existed prior to television). With these advantages the advertiser can show and demonstrate the product. If it is a packaged food, pack recognition is established so that the buyer knows what he or she is looking for in the shop, or there is quick recognition even if the advertisement has been temporarily forgotten.

(b) *Receptive audiences.* Being received in the home in an entertainment atmosphere, commercials are well received, especially as they are produced to high technical standards and the presenter is often a well-known personality or at least a good actor or actress who presents the product authentically.

(c) *Repetition.* The advertisement can be repeated to the point when a sufficient number of viewers have seen it enough times for the advertisement to have impact. Nowadays, advertisers do not indulge in saturation advertising, which is not only expensive but offensive. A good advertisement should be capable of being shown again after a rest without boring its audience.

The classic example of this is the chimp series which has been shown for some 25 years, advertising Brooke Bond PG Tips tea. The series that was launched in 1984 actually has flashbacks to sequences in old chimp commercials. One of this series, 'Mr Piano Shifter', has been shown so many times on television it has won a place in the *Guinness Book of Records*. Advertising agents, using the ratings supplied weekly by the Broadcasters' Audience Research Board (BARB, *see* 15:**19**), are able to calculate when sufficient audience volume has been attained so that the commercial can be taken off.

(d) *Zoning and networking.* In Britain, there are currently 15 ITV area contractors licensed by the Independent Broadcasting Authority (IBA), two being in London. A full list of the ITV companies currently licensed for eight years from January 1982 is given in Table 4.2 below. The ITV area contra :tors also sell the advertising time for the national Channel 4 service in their own areas. Consequently, an advertiser can use one or any combination of stations, or network them all if he wishes.

(e) *Appeal to retailers.* Television advertising can reach retailers as well as consumers, both because retailers watch television just like anyone else, and because commercials can be addressed solely to them. Retailers know that if something is advertised on television there will be demand and it will sell. It can sometimes be very difficult for sales representatives to sell products to retailers unless they can promise the back-up of television advertising, and this can be imperative when dealing with supermarket chains with hundreds of outlets. These are fast-moving goods, and nothing moves faster than television advertising.

(f) *Linked with other media.* The TV commercial may be fleeting, but if fuller information, or a means of returning an enquiry coupon is required, this can be done by advertising in the weekly programme magazine *TV Times,* or newspapers carrying supportive advertisements can be named in the commercials. Press ads may refer to 'as on TV'. The television companies also offer telephone enquiry services, and computerised ordering facilities, the number being given in the commercial.

20. Weaknesses of commercial television

If commercial television was the last word in effective advertising media one would be entitled to ask how have all the other media survived, and how is it that the press continues to dominate? Of course, realistic and powerful as it may be, television does have its limitations.

(a) It tends to reach mass audiences, whereas one can be more selective with the press.

(b) If a lot of detail is required by prospective buyers, the press wins again.

(c) Little else can be done while watching television, compared with radio, although 'zapping' is possible when irritated viewers (using their remote control pad) eliminate the commercials or at least the sound.

(d) Because of the audience size it is costly, and there are thousands of advertisers who appeal to smaller markets and cannot justify the cost of television.

There are pros and cons regarding each medium discussed in this book, and the media planner has to choose the medium which is likely to be both effective and economical in achieving the objectives of the campaign.

Table 4.2 *Regional TV companies*

Contractor	Region
Anglia Television	East of England
Border Television	The Borders
Central Television	East and West Midlands
Channel Television	Channel Islands
Grampian Television	North Scotland
Granada Television	North West England
HTV	Wales and West of England
LWT (London Weekend Television)	London: Friday 5.15p.m. – Sunday
Scottish Television	Central Scotland
Thames Television	London: Monday – Friday 5.15 p.m.
TSW (Television South West)	South West England
TVS (Television South)	South and South East England
Tyne Tees Television	North East England
Ulster Television	Northern Ireland
Yorkshire Television	Yorkshire

21. Regional TV companies

Table 4.2 lists the 15 regional television companies responsible for providing the ITV programme service, and for selling airtime in the commercial break of both ITV and Channel 4 in their own areas. TV-am is a separate ITV company providing a nation-wide breakfast-time television service.

The above contractors existed at the time of writing, but under the Broadcasting Act 1990 new conditions may appear as a result of the new system of bidding for stations.

Figures 4.1 and 4.2 show the independent TV areas and transmitting stations.

Alternative television

22. Introduction

Now we come to the bogey of mass audience commercial television, and what Alvin Toffler in his book *The Third Wave* (Pan Books, London, 1981) has described as the de-massification of the

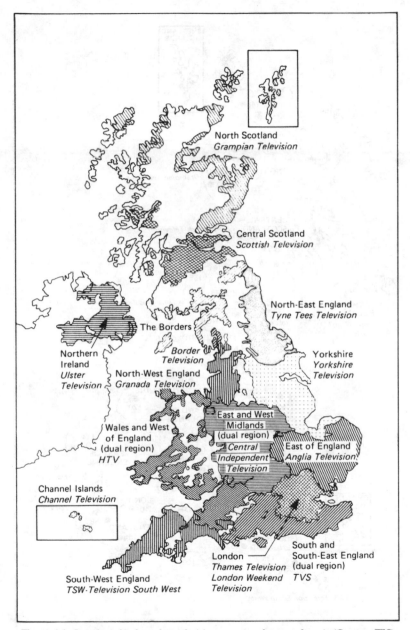

Figure 4.1 *Location of independent television areas (overlaps not shown). (Courtesy ITC)*

Figure 4.2 *Location of independent television transmitting stations. (Courtesy ITC)*

media. It is a change which is happening fast. An early example of de-massification was the community newspaper circulated to the residents of a small area in competition with both local newspapers and free newspapers. In television, however, the revolution is likely to be as decisive as the death of the 3,000-seater Odeon cinemas. Before television became popular there were big cinemas which attracted large audiences, but television stole these audiences and the cinemas were closed, altered to provide two or three small cinemas in the same building, or converted into bingo halls.

Alternative television presents a similar threat to the type of mass audience television offered by the fifteen regional contractors in Britain. The effect of alternative television is to dissipate the mass audiences for BBC and commercial programmes because viewers will be able to use their television sets to view a wide choice of other programmes, or even turn to totally different uses of their sets.

23. Effect on advertising

At present television advertising appears only on commercial stations, airtime being sold by the contractors to appear in commercial breaks in their programmes. There will be two effects of alternative television.

(a) The commercial television audience will diminish so that it becomes increasingly less possible for advertisers to reach large audiences, and the rates for airtime will need to fall to compensate for smaller audiences.

(b) Most of the forms of alternative television will have no advertising. There will be some but it will tend to be more local and limited to small audiences not easily measured because of the ability of viewers to watch what they like when they like.

Thus, the whole concept of television will be revolutionised, although this process will take a number of years to complete. Nevertheless, the changes are already evident in many homes, to mention only the popularity of the video-cassette-recorder (*see* **26**). In fact the VCR is popular in countries like Malawi which do not yet have television (*see* **33**), or Botswana where viewers can normally watch only programmes from South Africa.

24. Cable television

In the USA cable television was welcomed because it offered programmes superior to those put out by the large number of small local TV stations. However, the situation was different in Britain where a rent (on top of the BBC annual licence fee) had to be paid when a few large television companies were transmitting good quality programmes. The arrival of satellite television, with even greater choice of programme, gave cable television a much needed boost in 1990. Miles of streets throughout urban Britain were dug up and cabled in the 1980s but for a long time the take up was slow and disappointing, although 14.5 million homes could be reached.

By 1993 between five and eight million households should be capable of receiving cable services, with well over half the population of Britain able to receive cable services. This could dramatically affect the way in which people could choose their entertainment, make their telephone calls, and receive cabled information.

The Cable Authority was set up in December 1984 as a licensing body but not as a regulatory body like the IBA. However, the Cable Authority was absorbed into the Independent Television Commission, successor to the Independent Broadcasting Authority under the Broadcasting Act 1990.

The Cable Television Association is the trade association of the cable operators, cable hardware manufacturers and suppliers. Operating companies numbered 18 in 1990 of which US West, Pacific Telesis and United Artists were the three largest.

The channels available on cable television consist of:

All terrestrial channels	*Satellite channels*
BBC1 and 2	Sky One
Channel 3 (ITV)	Sky News
Channel 4	Eurosport
Channel 5 (when it begins)	Sky Movies
	The Movie Channel
	The Sports Channel
	The Power Station
	Screensports
	MTV Europe
Cable only channels	Lifestyle
Discovery Channel	Children's Channel

CNN	Japan Satellite TV (Europe)
Super Channel	TV5 (French)
Bravo	Sat-1 (German)
Home Video Channel	RAI (Italian)
Indra Dhush (Hindi)	VOA Europe
Cable Juke Box	Worldnet

Many homes have access to 'broadband' cable which has capacity to receive up to 40 channels of television without need for dish or aerial.

25. Satellite television

The extent of satellite television is shown in the previous section on cable television, pioneered by Sky Channel which was founded in 1981 as Satellite Television plc with first transmission on 26 April 1982. In June 1983 News International plc (headed by Rupert Murdoch) acquired 65 per cent of Satellite Television's capital. The name Sky Channel was adopted in 1984.

In 1990 the British-based British Satellite Broadcasting satellite channel was launched. Both Sky and BSB were suffering huge financial losses. On November 2, 1990, the shock decision was announced that the two satellite channels were to merge, Sky taking over BSB and the combined channel being called BSkyB.

26. Video-cassette-recorders

The first competitor to regular TV programmes is the VCR and such viewing is now surveyed by BARB (*see* also 15:**20**). Time-switching occurs when viewers record programmes and play them back at some future time, probably to the elimination of another regular programme and the advertising during its commercial break. In fact, advertisers on both programmes may suffer. That is not all, however: the viewer may use normal programme time to play back video films he has bought, borrowed or hired, and he may have a video camera himself and play back his own videos. With a VCR, now common in thousands of homes, the viewer can show what he or she likes and either ignore off-air programmes or be very selective about what programmes are switched on. This form of alternative television, and this degree of de-massification, has existed for some time, receiving a big boost with the Royal Wedding in 1981 when more VCRs had been sold in Britain by

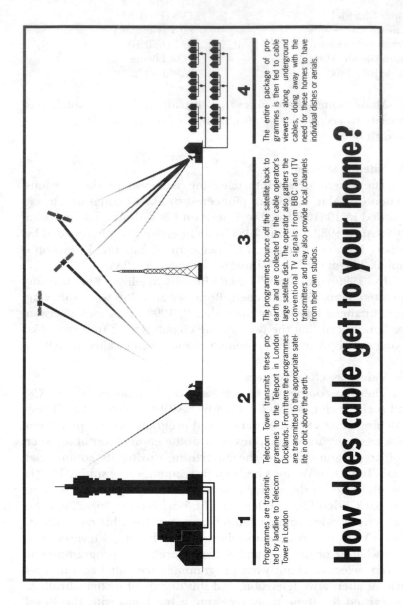

1

Programmes are transmitted by landline to Telecom Tower in London

2

Telecom Tower transmits these programmes to the Teleport in London Docklands. From there the programmes are transmitted to the appropriate satellite in orbit above the earth.

3

The programmes bounce off the satellite back to earth and are collected by the cable operator's large satellite dish. The operator also gathers the conventional TV signals from BBC and ITV transmitters and may also provide local channels from their own studios.

4

The entire package of programmes is then fed to cable viewers along underground cables, doing away with the need for these homes to have individual dishes or aerials.

How does cable get to your home?

Figure 4.3 *How does cable get to your home?*

July than had been forecast for the whole year! Britain has more VCRs per household than any other country.

27. Video games

Although these may have been over-sold, video games remain an important aspect of the video scene, and some of the more ingenious and popular software such as chess will doubtless survive as usurpers of regular screen time.

28. Home computers

The popular micro-computers such as the BBC Acorn require a visual display unit, and unless the user has a second TV receiver or a monitor, he will use the domestic set. A lot of time can be consumed operating a home computer—at the expense of regular TV!

29. Videotext

Again, this form of alternative television has been with us for some time and while British Telecom's Prestel Viewdata, introduced in 1979, has not been widely taken up by domestic viewers, an increasing number of sets equipped to receive the BBC's Ceefax and commercial television's Oracle systems have entered British homes. With these systems pages of information can be called up and viewed, and while they are being watched the regular programme is eliminated. When the commercials are on it is very convenient to transfer to Oracle or Ceefax to check on the latest news, the weather forecast, sporting results or even one's horoscope. The sound can be left on so that one knows when the programme is resumed after the commercials. Again, the advertiser has been penalised.

Prestel and Oracle can be used for advertising purposes, but only in computer-held text form and not with film-like commercials. Prestel, however, lends itself admirably to home shopping. We shall return to this in Chapter 8 when discussing direct response, but mention can be made here of the use made by Harrods and Debenhams to sell goods either from the shop or by using a response frame ordering facility, of tele-booking services for booking hotel rooms, and tele-ordering systems for mail-order clubs, all using the telephone-linked Prestel Viewdata response facility.

30. Advertisements on video

There are advertisers who offer videos about their products or services, and obviously they can only be viewed to the exclusion of the regular programme. This means that a small advertiser who would never use television can virtually absorb television time on domestic sets at no airtime cost to himself. A number of advertisers have offered videos in their press advertisements. Tourist organisations often supply videos through travel agencies which may be borrowed by potential holiday-makers.

31. Public relations videos

There are also numerous public relations videos ranging from house journals which employees can enjoy watching at home to those issued by voluntary bodies as diverse as the Royal Society for the Protection of Birds to the British Diabetic Association. These can absorb a considerable amount of normal viewing time.

32. Learning programmes

There are also video versions of distance learning courses which can be watched via VCR and TV receiver.

33. Developing countries

Video has its special uses in developing countries, and a clever use of video has been made in Malawi where there is no television. The Lonrho textile company David Whitehead & Sons (Malawi) Ltd has created its own video studio to make tapes of fashion shows which it takes round the country to show villagers the range of materials available for dressmaking. The company has a special demonstration vehicle, and one side drops down to make a stage on which models display dresses made from Whitehead materials.

Cinema

34. Introduction

In Britain, the size of the cinema audience and the number of cinemas fell dramatically with the arrival of television in the 1950s, and the make-up of audiences became a predominantly young one which made the cinema a special medium for advertisers wishing to reach young people.

However, cinema admissions began to rise in the 1980s and 1989 saw the fifth consecutive year of growth with an annual total of 88 million for those cinemas taking screen advertising according to the Cinema Advertising Association. This represented a weekly average of 1.69 million admissions which was 12.7 per cent up on 1988. Admissions continued to rise in 1990 and by June of this year the moving annual average was 1.77 million a week. The number of cinema screens has also increased mainly due to the opening of multiplex cinemas. First introduced in the USA by AMC, multiplex cinemas were first introduced into Britain with the Point at Milton Keynes in 1985, and consist of purpose-built cinema sites with from six to 14 cinemas with seating of around 150–250, supported by adjacent facilities such as shops and cafés.

By the end of 1989 the number of UK cinema screens taking advertising had risen to 1,424 and 1,530 by June 1990. Currently there are more than 1,600 cinema screens recording more than 95 million admissions annually.

35. Advantages of the cinema

There are certain characteristics which distinguish the cinema from other media although it shares many of the advantages enjoyed by television such as its realism through the combination of sound, colour and action.

(a) *Captive audience.* There is truly a captive audience since the cinema is purpose built and there are none of the distractions surrounding the home viewing of television.

(b) *Longer film.* The cinema commercial can be longer than the TV commercial, and so is less abrupt and kaleidoscopic.

(c) *Larger screen.* Being shown on a larger screen than that of the TV set, the picture is more dramatic, realistic and impactive.

(d) *No interruption of programme.* There are no commercial breaks, the commercials being shown as a complete segment before or after films, and since they are shown the same number of times as the films, they are seen by each audience.

(e) *Zoning.* While TV commercials can be shown in selected regions, cinema commercials can be shown in selected towns.

(f) *Entertainment atmosphere.* Cinema advertising is seen in a pleasant, receptive entertainment atmosphere, whether this be in a public cinema, in the shipboard cinemas as found on cruise ships, on aeroplanes with in-flight movies, in Forces cinemas, or on mobile cinema circuits.

36. Weaknesses

Like broadcast media, it is a transient medium and it relies on people remembering the message, and this may depend on how often the commercial is seen. However, research has shown that the recall rate can be as high as 50 per cent of cinema-goers interviewed being able to recall correctly a cinema commercial seen seven days earlier.

37. Characteristics of cinema audiences

The Cinema Advertising Association has since 1983 conducted annual audience research surveys through Carrick James Market Research. This study is known as the Cinema and Video Industry Audience Research, or CAVIAR. The following tables are reproduced from the CAVIAR 7 report for 1988–1989.

Frequency of cinema-going

Age	7–14	15–24	25–34	35+
Twice a month or more	6%	15%	4%	1%
Once a month	10%	15%	7%	2%
Once every 2–3 months	13%	18%	10%	3%
Two to three times a year	26%	19%	18%	8%
Once a year	16%	9%	13%	10%
Less often	13%	10%	20%	21%
Ever to go cinema	85%	86%	72%	44%

Annual trends

	1984	1986	1988	1989
All ever go to cinema	38%	53%	56%	60%
Ever go 7–14	73%	87%	84%	85%
Ever go 15–24	59%	82%	81%	86%
Ever go 25–34	49%	65%	64%	72%
Go once a month or more 15–24	15%	25%	27%	30%
25–34	4%	7%	10%	11%

These figures bear out the general observations made in **34**.

38. A special cinema service

Pearl and Dean and Rank Screen Advertising offer to advertisers their Audience Delivery Plan (ADP) whereby a specified audience is delivered at a fixed cost. The contractors monitor weekly cinema attendances and control the duration of a cinema screen advertising campaign so that the specified audience volume is achieved. This is rather like showing a TV commercial until sufficient audience ratings have been obtained, after which it is withdrawn.

General instructions on the length of the commercial, campaign areas, campaign period and number of cinema-goers to be reached are supplied by the advertiser. A minimum of one million cinema admissions nationally, or on an equivalent scale in ITV areas, must be booked and the campaign should be run for six to eight weeks. Weekly estimates of admissions are provided by Gallup, who are appointed by the Cinema Advertising Association for this purpose. The sample is made up of ten main circuits and 40 independent cinema owners who are checked every month.

Outdoor and transportation

39. Introduction

Outdoor advertising is probably the oldest form of advertising, and evidence of its use has been found on Greek and Roman remains. This is not surprising because even in those days public announcements had to be made, and a wall was as good a place as any on which to carve a message. It is believed that the spread of the Fire of London was assisted by the wooden signs which reached across the narrow streets of the City from one building to another.

In the 1930s the well-designed posters on the hoardings were nicknamed the 'poor man's art gallery'. Today, outdoor advertising has seen innovations such as the moving, illuminated newscaster, spelling out its message high up on a building, or the spangled flutter signs, common in Asiatic cities, which are now to be seen in London. There are also novel sites on which a number of different advertisements are produced on slats which revolve to show a succession of advertisements (e.g. ultravision sites). Thus movement is introduced into an otherwise static poster site.

Together with transportation advertising, this medium has shown great resilience and ingenuity as times, fortunes and regulations have had their impact on it. In developing countries it has proved to be an excellent means of advertising to multi-language, multi-ethnic or illiterate people. Even in countries like the Soviet Union and China, where commercial advertising might be least expected, there are illuminated signs and large posters. The streets of Hong Kong are overhung with scores of advertising signs erected on bamboo frames, and lit up at night. It is a universal medium.

40. Outdoor and transportation distinguished

The two are often put together and described collectively as 'outdoor' but a distinction is necessary. Outdoor advertising consists of posters of various sizes, and painted, metal and illuminated signs displayed on outdoor sites. Transportation advertising consists of similar advertising on the outside and inside of vehicles (which are moving sites), and on transportation property and premises which can include *indoor* sites such as within bus and railway stations, airports and seaports. The advertisements inside public transport vehicles and trains, and inside buildings where people are waiting, allow for more detailed messages or copy than is possible on posters and signs seen by passers-by.

41. Importance of outdoor advertising

This medium has special qualities different again from other media described in this book, and like all the others it has changed with the times, especially regarding its users. Its main use is for reminder advertisements, as with brands of FMCGs, or as secondary media to support press or TV campaigns on highways leading to the point-of-sale and so reiterating the main media campaign. Outdoor advertisements usually remain in position for weeks, months or even years, posters generally being pasted for periods of 13 weeks, while many painted or illuminated signs are more or less permanent fixtures. This long life in prominent positions gives the advertisements repetitive value.

42. Characteristics of outdoor advertising

There are many sizes of poster ranging from the small double crown bills to the large ones on hoardings or bulletin boards which are also known as supersites (*see* **44**). The characteristics of the medium may be summarised as follows.

(a) *Size and dominance.* Because of its size the poster dominates the view.

(b) *Colour.* Most posters are in full colour, with realistic scenes and pictures of products.

(c) *Brief copy.* Since the appeal is to people on the move, and the posters may be seen from a distance, the copy is usually confined to a slogan and a name printed in large letters.

(d) *Zoning.* Campaigns can be organised in selected regions or towns, but national campaigns can be planned using a minimum number of posters per town to secure maximum opportunities to see.

43. Weaknesses

Chiefly, the weaknesses of outdoor advertising are the inability to use much copy, possible damage by vandals or the weather, the lack of concentration on the message by passers-by, and the time it takes to design, print and exhibit posters.

44. Poster sizes and sites

The following are the standard poster sizes and kinds of site.

(a) *Double crown* : 762 mm × 508 mm (30 in. × 20 in.). This is the unit size for larger sizes, e.g. 16-sheet is the equivalent of 16 double crowns. Double crowns are used on billboards (e.g. newsbills outside newsagents shops) and on public information panels located on pavements and in shopping precincts. Note that in Britain 'billboard' refers to a small poster, whereas the Americans refer to large posters as billboards. It is also the size of the typical travel and airline poster displayed on travel agency premises.

(b) *Quad crown* : 762 mm × 1,016 mm (30 in. × 40 in.). This is a size often used to advertise entertainments.

(c) *4-sheet* : 1,016 mm × 1,524 mm (40 in. × 60 in.). Often printed on vandal-proof vinyl and nicknamed the 'pedestrian housewife poster' because of its use in shopping precincts.

(d) *16-sheet* : 3,048 mm × 2,032 mm (10 ft. × 6 ft. 8 in.). The standard upright poster seen on the hoardings.

(e) *32-sheet* : 3,048 mm x 4,064 mm (10 ft. × 13 ft. 4 in.).

(f) *48-sheet* : 3,048 mm x 6,096 mm (10 ft. × 20 ft.).

(g) *64-sheet* : 3,048 mm x 8,128 mm (10 ft. × 26 ft. 8 in.).

(h) For *bulletin boards* or *supersites* (which are specially built on large sites, often set out in gardens and sometimes floodlit at night) the measurements are slightly different from 64-sheet, being 9 ft. 6 in. deep by 27 ft. (2,897 × 8,230 mm), with even larger ones measuring 36 ft. (10,973 mm) or 45 ft. (13,716 mm) wide.

45. Scanachrome poster

A new style of poster, or rather display material, is that produced by Long Signs of Skelmersdale and Woking which uses the artistic Scanachrome process to produce backcloths, scenery, murals, exhibition displays and promotional advertising. It lends itself to the need for a single poster or for individual posters for different sites. Paper, fabric-backed vinyl and paper-backed vinyl fabrics can be applied like wallpaper or adhered to mounting plaques. Being durable, they can be used indoors or outdoors, and can be seen at underground railway stations and in shopping centres. Scanachrome is not a photographic process, but a system of making very large 'computer painted' colour enlargements.

46. Importance of transportation advertising

This medium is seen by the travelling public who have the time while waiting at terminals or stations or while travelling on public transport to absorb messages. In fact, reading advertisements may help pass the time. Consequently, transportation advertisements, unless perhaps where they are on the exteriors of vehicles (e.g. buses, trams, delivery vans or taxi-cabs), can be much more detailed.

In Britain, a very important part of transportation advertising is the extensive *London Underground railway system* which carries millions of passengers daily, and lesser systems in Liverpool, Newcastle and Glasgow. On the Underground there is a great variety of sites in the vestibules, corridors and lifts, on the escalators and on the platforms. On the wall across the tracks and facing the platforms are 16-sheet posters, but most wall posters are quad crown, with framed cards on the walls of the escalator tunnel. In the trains there are cards above the windows. Since many travellers are women going to and from work, this is a popular medium for women's goods, while the entertainment industry makes regular use of quad crown wall posters.

A number of countries like Hong Kong and Singapore also have underground railway systems. An innovation on the Hong Kong Mass Transit Railway (MTR) is the recycled plastic ticket, on which advertisement space is sold. MTR station walls also carry large illuminated photographic posters which are very attractive.

A special feature, found less in London today than in other parts of the world, is the painted bus or tram monopolised by a single advertiser as in Hong Kong. British Transport Advertising Ltd now calls the painted bus the ColourBus, and these buses are restricted to one trade in any one bus depot area. A second kind of bus available to a single advertiser is the UniBus on which the advertiser may have a single continuous advertisement band, 80 ft. in length (24.4 m), which encircles the bus, whether double deck or single deck.

Taxi-cab advertising, with plates on the nearside front door, is a popular medium in London and regional cities although a drawback is that such vehicles must not drive on roads through the Royal Parks.

47. Characteristics of transportation advertising

Some have been mentioned already, but ones special to the medium are as follows.

(a) *Variety of sites and sizes.* Throughout the road, rail, sea and air passenger and goods transportation system there is a great variety of sites and sizes so that the medium lends itself to the campaigns of many advertisers, local, metropolitan, national and—in some cases such as airlines—international.

(b) *Selectivity.* Because the medium has so many sites at different locations or routes it is possible to select the ones most suitable for a campaign. Like the special positions in the press, or the time-of-day segments on radio and TV, the costs of sites will relate to the volume of traffic. For example, it costs more to advertise at Piccadilly Circus Underground station than at a station on the outskirts of London. This facility also makes zoning possible if the advertiser wishes to concentrate a campaign on a certain area of London or of the country.

(c) *Short-term campaigns.* Short-term advertising is more possible with transportation than with outdoor advertising, as posters are usually exhibited for 13 weeks, and advertisers may seek to obtain particularly prominent outdoor sites on a 'till cancelled' or permanent basis. Transportation, on the other hand, is useful for local traders, cinemas and theatres who may change their posters every week, or for exhibitions which may be advertised for perhaps only a month.

(d) *A mobile medium.* A special feature of buses, trams, taxis and trains is that as passengers change there is a cumulative audience who see the interior advertising, while exterior advertising is seen by yet another cumulative audience as the vehicle travels along its route. This is very different from the regular readership of various publications. While there is no control over who might see transportation advertising, it is likely to reach a large number of people repeatedly over a period. In a highly urbanised country like Britain, where 80 per cent of the population live in towns and either use or are aware of public transport, this medium offers penetration and coverage of the mass market, yet it also offers opportunity for specialists as already shown regarding the London Underground.

48. Weaknesses

On above ground and underground railway stations it is necessary to display sufficient posters for people to notice them, and the same applies to roof cards since they appear in separate compartments of the train. On some routes it is possible that there are irregular volumes of passenger traffic, and that at peak times when most people are travelling it is less easy to see advertisements in crowded compartments.

An advertisement rate may appear to be modest, but it will be expensive if the advertisement appears in empty compartments or on deserted platforms. The same production costs apply whatever the size of the audience or the attention paid to the advertisement. However, in central London the Underground has become increasingly busy throughout the day, and is less affected by the fluctuations of commuter traffic than above ground trains.

Progress test 4

1.   What classes of media may be called (*a*) above-the-line and (*b*) below-the-line? (**2**)

2.   What are primary and secondary media? (**3**)

3.   Name the British national newspapers, and give an approximation of their individual circulations. (**7**)

4.   What are the main advantages of the press as an advertising medium? (**9**)

5.   What are the main disadvantages of the press as an advertising medium? (**10**)

6.   Explain the expression 'Independent Local Radio'. (**11**)

7.   What are the advantages of television advertising? (**19**)

8.   Describe some of the forms of alternative television. (**24–32**)

9.   What is the predominant characteristic of the British cinema audience? (**34, 37**)

10. Distinguish between *outdoor* and *transportation* advertising (**40**)

11. Describe the special characteristics of underground railway advertising. (**46**)

5
Advertising media: below-the-line

Introduction

1. Definition

Traditionally, 'below-the-line' is the term used to describe all the other advertising media which exist in addition to the five described in Chapter 4. The difference between above-the-line media (sometimes called media advertising) and below-the-line media is explained in 4:**2**. Separate chapters are given to *sales promotion, sponsorship, direct mail* (with direct response marketing), and *exhibitions.* This still leaves us with a great many other media to discuss in this chapter. They range from essential media such as catalogues to those which exploit special opportunities and some which may be considered as fringe media.

The mistake is sometimes made—even in the trade press—of including public relations under below-the-line. Since public relations is not a form of advertising, has its own budget, and is usually conducted by separate personnel (either in-house or consultancy) it has no place in below-the-line advertising media.

2. Importance

The reader is reminded that below-the-line are not necessarily inferior or minor media, and for some advertisers they may be more effective than above-the-line media. It is up to the advertiser to decide whether a medium is value for money and fits his campaign, and not simply be persuaded by a salesman.

Types of media and their applications

3. Sales literature

Many goods and services are more easily sold if the customer can be given explanatory literature. This may be offered in an advertisement, accompany a mailing shot, be supplied with a product, or be available at the point of sale. There are many forms of sales print, including the following.

(a) *Leaflet.* This is a single sheet of unfolded paper.

(b) *Folder.* As the name implies, this is a sheet of print—which may be quite large—which is reduced to a convenient size by means of folds, or which may be folded concertina fashion to form a number of separate pages without need for binding. A good reason for folding may be so that the item fits into an envelope for mailing, or is easy to carry in the pocket.

(c) *Brochures and booklets.* If multiples of four pages are used they can be bound by some form of stitching, while single sheets can be bound by the process of 'perfect binding' when the left-hand edges are glued and the whole bound in a cover.

(d) *Broadsheet.* This is really another kind of folder which unfolds to a size similar to a large newspaper page. Maps, charts and small posters may be produced in this style. Note that this term also refers to a large page newspaper as distinct from a tabloid.

(e) *Catalogues.* These are brochures which describe and often illustrate the range of products available and give their prices. They can be of any size from pocket-size to something resembling a telephone directory according to the nature of the business.

(f) *Timetables.* These are generally brochures, and may be of handy size like airline timetables, or even small folders like those for bus and railway services, while those embracing all rail or air services are large, bound books.

(g) *Picture postcards.* Useful publicity can be gained by supplying customers with postcards as with hotels, airlines and shipping lines. People also collect them.

(h) *Hotel stationery.* Letterheadings and printed envelopes placed in hotel rooms are not only a service but a useful form of advertising.

(i) *Stuffers.* These are leaflets placed (or 'stuffed') in the package.

They contain instructions on how to use a product, and can also be used to advertise the product or sister products.

(j) *Diaries.* Whether desk or pocket, they are of long-lasting advertising value since they are referred to throughout the year, and refills or new diaries can be supplied every year as a timely Christmas gift.

(k) *Telephone number reminders.* These can be supplied as hanging cards, or message pads, and can occupy a permanent place by the telephone.

(l) *Swing tags.* Attached by card to products of many kinds, they identify the product and may give advice on how to use or take care of it.

(m) *Guarantee cards.* In addition to requiring the customer to register ownership for guarantee purposes, these cards can be used to request purchasing details for research purposes. It can be very useful when planning advertising to know *who* buys the product, for whom, and whether it is the first or a succeeding purchase of the company's products.

(n) *Price lists and order forms.* These may be combined or separate items. Order forms need to be designed so that they are easy to complete and produce accurate information such as the correct total amount of the order or payment, and the full address of the sender. Orders cannot be fulfilled if the information given is incomplete. For use with computers, it is necessary to request information clearly so that the customer is not confused. If credit or charge card facilities are offered, it must be simple for the customer to state their card number, and it may be necessary to illustrate the cards which are accepted.

(o) *Competition entry forms.* These are important pieces of sales literature requiring very careful writing and design so that they are easy to complete. (*See also* 6:**5**).

4. Point-of-sale (POS) display material

Some of the sales literature described in **3** may be distributed as give-away material at point-of-sale (point-of-purchase), but in this section we refer to material which is designed specifically to attract attention and encourage sales. It may also identify the premises as a source of supply.

Display space is scarce in shops, and some goods or services are seasonal so that the possible period of display is also limited.

The supplier has to budget carefully and avoid waste. It is best if material is supplied against requests, or displays are arranged by the sales representative. Some suppliers produce broadsheets illustrating available display material, together with an order form. It can be very costly and often wasteful to distribute display material speculatively.

Again, many examples can be given, some being more suitable for certain advertisers than others.

(a) *Mobiles.* Not to be confused with travelling exhibitons and demonstrations (as occur in developing countries, including mobile cinemas), mobiles at POS consist of ingenious cut-out displays suspended on a string from the shop ceiling so that they move with the air currents. They are useful in supermarkets where there is limited display space.

(b) *Posters.* Crown and double crown posters are a familiar feature of shop displays, decorating walls, doors and windows. In addition to colourful pictorial posters, there are those produced by silk screen in bright colours which stores use to announce special offers. Some firms (e.g. insurance companies) supply stock posters bearing their names with blank space which can be overprinted to advertise local events such as amateur theatricals or flower shows.

(c) *Pelmets.* One of the oldest forms of display material which can have a very long life, pelmets are paper strips which can be pasted along the top edge of a window.

(d) *Dummy packs.* Empty display cases, packets and bottles are useful for window displays, especially when real products would deteriorate if left in a window for any period, or too much stock would otherwise be tied up in this way.

(e) *Dumpers and dump bins.* Decorated with the name of the product, they are filled with the branded product and placed near check-outs in supermarkets to induce impulse-buying.

(f) *Wire stands.* Either self-standing or small enough to stand on the counter or hang near the cash register, these contain a stock of the product and encourage self-service. They should carry the manufacturer's name-plate to encourage refilling with the same brand, otherwise there is a danger of the retailer finding them convenient for the display of other or rival goods.

(g) *Showcards.* Strutted or hanging, and printed on card or metal, these are portable displays which a retailer can move about the shop or use from time to time, and they can often have a very long life, especially if strongly made. Some, such as those advertising credit card and other services, may remain permanent displays on, say, a hotel reception desk.

(h) *Dispenser boxes.* Rather like showcards, they are portable and may remain in position permanently if they contain leaflets which satisfy a regular demand. A typical use is for the display of insurance prospectuses, tourist leaflets and official forms. There are also very attractive free-standing or wall-mounted ones made of clear acrylic which reveal contents, unlike cardboard or wooden ones which reveal only the top of the literature. They are supplied by Showcard Systems of Letchworth.

(i) *Clocks.* Again, this is a popular and permanent form of POS display, every glance at the time disclosing the advertiser's name.

(j) *Trade figures.* Johnnie Walker, the Michelin Man and the Sandeman figure have been used in displays for decades. They appear as moulded figures and cardboard cut-outs, with various versions of the Michelin rubber man. Some figures are static, others are moving models.

(k) *Models.* Very realistic because of their three-dimensional form are scale models, especially when the real subject is too large or impossible to display. Good examples are ships and aircraft.

(l) *Working models.* These always fascinate, for few people can resist stopping and staring at a model which is active. One which was very amusing was a model baby elephant which bounced up and down in an armchair to demonstrate how well the chair was sprung.

(m) *Illuminated displays.* In a similar way, as when the lights go on and off or change colour, the lighted sign in a window attracts attention, particularly of window-shoppers and passers-by after dark when the shop is closed.

(n) *Display stands.* According to the trade these may be standard or custom-built, and they may be enclosed, perhaps velvet-lined for expensive products. They give exclusiveness to goods. They can also be simple stands to hold small items like confectionery.

(o) *Dispenser cards/packs.* These may be complete in themselves for hanging on the wall like cards from which packets of nuts are detached, or they may be individual self-display dispenser bubble packs, bags or sachets hanging on hooks for items like toys, razor blades, music cassettes, ironmongery, confectionery, or ball-point pens. The hooks may be on the retailer's wall or on a special stand or fitting supplied by the manufacturer who thus provides permanent POS material that permits self-service.

(p) *Display outers.* Very useful for small items like confectionery sold in units, packets of soup, or other compact single items, display outers consist of containers holding a quantity of items, the lid folding back to produce a display. The carton can then be placed on the counter or shelf and goods sold from it. This is very economical and effective since the original container becomes its own display piece.

(g) *Crowners.* When bottled goods are displayed, collars or crowners can be slipped over the necks, either to state the price or to display a slogan. They are used mainly for soft and alcoholic drinks.

(r) *Stickers and transfers.* Often these are carried by the sales representative who positions them on various surfaces such as walls, doors, windows and even cash registers. They are supplied in a pull-off form.

(s) *Cash mats.* Because of their utility—preventing coins from rolling off the counter—they are likely to be welcomed by retailers and kept in a regular position.

(t) *Samples.* Sampling will be referred to again under sales promotion (*see* 6:**20**), but it may be point-of-sale strategy for the manufacturer to supply free samples, perhaps in special packs like sachets of coffee or miniature bottles of wine.

(u) *Drip mats/coasters.* Whether made of cork, aluminium or paper, these can be used in bars, cafés and other catering situations such as on board airliners, placing prominent advertising in a very convenient form. They have become popular as collector's items, perpetuating their advertising value.

(v) *Ashtrays.* These are much used by drinks and tobacco manufacturers, and are freely distributed to bars and restaurants where customers drink and smoke. The advertisements are usually silk-screen printed on to the various shaped trays made from a variety of materials.

(w) *Tickets.* Advertisers such as Coca-Cola take space on transportation tickets including airline boarding passes, which is very appropriate when the product is immediately available.

(x) *Shelf edging.* This has become a very popular POS display on the edges of shelves facing customers across the counter or bar.

(y) *In-store advertising.* Using videos and TV screens, public address systems, electronic newscasters with colourful LED letters, trolley ads and other devices, products and special offers can be announced to shoppers in the shop. Video ads may also be introduced into juke boxes when these are played.

(z) *Menu cards.* The supply of menu cards printed with the advertiser's name, logo and slogan is a method of advertising long used in the food and drinks trades. Some are more elaborate with magazine material which is changed from time to time to maintain the interest of regular customers. Menu cards provide a service to both caterer and customer.

5. Aerial advertising

While this may be regarded as 'outdoor' advertising, it is not usually classed as above-the-line. It is a medium which exploits elements of drama and surprise, involving curiosity. The forms of aerial advertising available in different countries depend on the laws which apply, especially as regards low flying over urban areas, on the ingenuity of promoters, and sometimes on what is peculiar to or possible in certain countries. For instance, if there is a coastline it is possible to carry aerial advertisements low over the sea in view of holidaymakers on the beach. The following are examples of this medium.

(a) *Sky writing.* Emitting a trail of smoke, an aircraft writes a word or words in the sky. This does, of course, require a clear sky and is limited by the weather.

(b) *Sky shouting.* In the aftermath of Rhodesian UDI, when the army used helicopters and loud-hailers to address villagers, this technique of shouting messages from the sky has been converted into an advertising medium in Zimbabwe.

(c) *Sky banners.* One of the oldest forms of aerial advertising is the use of a slow aircraft to trail an advertising banner. A spectacular form seen in Holland is to have three aircraft tied together, each trailing a banner.

(d) *Lighted aircraft, airships.* At night aircraft can carry illuminated messages on the undersides of wings, while the Goodyear airships are a familiar sight in the USA and in Europe. Normally, Goodyear airships do not carry advertising over Britain but on the eve of the Royal Wedding in 1981 London read 'Loyal Greetings' in lights on the side of the Goodyear *Europa.*

(e) *Projected advertisements.* A few attempts have been made to project advertisements on the night sky with laser beams, or with a searchlight effect on low cloud.

(f) *Tethered inflatables.* Inflatables can be balloons or small airships (like military observation balloons), or designed in the shape of trade figures or product containers such as bottles. A large coloured balloon is a very noticeable object, and it can be a short-term advertising device to draw attention to an event. Sussex farmers have used balloons to attract motorists to pick their own fruit. They can also be used to advertise to crowds at outdoor events, which may have the added advantage that they are picked up by television cameras. Spherical balloons can be tethered to marker buoys in the sea off holiday beaches.

6. Calendars

Here we have a very old medium, one that is popular all over the world and has produced some famous calendars which have become collectors' items with collections like Pirelli's reaching the auction rooms. It is significant that Pirelli gave up using the famous calendars a few years ago only to return with a new series. They must have been missed! Calendars have a mixture of public relations goodwill and advertising reminder value, and so may be used for either or both purposes. They last a year, and are displayed prominently, and referred to repeatedly.

Some advertisers may reproduce individual calendars, while others take advantage of stock calendars on which they can have their name and business details overprinted. Firms like Bemrose, Eversheds and K. & J. Lockwood offer excellent designs which they change each year. Evershed have won international awards with their designs. Calendars take the following forms.

(a) *Pictorial.* Probably the most popular, the pictorial calendar can be of one, six or twelve sheets with a similar number of pictures. For some trades, the glamour girl calendar may be appropriate, for others, landscapes, paintings or cartoons may be preferred. For international use, months can be printed in more than one language.

(b) *Block.* This kind of calendar consists of a block of tear-off dates.

(c) *Digital.* Possibly combined with a clock and usually electric or electronic, the digital calendar can look modern and efficient.

(d) *Scroll.* Hanging vertically like a scroll, this type displays all the dates of the year.

(e) *Quarterly.* Here we have a clever idea because the quarterly calendar can be issued during the year at the right time, and avoids competition with the conventional calendars distributed at Christmas.

7.   Plastic records, audio and video cassettes

Increasing use is made of these devices, especially with the widespread availability of tape and video recorders. They can be used for sampling purposes as *Reader's Digest* and Linguaphone do (*see* Chapter 8, Fig. 8.2), or as Record Tokens have done with the offer of an audio tape on promotion tapes. Plastic records are easily sent with direct mail shots, and audio and video cassettes can be offered in press advertisements (*see* Fig. 5.1).

8.   Adbags and carrier bags

Both can carry advertising messages, adbags being the more durable type of in-flight or sports bag, the carrier bag being a plastic one supplied by a retailer to carry home shopping and having a shorter life. Both convey the advertiser's name to countless people who see the bag being carried about. This advertising can be well-placed if a sportsman carries his gear to a match.

9.   Body media

This is perhaps an astonishing medium because people, especially teenagers, are willing to buy and wear clothing advertising radio stations, drinks and other commercial interests. Guinness have advertised their named shirts in the weekend colour magazines.

Specialist firms provide a comprehensive range of promotional leisure clothing such as T-shirts, sweatshirts, caps, hats, headbands, visors, pullovers, jogging suits, bodywarmers, anoraks, scarves, umbrellas, rain-suits, ties, squares, aprons, rally jackets, sportshirts, light-weight jackets, tracksuits, ski wear, sashes, towels, and bar towels as well as various bags and cooler bags.

Figure 5.1 *This advertisement for Fidelity International shows how audio cassettes can be used in direct response marketing.*

Staff and members' ties are another popular form of body media which are mainly a way of creating corporate identity. They may have emblems printed by silk-screen on polyester, or woven into fabrics such as silk.

10. Flags

This is a medium which is particularly popular in certain countries like Germany where premises such as motor-car showrooms fronting a main highway attract attention with a long row of masts with large flags run up. On a lesser scale are the smaller flags projected from shops and kiosks advertising, say, ice-cream. There are also company flags which adorn and identify factories and other company premises. Not only are they colourful but they flap in the breeze, and therefore have attention-getting movement.

11. Playing cards

Another old medium, with Carta Mundi and Waddington as well-known suppliers, are packs of playing cards bearing advertisements on the backs of the cards.

12. Bookmatches

In a similar way to menu cards, bookmatches provide a service to the customer, as well as advertising the proprietor such as a hotelier or restaurateur. They are a form of point-of-sale material. Designs can be clever and of different size and shape container with various kinds of matches.

13. Give-aways

Under this heading come numerous gifts and novelties, some of which may have genuine usefulness and therefore long life. Probably the most popular are pens and key-rings, but there are many more to mention only pencils, rulers, paper-knives, penknives, bottle openers, wallets, card-holders, calculators, drinking mugs and acrylic blocks containing souvenirs.

14. Paper-clips

Perhaps one of the best ideas in recent years is the plastic ad-clip, a colourful advertising paper-clip which can convey an advertising message with correspondence and become reusable since the modest paper-clip is rarely thrown away. (People even make chains of paper-clips for fun.) Produced by Westfield of Birmingham, they are supplied in tubs containing 100 Super Ad-Clips. There are also larger Midi Ad-Clips, and even bigger Giant and Giant Heart Ad-Clips.

15. Video media

Video is becoming the most versatile medium, emerging as an alternative mode of domestic television, and appearing in various ways at the point-of-sale to demonstrate, for example, new motor-cars or give 'film' presentations of holiday attractions.

The Post Office videoservice is an ingenious example of the use of video in retail premises. In large post offices where there is a single queue leading up to an indicator light which directs customers to the free counter clerk, a large TV-like monitor gives a continuous presentation of video ads. Some are for Post Office services but other advertisers have included Servowarm central heating, Pentel pens, Canon cameras, Stork margarine, CreditPlan loans, Pilot pens, Ordnance Survey maps, Thomas Cook, Truprint and Bonusprint film processing. The video commercial usually refers to leaflets which are displayed in dispensers on the premises.

16. Book advertising

Advertisements were common in novels many years ago, and when Penguins were first introduced by Alan Lane in the 1930s, advertisements were included in the paperbacks. Now *Burke's Peerage* have reintroduced advertising into popular books and, by so doing, have helped to subsidise the prices of the books. Another form of book advertising is the insertion of a loose card, as conducted by some insurance companies, readers often retaining this as a bookmark.

17. Milk bottle advertising

A fairly new medium is advertising on glass milk bottles, so that the advertisement is delivered to thousands of homes. The advertisements are silk screen printed on the bottles by the manufacturers (e.g. Rockware) who use a Strutz decorating machine. These are short-necked bottles which have a better survival rate than the former tall ones, and so the message persists for up to 24 trips. It is a means of repeatedly advertising in 17 million doorstep delivery homes in Britain with a potential of 36 million adults. Minimum quantities of Rockware doorstopper milk bottles for a regional campaign is 250,000, or 1 million for a national campaign. The dairies benefit because bottles carrying advertisements cost them less to buy. A typical milk bottle advertisement is shown in Fig. 5.2. This advertisement was produced in the red, brown and yellow of the Mars bar wrapping and the Mars logo was used for the brand name.

COOL 'EM
Mars
Cool and Delicious
Straight from
The Fridge

Figure 5.2 *Milk bottle advertisement.*

18. Badges
The badge, usually bearing a logo, has a multiplicity of uses such as product identity (e.g. the badge on the bonnet of a motor-car), personal identity, enamelled plaques and so on. Probably the best known producers of badges of every type are Fattorini of Birmingham.

19. Stickers
Again, these have a variety of uses such as on shop windows, motor-car windows or for application to stationery. A variation on this is the transfer.

Progress test 5

1. List the main classes of below-the-line media. (**3–19**)
2. What are (*a*) mobiles; (*b*) dumpers and dump bins; (*c*) display outers; (*d*) crowns; (*e*) shelf edgings? (**5**)
3. Describe the various kinds of aerial advertising. (**5**)
4. What is the advertising value of the calendar? (**6**)
5. How can audio cassettes be used as advertising media? Give an example. (**7**)
6. What are body media? (**9**)
7. How can flags be used for advertising purposes? (**10**)
8. Describe some uses of video tapes as advertising media. (**15**)
9. How has advertising been introduced with glass milk bottles? (**17**)

6

Sales promotion

Growing importance of sales promotion

1. Definitions

The term 'sales promotion' has become widely accepted as covering special promotional schemes, usually of limited duration, at the point-of-sale or point-of-purchase. Such schemes were formerly referred to as 'merchandising', and the old term is still used in some quarters, for example by the sales departments of television companies. However, with the growing influence of the Institute of Sales Promotion, the existence of the British Code of Sales Promotion Practice (*see* 16:**40**), and the appearance of sales promotion features in the trade press, plus specialist journals such as *Sales Promotion*, the old expression 'merchandising' in the promotional sense is falling into disuse.

The advent of the single European market, in which countries some forms of give-away or premium offer sales promotion are illegal, led in 1990 to the creation of a European Code of Conduct under the European Federation of Sales Promotion. (*See* also 16:**42**.)

2. Reasons for growth

Sales promotion has grown enormously in recent years, and sales promotion consultancies have reported record business. The chief reasons for this are outlined below.

(a) The desire of advertisers, often worried by the high cost of media advertising (e.g. TV), which has increased faster than the rate of inflation, to find more cost-effective forms of promotion.

(b) The growth of huge supermarket chains and out-of-town superstores and the need for aggressive on-the-shelf competitive promotions, both to sell in and to sell out.

(c) The opportunities provided by supermarkets, hypermarkets and large-scale mixed retailing to promote on the premises.

(d) The need to propel sales, both to satisfy the cash flow of retailers and to maintain output from high volume production plants.

(e) The availability of greater expertise in creating sales promotion schemes, as demonstrated by the emergence and growth of successful sales promotion consultancies. They have filled the gap left by traditional advertising agencies which were reluctant to indulge in other than commission-paying above-the-line media advertising.

(f) The goodwill aspect of sales promotion which tends to bring the manufacturer closer to the retailer. Media advertising tends to be remote whereas sales promotion is more personal, linking the manufacturer with the customer at the place of sale wherever this may be.

(g) The introduction of a certain fun and excitement into promotions which customers can enjoy as participants. This, again, is quite different from media advertising with its strident clamour to buy.

(h) The ability, with small unit FMCGs, to encourage impulse buying and attract first-time buyers.

(i) The extension of sales promotion into new areas such as financial institutions promotion (e.g. banking and charge cards), and to the promotion of consumer durables from cameras to motor-cars, plus many services such as holidays, travel, hotels and restaurants. It is by no means limited to the supermarkets and High Street stores (*see* **3**). It has also been extended to multinational and international marketing of products such as beer.

(j) The growth of direct response marketing which often uses sales promotion devices and gimmicks as inserts in mailings, or as rewards and bonuses to buyers. There has been an interesting marriage between the two as when an insurance company offers a free camera or clock if an insurance policy is taken out.

3. Sales promotion consultancy clients

The importance today of sales promotion is borne out by the fact that the clients of British sales promotion consultancies include names as diverse as Allied Breweries Overseas Trading, American Express, Bass, Birds Eye, Booker Health Foods, Boots, British Airways, Citicorp Travellers Cheques, Dunhill, Duracell, Guinness Overseas, Hertz, The Jamaica Tourist Board, Lloyds Bank, LRC Products, L'Oreal, Pan Books, Peugeot Talbot, Royal Worcester, Sterling Health, Seiko, Smirnoff (Europe), Times Newspapers and Hiram Walker.

Types of sales promotion scheme

4. Variety of choice

A remarkable variety of sales promotion techniques is available, and a walk around a supermarket will reveal the large number of very different schemes which are operating simultaneously. Equally, at one's bank, travel agency, building society, filling station, hotel or corner shop all manner of schemes will be apparent. Often, they work on the principle that few people can resist a free gift, price reduction or special offer. The appeal is basically to greed!

In recent years there have been changes in the popularity of certain types of offer, while some older kinds have returned. There are still premium offers which require the sending in of cash and proof of purchase, but competitive prices in High Street shops have made some of the offers of household articles less attractive (*see* **3:24**). Moreover, offers with immediate take-up while shopping have become more popular than those requiring the effort of mailing in. There has also been the innovation of charity promotions (*see* **16**), while free draws have been introduced by Woolworth and some petrol companies such as BP, Esso, Mobil and Shell (*see* 16:21). The matching halves of coupons idea has been revived with original versions such as Mobil's Scrabble and Shell's Mastermind.

While sales promotion schemes may induce habit buying or the buying of quantities to the exclusion of other brands, they can also induce frenetic brand switching and the loss of brand loyalty. The 'cherry picker' is the person who goes round a store selecting the special offers, probably irrespective of brand. On the other hand, sales promotion encourages greater competitiveness at the point-of-sale which can, of course, widen consumer choice and encourage people to make experimental first-time buys. All these implications have to be considered carefully by the promoter of any of the sales promotion schemes discussed below.

5. Competitions and free prize draws

Prize contests depend for success on the value or originality of the prize, and perhaps on the additional chances of winning offered by consolation prizes. The entry requirement can be proof of purchase such as a token or entry coupon detached from the pack, extra entries requiring extra purchases. To be legal, contests require an element of skill (*see* 16:**22**), there should be sufficient permutations of, say, answers to avoid division of the prize and a secondary part of the contest (such as 'why I wish to win' statement) may be adopted as a tie-breaker in the event of the main contest producing more than one winner. Contests should be organised with adequate time for proper adjudication, and there should be publicised announcement of results.

Competitions should not be inhibited by the nature of the prize. For example, a cash prize or a motor-car may be more attractive than something like a holiday which may not suit the winner's personal affairs and may be an embarrassment. With some prizes such as holidays, cash alternatives are seldom possible. However, it depends where the contest is being held; in a developing country a motor-car might be inappropriate whereas a holiday abroad could be very attractive. Money prizes are usually universally acceptable, as evident by the international success of football pools, sweepstakes and public lotteries.

There is a distinction between a prize *competition* which requires an element of skill, and a *free draw* which depends on chance. To avoid the illegality of a lottery, no proof of purchase or in fact any purchase is required, and the promoter offers prizes to lucky entrants. One football pool promoter, for instance, offers free flights on Concorde whether or not the entrant invests in the pools.

6. Self-liquidating premium offers

The meaning of the expression 'self-liquidating' is not that slow selling goods or old stock are sold off cheaply, but that special lines are bought by the promoter and offered at a premium (i.e. less than normal retail price) which will liquidate the cost. Many such lines are, however, made up specially and are not available in the shops, and care has to be taken not to make a false reference to retail value. Premium offers have the irresistible appeal of the bargain that must not be forsaken.

7. Mail-in free offers

Here, no payment is required, only proof of purchase or perhaps a token payment to cover postage and packing. Care is necessary to control demand and supply, and it is best to limit the offer in some way. John Player & Sons met disaster with their King Size cigarette offer of a free lighter. To their cost, they were obliged to distribute 2,250,000 lighters each costing the company £1! (*See* also **32**.)

8. Free gifts with goods

The gift is usually attached to the product, as with a toothbrush attached to a carton of toothpaste. Toys (carefully packed separately) may be inserted in packets of breakfast cereals. Alternatively, the customer may have to request the gift from the retailer, e.g. wine glasses with petrol purchases.

9. Picture cards

Originating with cigarette cards of years ago, these require collecting and so encourage repeat buying in order to obtain the set. They may be inserted in packs, or printed as cut-outs on cartons. Such cards are contained in boxes of tea bags.

10. Gift coupons

Again, these have to be collected in order to qualify for gifts, and so require repeat purchasing. A catalogue of gifts must be made available. This has been a favourite with cigarette companies.

11. Cash dividends

Cash refunds against the collection of tokens with a cash value also induce repeat purchase.

12. Matching halves

Popular with the petrol companies, coupon halves are given with the purchases, and certain matching halves have claimable cash values.

13. Cash premium vouchers or coupons

These can be redeemed at the retailers as a price reduction. They may be printed in press advertisements, delivered door-to-door, or printed on packs as money off the next purchase.

An example of door-to-door delivery of coupons is the very successful *The Coupon Book* in which advertisers such as Brooke Bond, Colgate Palmolive, Colmans, Johnson Wax, Procter & Gamble, Lever Brothers and Dulux have taken space for coupon offers. This method is claimed to be very economical, production costs being 50 per cent less than for door-to-door leaflet distribution, while the cost of redeeming a coupon is 7.5p compared with 40p from the national press.

14. Cross-couponing offers

This is a popular co-operation scheme whereby an on-pack coupon or token enables the customer to buy another product (not necessarily made by the same manufacturer) at a reduced price. A great variety of offers have been made such as free railway tickets, reductions on package holidays, or reductions on products associated with the one making the offer. The reference to another brand on a pack, whether as an advertisement or as a premium offer, is also known as 'cross-branding'.

15. High Street redemption schemes

This is a fairly recent on-pack idea, whereby a product carries a premium coupon entitling the customer to a discount at a named store. This is liked by the store because the discount can lead to other purchases.

An interesting scheme which combined **14** and **15** was that which offered a free 250ml trial size of Crown Solo paint on packs of Kellogg's Bran Flakes. Eight tokens and 40p to cover postage had to be sent to the fulfilment house (one in the UK, one in Ireland), and the large 750g carton carried three tokens. The association of paint and cereals may seem strange, but actually some serious thinking went into the promotion. Steve Duncan,

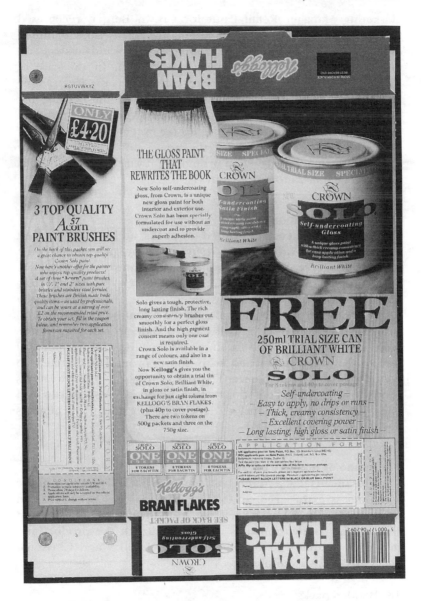

Figure 6.1 *The Kellogg's Bran Flakes pack, as printed flat before folding, and described in 16.*

Marketing Manager Retail Paint for Crown Berger, recognised that Bran Flakes has an adult target market as does painting, especially gloss painting. Both products were brand leaders and the promotion offered both parties a benefit. In the case of Kellogg's there was a high perceived value offer, the free sample being worth £1.89. Crown Berger liked the scheme because the distribution channels were not common, the daily traffic of consumers through grocery multiples far exceeding that of a DIY superstore. Thus the profile of the new paint was raised more significantly than by relying on promoting it within the retail paint market. See illustration of pack in Fig. 6.1.

16. Charity promotions

Cash value tokens are printed on packs, and if these are sent to the charity it can redeem them with the promoter of the scheme. However, the redeemable amount must be worthwhile. One food manufacturer ran a scheme which offered to help finance school sports funds, customers giving their children the tokens to take to school. The value of the tokens was so trivial, and so many tokens had to be collected to redeem cash, that there were protests from schools. It is also vital to avoid political overtones as has happened with some promotions linked to controversial Olympic Games. There is an integral public relations element in charity promotions which could have a good or bad effect on the company image, depending on how the scheme is devised and managed.

17. Jumbo or multiple packs

This means that a number of items are packed together or the container is extra large, and offered at a special price. It is an economical way of both packing and buying such items, and ensures that the customer is well stocked with the product and may thus become a habit buyer. Special holiday and Christmas packs are typical examples.

18. Banded packs

Similarly, a number of items are banded together and sold at a bulk price, e.g. bars of soap, bars of chocolate.

19. Flash packs

Special offers, or money-off offers, are 'flashed', that is, printed on the wrapper or carton, a sure way of inducing impulse buying. The Trade Descriptions Act 1968 must be observed by stating the normal recommended price when a price cut is 'flashed'. This is one of the most popular sales promotion schemes, and very easy to operate.

20. In-store demonstrations

Here, a demonstrator will have a booth in the store and demonstrate the product (e.g. an ironing board) or offer samples (e.g. drinks), and either sell the product directly or pass sales to the regular shop assistant.

21. Promotional games

These have become popular in recent years, and include scratch cards revealing a possible cash claim which the promoter will redeem. Some resemble football pools or bingo.

22. Advertorials

An old favourite when a new product is launched is to supply it to a newspaper or magazine which provides an editorial feature and makes readers a special introductory offer. This has been used to launch lipsticks and shampoos through mass-circulation women's magazines, and it has been developed in many other joint ventures with publishers offering a wide variety of products and services from camera lenses to holidays. For some publishers it has become an additional business activity while providing a reader service.

23. On-pack direct marketing

A number of product packs, such as Swan Vestas matches and Tate & Lyle sugar bags, carry offers which are perhaps more than premium offers, and are really an extra form of trading. McDougall's famous cookery book has been advertised with a mail order coupon on flour bags.

Terminology

24. Bolt-on promotion
This is a ready-made promotion, often specially produced and offered to manufacturers, such as scratch-card games.

25. Fulfilment house
This is a specialist firm which warehouses sales promotion gifts or premium offers, and despatches them to applicants. The address of the fulfilment house usually appears on the offer. It should not be confused with a sales promotion agency which organises the scheme. Fulfilment houses also handle requests for catalogues and brochures which have been advertised.

26. Contract packer
This is a firm which not only packs normal retail packs (e.g. aerosols, blister packs, sachets) for manufacturers, but produces special promotional packs.

27. Redemption
This means the payment of cash in response to cash premium offers, or the acceptance of premium vouchers.

28. Misredemption and malredemption
Acceptance of premium vouchers or coupons as part payment for goods other than that of the product being promoted is referred to as misredemption (*see* **35**). Malredemption means criminal misuse of premium vouchers such as by theft. The terms mis- and malredemption are loosely used to mean the same thing, but strictly speaking malredemption refers to a malpractice.

29. Extrinsic
Additional in value to that of the basic product, e.g. garden bulbs or Christmas cards offered free to purchasers of, say, a brand of tea.

Problems and risks

30. Disappointed customers
An important public relations aspect of sales promotion is

that while money-off offers can be welcome, and premium offers can be enjoyed, and it may be entertaining to enter for a prize contest, promotions have a magnetic appeal which in itself poses risks of damage to company goodwill and product images. If, for some reason, customers are offended or disappointed, the promotion can turn sour, or if the fulfilment house is slow to deliver, this is bad public relations.

There have been many examples of stocks being exhausted by unpredicted demand, long delays in the delivery of merchandise, arrival of damaged goods owing to poor packing, or in the case of contests inefficient announcement of results.

In an article, 'Special Offers Out of Control', *Campaign* (27 April, 1984), Brian Oliver described the experience of Smiths Foods who ran a James Bond watch offer for £6.99 plus proof of purchase of Monster Munch. Demand was so incredible that initial stocks and repeat orders of the watch were exhausted, and it became impossible to obtain further stocks. Refunds had to be sent to disappointed youngsters. Fisher-Price dolls were offered in a promotion for Sterling Health's Baby Wet Ones, but supplies ran out and apologies had to be mailed to disappointed applicants.

31. How to avoid disappointing customers

While this may not be easy with FMCGs which have rapid sales to the mass market, certain precautions can be taken, such as the following.

(a) Make sure that the supplier can supply on time and in repeat quantities if necessary.

(b) Limit the offer to a given number of applicants.

(c) Put a time limit on the offer.

(d) If possible, include in the offer a substitute if stocks run out. A cash voucher is seldom satisfactory.

(e) Warn applicants not to expect delivery until, say, 28 days after sending in the application.

(f) Employ a reliable fulfilment house (*see* **25**) to handle despatches.

(g) Demonstrate thoughtfulness by including in the package a note offering to replace any item damaged in the post. Thank you notes, hoping applicants will enjoy a premium product, are always good public relations. While sales promotion in itself is not public relations, there are public relations aspects in the extent to which goodwill is gained or lost.

32. Retailer attitudes

It is important that the retailer likes a sales promotion scheme and is prepared to co-operate with it. As Brian Oliver said in an article 'Offers They Cannot Refuse' in *Marketing* (26 April 1984): 'If retailers see the premium as a competing product, they might not give the promotion the display space you're after. They might even refuse to stock the product.' In the John Player example referred to in **7**, the mistake was also made of alienating traders who suffered a loss in demand for lighters because of the free offer.

33. Sales force enthusiasm

A sales promotion scheme can fail if it is not fully supported by the company's own salespeople. In another article in *Marketing* (26 April 1984) Peter Hood stated: 'The communication begins at home: if the promotion is not sold to the company's own management and sales force there can be little chance of them selling it to anyone else.'

34. Too enthusiastic consumers

It is also necessary to ensure that the enthusiasm of consumers for a promotion does not create problems which both harm the promotion and embarrass the company. Some ideas can be too clever, as occurred with the Cadbury's chocolate cream Easter egg treasure hunt scheme. There was a treasure hunt for 12 'gold' eggs worth £10,000 each. One hundred thousand people wrote in for the storybook containing the treasure hunt clues. One of the 'golden eggs' was hidden in a field, and when some participants started digging up an archaeological site in Cornwall, Cadbury had to cancel the hunt for this particular egg.

35. Misredemptions

A serious problem with cash premium vouchers which can be redeemed at the shop when purchasing the promoted product is that the response can be misleading if retailers accept them as part payment for other goods. Some manufacturers print warnings on the vouchers that they may be redeemed only for the specific product (*see* **37**), but this is ineffective when leading supermarket chains openly announce that they will accept any premium vouchers against any purchase provided the promoted product is stocked. Consequently, when the retailer seeks payment from the manufacturer the latter may have no idea of the effect of the scheme upon sales other than perhaps the level of reordering. Thus, the vouchers could have been redeemed for rival brands, and the level of reordering could have been static so that the effect of the promotion had been either nullified or less than forecast.

One method of discovering the extent of misredemption is discussed in **36** below.

36. Coupon redemption analysis

An interesting example of the application of marketing research to sales promotion is the RETAL service which has been developed by Nielsen Clearing House (NCH) of Corby. The company acts as a clearing house for premium coupon redemptions, and handles more than one million redemptions a day. It enables clients to see a summary of coupon redemptions by individual retailers. The analysis offers subscribers three benefits. First, it identifies major sources of coupon redemption. Second, it enables comparisons to be made between products sold into outlet and coupons redeemed. Third, it enables comparisons to be made between individual retailer contribution to coupon promotions.

The RETAL report shows the total number of coupons contained in all claims processed by NCH during the selected period for the named retailer. It gives the value of coupons paid for all claims processed by NCH in the selected period for the named retailer. There is an analysis of the individual coupons or group totals for the named retailer and an individual analysis of the number of coupons redeemed within each code or group by retailer within the given period. This includes a percentage of all coupons within each code or group within the period.

Thus promoters of premium coupons can see how their sales promotion scheme performed in respect of different retailers and also in relation to stocks supplied to these retailers. This can also reveal the extent, if any, of misredemption, as when coupon redemptions exceed supplies to a retailer.

37. Example of redemption

The new sanitary cleaner, Vortex, was launched with TV advertising plus door-to-door delivery of an explanatory leaflet bearing a coupon 'worth 10p when you buy Vortex'. The coupon bore a code number and the following instruction and warning to the retailer:

'*To The Retailer.* Procter & Gamble Limited will redeem this coupon at its face value, provided you have accepted it from your customer in part payment for a purchase of Vortex, and not otherwise. Only one coupon may be accepted per pack purchased. Coupons for redemption should be sent to "Proctor & Gamble Limited, Coupon Redemption Centre", PO Box 160, Corby, Northants.

Procter & Gamble Limited reserve the right to withhold payment if they have cause to believe that this coupon was redeemed against any item other than Vortex.'

The address is that of Nielsen Clearing House at Corby.

Progress test 6

1. Define sales promotion. (**1**)
2. Why has sales promotion become so important? (**2**)
3. What changes have occurred in sales promotion practice? (**4**)
4. Why is the nature of the prize so important when running a competition? (**5**)
5. Explain the terms: (*a*) self-liquidating premium offer; and (*b*) mail-in free offer. (**6, 7**)
6. What is a cross-couponing offer? (**14**)
7. What is a High Street redemption scheme? (**15**)
8. How are charity promotions conducted? (**16**)
9. Explain the use of flash packs. (**19**)
10. Distinguish between misredemption and malredemption. (**28**)
11. How can the sales promotion organiser avoid disappointing customers? (**31**)
12. Describe the essentials of the RETAL system of researching sales promotion. (**36**)

7
Sponsorship

Definition and examples

1. Definition

Sponsorship consists of the giving of monetary or other support to a beneficiary in order to make it financially viable, sometimes for altruistic reasons, but usually to gain some advertising, public relations or marketing advantage (*see* **7–10**).

The support could consist of money, as in the case of prizes, but may comprise trophies or other gifts in kind. The beneficiary could be an organisation or an individual. While some sponsors may simply wish to be philanthropic this is seldom so today when the object is more often deliberately commercial.

2. Growth of sponsorship

Sponsorship has become an industry on its own and according to Mintel 'Sponsorship 1988' £182 million was spent on sports sponsorship alone, £55 million being on motor sport.

Arts sponsorship has become increasingly popular in recent years with more than 1000 businesses sponsoring arts interests. It is popular world-wide with large and small advertisers. Historically, its origins go back to the sponsorship or patronage of artists and musicians by royalty and other wealthy benefactors. We still see this today with the commercial sponsorship of symphony orchestras, art exhibitions and the theatre. However, the bulk of sponsorship money is spent on sport, and while this support is given mainly to the major sports of motor-racing, horse-racing, show-jumping, football, cricket, tennis and golf, a number of other sports have become popular through sponsorship and television coverage, to mention only bowls, snooker and darts.

In recent years major sports and sporting events have become sponsored when this would have been unheard of in the past. We now have test cricket, the Football League and the Derby sponsored by Cornhill Insurance, Barclays Bank and Ever Ready respectively (*see* 13:**22–31**). The Colt Car Co. Ltd, the *Sun* and Seagram have financed the Grand National, and Gillette and Mars have backed the London Marathon. International events such as yacht races, car rallies and safaris also have their sponsors. Sometimes there are multiple sponsorships embracing the event itself, section prizes, and the individual competitors or their vehicles, horses or boats.

Canon were the original sponsors of the Football League, and at the end of their three-year sponsorship costing £3 million they were able to boast that there was hardly an office in Britain which did not have a Canon machine. The strength of this sponsorship was that British football is played for many months of the year by 92 teams, thus producing constant media coverage.

3. What can be sponsored?

While the biggest, costliest and probably most cost-effective sponsorships are those which make popular news, and are mainly in the realms of sport, there are many categories of sponsorship, and some may suit particular sponsors better than others. It is not necessary to spend a fortune, and support for a local event in the vicinity of the company's headquarters may be of minimal cost but have maximum effect on, say, staff relations or recruitment. The main categories of sponsorship are as follows.

(a) Books and other publications such as maps.

(b) Exhibitions which may be sponsored by trade associations and professional societies, or by newspapers and magazines, or company-sponsored private exhibitions.

(c) Education, in the form of grants, bursaries and fellowships.

(d) Expeditions, explorations, mountaineering, round-the-world voyages and other adventures.

(e) Sport, as already described and spreading to many of the minor sports.

(f) The arts such as music, painting, literature and the theatre.

(g) Causes and charities, especially by helping them to promote their activities. For instance, pharmaceutical companies produce videos to explain the causes, nature and treatment of illnesses.

(**h**) Local events can be supported with prizes, as with horse shows, gymkhanas, sports meetings and flower shows.

(**i**) Professional awards for people associated with the sponsor's industry such as photographers, journalists, architects and others. Canon, for instance, in conjunction with *UK Press Gazette,* sponsor a Press Pictures of the Year competition which is very appropriate for a *camera manufacturer.* Nikon also have a contest for press photographers.

4. Examples of sponsorship
The following are some examples of sponsorship:

1. Barclays Bank: tour of London City Ballet.
2. Digital Genie Ballet Awards.
3. Guinness Scotland Ballet season.
4. The Booker Prize.
5. Bovis/*Architectural Journal* Award for Architecture.
6. Sainsbury's Choir of the Year Competition.
7. Royal Insurance: Royal Shakespeare Company.
8. Cadbury's National Childrens Art.
9. Royal Bank of Scotland: Bournemouth Symphony Orchestra.
10. Toyota (GB) Ltd: National Youth Orchestra.
11. Kodak: Royal Philharmonia Orchestra.
12. Martini Royal Photographic Competition.
13. Nabisco International Under 15's Soccer.
14. Peugeot Talbot Athletics, The Peugeot Games, Crystal Palace.
15. Carlsberg Basketball League.
16. Bristol & West Building Society, Champion of Champion Outdoors Bowls.
17. National Dairy Council Milk Race (cycle).
18. Everest Double Glazing Championship, Horse of the Year Show.
19. Alfred Dunhill Ltd, the Dunhill (Golf) Cup.
20. Coral Eclipse Stakes.
21. Whitbread & Company: Whitbread Gold Cup.
22. Honda Marlboro McLaren Formula 1.
23. Shell British Grand Prix.
24. Mitsubishi Motors British Powerboat Grand Prix.
25. Embassy World Professional Snooker Championships.

An AGB Sportswatch/BARB survey published in *Marketing*

Week (7 April 1989) showed that the following sports gained the highest television audience figures in 1988. It will be noted that a number of these *events* were sponsored, but so were some of the individual players or performers.

1988 TOP TEN SPORTS PROGRAMMES

1. Seagram Grand National.
2. Tennents UK Professional Snooker Champs Final (BBC).
3. Grandstand, 2 July (BBC).
4. Sports Review 1988 (BBC).
5. Mars London Marathon Highlights (BBC).
6. Benson & Hedges Masters Snooker Final (BBC).
7. International Boxing Special: Barry McGuigan *v.* Julio Miranda (ITV).
8. Wimbledon Ladies Final (BBC).
9. Match of the Day: FA Cup, Everton *v.* Liverpool (BBC).
10. Olympics Today, 29 September (BBC).

5. Sponsorship agencies
The planning and conducting of sponsorships, including the preliminary liaison between interests seeking sponsors and likely sponsors, and between potential sponsors and the bodies representing things which might be sponsored, is a very complicated and skilled business. Consequently, a number of specialist consultancies exist (*see* also **3:25**). Two which are responsible for many of the major sponsorships are the Alan Pascoe Associates and CSS Promotions. On the other hand, leading Japanese advertising agencies such as Dentsu and Hakuhodo have sponsorship divisions.

For fuller information about subjects sponsored, sponsors and sponsorship agencies the reader is recommended to study the comprehensive sponsorship section in *Hollis Press and Public Relations Annual.*

Objectives

6. An investment
As stated at the end of the definition in **1**, the aim of a sponsorship is to gain results associated with the advertising,

public relations or marketing strategy. It is an investment to gain a desired positive result. Before becoming committed to any sort of expenditure, large or small, the prospective sponsor needs to check that these results are attainable.

It is not uncommon for a sponsorship to have a blend of advertising, public relations and marketing objectives and benefits, which could be quite different. Although this book is concerned mainly with advertising, all three aspects of sponsorship are analysed in **7–10** below. This analysis will show both the scope of this activity, and distinguish between the three aspects. It would be wrong to think that all the benefits of sponsorship were in terms of advertising.

7. Advertising objectives
There are many possible advertising objectives as follows:

(a) *When media advertising is banned.* The product may be banned by certain media, e.g. cigarettes cannot be advertised on British TV, although this may not apply in other countries. This is a controversial question, but cigarette manufacturers have succeeded in gaining considerable TV programme coverage by sponsoring cricket, golf and motor-racing, the John Player Special being a well-known racing car.

(b) *Associated advertising.* In association with sponsorship, arena advertising in the form of boards and bunting can be displayed at racecourses, sports stadiums, motor-racing circuits and other venues so that they are inevitably picked up by the TV cameras covering the event, apart from being seen by spectators on the spot. The Marlboro cigarette displays are familiar at grand prix motor races, and the Coral boards at horse-races sponsored by the bookmakers.

(c) *To promote products.* When Yamaha sponsored snooker they used the main display to establish that it was Yamaha Keyboards and not Yamaha Motor-cycles which was responsible for the event, while Canon have used perimeter boards at football stadiums to show that they are makers of office equipment and not only cameras.

(d) *To exploit other advertising opportunities.* These would not always be available. They include free programme advertising, or facilities for product displays and demonstrations at the venue.

Daihatsu launched a new golf cart simply by supplying them to players in a golf tournament.

The opportunity may also be taken to incorporate references to a sponsorship in press and poster advertising, for instance, giving the dates of sponsored events and encouraging customers to take an interest by, say, watching on TV the grand prix motor race in which the company is involved in sponsorship.

An interesting example was the way in which the John Player Special racing car was linked with holiday promotion. JPS Grand Prix Holidays, organised by Page & Moy Ltd, with the authority of the trademark holders Imperial Group plc, offered exotic package holidays to grand prix venues such as Monaco and Monza. In half-page full colour ads in publications such as *TV Times*, almost the whole of the top half of the ad pictured the famous black and gold racing car sponsored by Players. The wording of one such ad was as in Fig. 7.1.

**FOLLOW THE ACTION, FOLLOW THE SUN,
ON A JPS GRAND PRIX HOLIDAY**

If you're tired of ordinary, run-of-the-mill holidays, try the glamour and excitement of a JPS Grand Prix holiday.

Take off with us and experience the non-stop, action-packed world of the international racing circuit.

Take your pick of the world's top venues. And of course your holiday won't be all racing.

Choose Monaco as your destination and enjoy the freedom of days on the famous Côte D'Azur beaches and nights out on the town in the top casinos of Monte Carlo.

On our Canadian and Detroit package you'll take in the beauty of the Great Lakes as well as experience all the sightseeing and entertainment that the big cities like Montreal and Toronto offer.

If you're after variety book up now for the Italian Grand Prix at Monza. Travel in style on the legendary Venice Simplon Orient Express and contrast the excitement of racing with the gentle, relaxing scenery of Lake Como.

We'll make every effort to give you a memorable holiday in some of the most fascinating places under the sun, climaxing in the unforgettable experience of a Grand Prix race.

Whichever destination you choose, on a JPS Grand Prix holiday you'll find you always come first.

Figure 7.1 *John Player Special holiday advertisement.*

8. Controversy

Confusion and controversy have raged regarding the permissible extent of visible publicity, and a muddle of acceptance and limitation has existed over the years, especially concerning displays (and mentions) during broadcast programmes. Names have been allowed on athletes', footballers' and cricketers' apparel, yet not on boxers' shorts, although permitted on the dressing gowns they wear to the ring. There have not been objections to the naming of sponsored events, and in motor-racing, yacht racing and motor-boat racing each entrant has been clearly identified with its sponsor's or sponsors' names.

The media, the authorities (government, BBC, ITC) and pressure groups representing anti-smoking, teetotal, health and religious interests may regard all the publicity generated by sponsorship as *advertising*, but as will now be explained, the sponsor's aims may be defined differently. The purpose of advertising is to make known in order to sell, but a sponsorship may have other purposes besides selling.

9. Public relations objectives

These objectives do not seek to advertise (even by reminder advertising) in order to persuade and sell, but aim to develop knowledge and understanding of the organisation. This in turn may *contribute* to advertising so that it becomes easier or more economical to advertise and sell. The principle is applied that people like what they know, that 'familiarity breeds content', to reword the phrase in an advertising sense.

(a) *Goodwill.* An important public relations objective may be to create goodwill towards the company, locally, nationally or internationally. A large corporation, making big profits, may adopt a social conscience by donating funds or gifts to society. It might give financial aid to a library, college, theatre, hospital or medical research fund. By sponsoring sports or arts it may be seen to be acting in the public interst, or in its customers' interests. When a foreign company enters export markets, where it may be unknown or possibly greeted with prejudice or suspicion, sponsorship can help create a friendly attitude without which it would be impossible to sell. Goodyear has done this by using its airships to make public announcements at night with illuminated messages.

Japanese firms the world over have used sponsorship in this way. There was a time when Japanese motor-cars were burned in the streets of Asiatic countries which had been victims of wartime occupation. Today a British motor-car is a rare sight in Bangkok, Hong Kong, Jakarta, Kuala Lumpur or Singapore.

(b) *Corporate image.* Allied to what has been said above about goodwill, there may be a need to create understanding of the character of the company. A name may just be a name, but what does it represent and what does it do? Until a few years ago, 80 per cent of the British male population had a poor image, if any at all, of Cornhill Insurance. Sponsoring test cricket has changed that.

(c) *Corporate identity.* Sponsorship can help to identify a company by making its logo and colour scheme familiar to people. This has been well achieved by firms such as Coca-Cola which sponsor athletics and swimming world-wide.

(d) *Familiarising the name.* This, of course, is implicit in **(b)** and **(c)** above, but sponsorships usually involve continuous repetition of the name, especially in media coverage when reports and commentators describe the event (or the prize or competitor) by the sponsor's name. When calculating the results of a sponsorship, these references can be monitored and assessments made. For instance, during the football season there are references almost every night to the various sponsors when match results are announced. Snooker championships occupy several days' play, and the sponsor's name is given with every report in the press and on the radio and television in addition to the actual televising of the play. This is a typical press or media relations aspect of sponsorship and it is public relations not advertising, although in addition the TV cameras will pick up advertising signs.

(e) *Hospitality.* While not to be disregarded when considering the costs of a sponsorship, hospitality can provide numerous opportunities for socialising. The managing director can invite a party of business friends or important customers to the sponsored event, whether it be a cricket or football match, golf tournament, show-jumping event or athletics meeting. In fact, the *ability* to offer such hospitality may be a major reason for sponsoring.

(f) *Encouraging interests of journalists.* Very popular is the presenting of awards to journalists for their skill and knowledge when writing about the sponsor's subject or industry. These awards are announced and reported in journals such as the *UK Press Gazette*, and a number have become annual events. Some examples are Nikon Press Photographer of the Month Award and the Nikon Awards for the Provincial Press Photographer of the Year, the Bank of Scotland's Press Awards, and the Blue Circle Awards for Industrial Journalism.

10. Marketing objectives

Here we have aims which are different again from advertising and public relations objectives, although the three may be blended together in a single sponsorship. The important thing is to understand the differences between the three, and their distinct purposes. The following are examples of marketing objectives.

(a) *Positioning a product.* The company may seek to identify the product with a certain segment of the market such as sex, age group, or income group. To do this it could sponsor a male or female interest; youth, young executive or mature person's interest; or a working-class, middle-class or upper-middle-class interest. Not every sponsor is interested in the whole audience. It is therefore clear that Coca-Cola and Haig whisky, the *Sun* and the *Financial Times*, and the Midland Bank (e.g. farmers) and Woolwich Equitable Building Society (e.g. young home builders) are aiming their sponsorships at very different market segments.

In 1990, seeking to position itself with younger borrowers and investors, Abbey National Building Society sponsored a Madonna concert televised by Sky. Because of the American singer's behaviour at a Wembley pop concert controversy arose, and some Abbey National shareholders (the building society had 'gone public') threatened to sell their shares. These shareholders were, on the whole, older people.

(b) *Supporting dealers.* A successful participation, as when a car wins a motor rally (or the winning car uses certain equipment such as tyres), provides excellent back-up for retailers with opportunities for topical displays coinciding with topical advertising placed by the manufacturer. Dealers are more likely to stock, display prominently and sell products whose performance is proven.

(c) *Establishing a change in marketing policy.* If a company is well established in a particular product field it can be very difficult, even through advertising, to obtain quick and widespread acceptance that the company has diversified into other product or service areas. A company which makes women's products like perfume may decide to make men's toiletries, as with Yardley some years ago, when for a time they sponsored the young men's sport of motor-racing. Or a firm well-known for cameras may produce office machinery (like Canon), or keyboard instruments as well as motor-cycles (like Yamaha). Again, it may wish to further the interests of different divisions as Dunlop has done with tyres and tennis racquets (although there have now been changes in the structure of that company). These are all marketing policy decisions which have used sponsorship for the purpose.

(**d**) *Launching a new product.* As part of the strategy of launching a new product, sponsorship may be an excellent vehicle, and also a kind of public test for its performance. This has been applied to many new products such as tyres, tennis racquets, golf carts, motor-cars and sports wear.

(**e**) *Opening of branches.* One of the spin-offs of the Canon Football League sponsorship, which involved 92 football clubs, was that when the company opened new premises it was able to call on the local football clubs to provide star players to perform opening ceremonies, often with follow-on local media coverage.

The strong point about the Canon sponsorship of the Football League, and also the *Sun* sponsorship of the Grand National, was that they worked at it and exploited every opportunity. Barclays Bank has not thrown itself so wholeheartedly into its sponsorship of the Football League.

(**f**) *International marketing.* Mention has been made already of using sponsorship for public relations purposes in overseas markets, but sponsorship can also be part of the marketing strategy to establish the product in these markets, to attract dealers and agents, and to prove the suitability of the imported product in a market with special conditions. For example, it may be good marketing strategy to sponsor local or national events in which the product can be seen to perform as well as or better than indigenous products with which the market is familiar. Foreign goods are not necessarily accepted because they come from a country with a good reputation for such things.

The Japanese are said to be 'golf mad', and some Japanese firms have sponsored British golf tournaments because the British television coverage of the events would also be shown on Japanese television!

(g) *Encouraging product use.* Activities can be sponsored to develop the market, as when London brewers Truman have sponsored darts championships, with TV coverage, to popularise the pub.

Again, a well-established foreign importer may find sponsorship a good way of fending off competition from a new importer. The Japanese have been quick to use sponsorship to win their way into foreign markets (including the British), and it may be a good idea for British firms to defend their overseas markets by adopting sponsorship as a tactic which earns recognition, praise and respect in markets under attack.

Cost-effectiveness

11. Justification for sponsorship

The attractions of sponsorship, and maybe the temptations, are great, but is it worthwhile? In this chapter many examples and reasons are given. It is not good enough to indulge in sponsorship merely to show off or to copy other people and to be in the fashion. However great or small the cost, it has to be justified as a trading cost.

12. Testing results

It is possible to assess the success or otherwise of a sponsorship. The following are typical methods.

(a) Monitoring media coverage to record not only the volume of column inches or centimetres and airtime, but also the quality of this coverage, by analysing which publications or programmes are reported or commentated, in what tone, and by whom. It would be valueless to have great coverage in media irrelevant to the market, yet very valuable to have even modest coverage in media which reached the particular market segment.

(b) By using market research techniques which can record the situation before, during and after sponsorship to show whether the objective had been achieved. This could range from opinion polls to dealer audit according to the purpose of the sponsorship. For instance, has name familiarity been improved, is there a better understanding of the corporate image, has there been acceptance in a new or foreign market, has a greater brand share of the market been achieved?

For example, Audits of Great Britain were commissioned by Lloyds Bank to evaluate their sponsorship of the BBC Young Musician of the Year competition which appeared week by week on BBC2 in 1990. One result was that 53 per cent of informants strongly agreed that it was a suitable and worthwhile event for Lloyds Bank to sponsor.

13. A new trend

Among the reasons for spending money on sponsorship is a new and interesting one, which may also in some cases explain the phenomenal increase in expenditure on public relations. The cost of advertising media has risen out of all proportion to the rate of inflation, and at the point when, for some companies, media advertising ceases to be cost-effective, public relations techniques, of which sponsorship can be one, have been found more cost-effective.

This does not mean that public relations is a substitute for advertising but that whereas public relations was mostly applied as a pre-advertising preparation of the market it is now being used for post-advertising consolidation of the market. In other words, there can be a point when advertising can do no more to sell the product but sponsorship can continue to maintain goodwill, reputation, understanding of the corporate image, reiteration of the corporate identity and name familiarity, thus strengthening the advertising which is conducted.

Progress test 7

1. Define sponsorship. (1)
2. What is the total value of the British motor sport sponsorship industry? (2)
3. What can be sponsored? (3)
4. Name some of the biggest sports sponsorships. (4)
5. What is the role of a sponsorship agency? (6)
6. What advertising objectives can be achieved through sponsorship? (7)

7. What controversies have occurred concerning sponsorship? (8, 10)
8. Explain the public relations aspects of sponsorship. (9)
9. What marketing objectives can be achieved through sponsorship? (10)
10. How can sponsorship assist international marketing? (10)
11. How can the effectiveness of sponsorship be measured? (12)

8
Direct mail and direct response

Introduction

1. Growth in importance

Shopping without shops or direct marketing has become very big business, aided by direct mail, TV commercials and teletext, off-the-page selling, the telephone, the computer, and the credit card. Mail order is nowadays better known as direct or direct response marketing. Direct mail is so involved in all this that the British Direct Mail Advertising Association changed its name in 1976 to the British Direct Marketing Association (BDMA). In Britain, direct mail takes third place to press and television and takes up 10 per cent of the total advertising expenditure.

Post Office figures quoted in The Advertising Association's *Advertising Statistics Yearbook 1989*, show that in 1988 1,766 million direct mail shots were mailed, and that direct mail's share of all media expenditure was 7.3 per cent. Total expenditure on production and postage was £530 million.

According to an independent report on direct mail published by Projection 2000 Ltd, spending on direct mail was expected to double between 1988 and 1991, from £530 million to £1000 million. The increased expenditure on direct mail was believed to derive from three factors: (*a*) cut back in above-the-line media expenditure; (*b*) the success of the Royal Mail's Mailsort scheme (*see* also **14**); and (*c*) growth in direct mail by people organising their own mailings as distinct from using direct mail houses or agencies.

The Post Office has vigorously promoted the medium and the annual Direct Marketing Awards are made by the BDMA and the Post Office. The value of direct mail is seen in a small country like Botswana where the press is negligible and broadcast media is mostly South African. It is also an excellent medium for international advertising when it is more economical to airmail selected prospects than to advertise in the press which may be very limited anyway.

Alternative mailing services, such as TNT, can be used very economically.

2. Definitions

Confusion of terms can be avoided by remembering that direct mail is an *advertising medium* but mail order (or direct response) is a *form of distribution*, that is, trading by mail whatever medium is used for advertising sales offers. Consequently, direct mail is not limited to direct marketing: a retailer can use direct mail to attract shoppers to his store.

Characteristics of direct mail

3. Controlled

It is not aimed at unknown readers, listeners, viewers, audiences or passers-by or travellers like all the above-the-line media described in Chapter 4. Instead it is addressed to selected, named recipients or at least to chosen people at selected addresses whether they be householders or managing directors. The quantity can be controlled, the message can be varied to suit different groups of people, and the timing can be controlled or at any rate estimated within postal limits.

4. Economical

Because of the controls mentioned in **3**, it is economical in the sense that even the selected lists can be culled of unwanted addresses. De-duplication can be applied when a number of lists are being used in which certain names are repeated. It is also economical because in a mail shot more copy and illustrations can be used than would fill a whole page broadsheet newspaper, and at a fraction of the cost.

5. Personal

Unlike any other medium, except possibly the telephone, it is a one-to-one personal medium, like a conversation on paper. Generally, people like receiving mail, and if the recipient is well-chosen the mail shot will be welcomed.

This medium is also personal in the sense that sales letters and envelopes can be addressed by name (personalised). Using special techniques like laser printing, dramatic and colourful effects can be achieved with the recipient's name inserted at various points in the body of the letter itself. This should not be overdone otherwise the letter will sound insincere, but neither should letters be addressed 'Dear Sir/Madam' which looks careless and indifferent. If a formal salutation is necessary it is better to have letters addressed separately, 'Dear Sir' and 'Dear Madam'.

6. Speed

A direct mail campaign can be mounted very quickly, in a few hours if necessary given the facilities to write and reproduce a sales letter, and pack and post it with or without an enclosure. It is therefore a very flexible medium which can be used in an emergency. Such an emergency might be to clear stocks, announce a special offer, out-do a competitor, or take advantage of a topical opportunity.

7. A primary medium

For those advertisers who (*a*) have or can hire a reliable mailing list and (*b*) need to supply considerable information, direct mail can be their first line or primary advertising medium. In fact, they may use no other, except perhaps sales literature as enclosures. Others may use press advertising to produce enquiries or initial orders which provide a mailing list for future use.

For instance, press advertising could be useless for some advertisers because the cost of adequate space to include all the necessary information would be prohibitive. If this detailed information cannot be given, the response could be negligible. All the affordable press advertisement can do is attract enquiries, but that is introducing another time-wasting and inconvenient stage in the marketing strategy. The direct mail shot can eliminate this stage and attract immediate *orders*, not enquiries, and is more productive and cost-effective.

8. Testing and evaluating

It is possible to pre-test mailings by sending out test mailings of either offers of different merchandise, or offers of the same merchandise at different prices to a sample of prospective customers, and then to record the response. For example, the price may be around 100 (pence, cents, etc.) but some variation on this price may prove to be more psychologically attractive. The product may draw more sales at, say 98 or 102. People judge by price and 98 may seem inexpensive while 102 may suggest quality, and 100 could have an indecisive effect.

Direct mail shots are easily evaluated by the response they produce, and this can be calculated on a cost-per-reply basis (the cost of the shot divided by the number of replies), and cost-per-sales (which can be either the cost of selling a given volume of stock, or the cost of selling one unit). Experience can then guide the planning and budgeting of the marketing strategy—what merchandise will sell to whom and at what price, what form the mailing should take, and how much should be spent on a mailing to achieve the sales target.

The sales letter and enclosures

9. Writing the sales letter

A sales letter is not just a business letter. It is a special form of copywriting with its own techniques. The length of the letter will depend on the extent to which the reader's interest can be sustained. There are some excellent sales letters which extend to as many as four pages, perhaps in a four-page folder style rather than two or four separate sheets, but generally there is a psychological value in a single-page letter when the signature is visible at the foot of the page.

This is a controversial topic, with 'experts' expressing different views, but when there is a lot of direct mail and it competes for attention, the short letter uncluttered by too many inserts, is likely to command the most attention.

The letter may present a complete selling proposition, or it can be a covering letter referring the reader to an enclosure. In the latter case the letter should not laboriously repeat the contents of the enclosure but highlight special features of it. Not all sales letters include a salutation, and this may be a way of avoiding uncertainty over the identity or sex of the recipient. Other letters may be personalised as already described in **5**.

10. A pattern to follow

If the sales letter presents a self-contained proposition a useful pattern is as follows.

(a) *Introductory opening paragraph.* This needs to capture the reader's attention, but it need not disclose the selling proposition. Various intriguing devices are used such as posing a hypothetical question or even telling an amusing anecdote. This should induce the recipient to read on. It is the sugar on the pill or the bait.

(b) *The proposition.* The heart of the letter should now set out the proposition.

(c) *Convincing the reader.* The next stage is to convince the reader. There may be a price concession if the offer is taken up quickly, or the offer may have a time limit.

(d) *Final paragraph.* The letter should close with instructions on how to respond or order. This may refer to an enclosed order form or card, and there may be an unstamped envelope, or reply-paid or Freepost envelope or card.

Adopting the above four-point formula, here is an example of how a sales letter might be written.

Dear Mr Brown

What do you do when your wife says the lawn needs cutting? Do you turn over a new leaf—in the book you are trying to read? Or maybe you take the dog for a walk? If you haven't got a dog perhaps you pray that it will rain?

That's if you have an old back-breaker of a lawnmower that's agony to push up and down the lawn on a hot day.

With the new Smith and Jones electric lawnmower you don't have to push. You simply steer! The machine does all the work. It's a pleasure, really.

Your wife will be surprised how willingly you take your Smith and Jones out of the garden shed. She'll probably have a drink waiting for you afterwards, not that you'll be hot and weary. It will just be nice to sit down with her in the deckchairs and admire that neat, trim lawn. Nice work, Mr Brown!

You can see the new Smith and Jones electric lawnmowers at the New Town Garden Centre—open all weekend so you can call in when it suits you. It comes in a box you can put in the boot, and it's very easy to assemble. Why not bring the wife along?

> Yours sincerely
> John Donaldson
> Manager

11. Appropriate language

When writing a sales letter it is necessary to use language which is appropriate to the medium, the product and the reader. The *Financial Times Industrial Companies Year Book* is no doubt an excellent reference work, but in a letter to potential advertisers it was rather silly of the advertising sales executive to write: 'We thought it would be a good idea for you to advertise your services in this exciting new book.' It was not exactly a holiday in Bali, and advertising clichés like 'exciting' need to be used less indiscriminately.

12. Enclosures

The contents of the envelope should be kept to a minimum. Some mailings consist of so many items of different shapes and sizes that the recipient is bewildered and may well discard the whole lot! Good enclosures are those which supplement the sales letter.

Some of the best examples of well-planned shots are the *one-piece mailers* which contain all the necessary information and the order form, making an accompanying sales letter unnecessary. One-piece mailers are usually in folder form, either folding out to make a flat sheet, consisting of a series of panes in concertina fashion, or following some other ingenious design which contains everything in a single piece of print. There are thus no untidy, loose bits and pieces, and the information and ordering facility is neatly and conveniently limited to one item of print.

13. Printed envelopes

Whether or not printed envelopes should be used is a decision which may depend on where and by whom the shot will be received. If the recipient is never likely to see the envelope because the letter will be opened by his secretary, or in a post room, a printed envelope can be a costly irrelevancy, unless it is likely to influence a secretary. If the recipient, such as a private individual or shopkeeper, opens his or her own mail, then the sales message can begin with the envelope. Good examples of this are holiday brochures and mail order catalogues. *Reader's Digest* have exploited the printed and the window envelope to command immediate attention and interest. But, of course, it could operate adversely if identification of the sender invites instant rejection and the mail is not even opened!

In a sense, a printed envelope can be an advertisement just like the packaging of a retail product. It is the first thing people see. It can attract attention and invite curiosity about the contents, and if sufficiently interesting to the recipient the printed envelope could achieve priority over other correspondence received at the same time.

14. Postage

While direct mail is in many respects an economical medium, there are certain special costs which must be considered and carefully controlled. A primary cost is postage, and while the Post Office does offer special rates for bulk mailings, the postage will depend on the weight of the shot. This weight problem can be controlled by the size of enclosures, and also by the weight of paper used for printed literature.

Mailsort has replaced earlier Post Office discount and rebate schemes. The discount is based on the proportion of the mailing that can be pre-sorted and according to the quantity mailed. The minimum quantity is 4,000 letters or 1,000 packets of which 85 per cent must be fully postcoded. There are three options:

Mailsort 1—1st class, target delivery next working day. Maximum discount 15 per cent
Mailsort 2—2nd class, target delivery within 3 working days. Maximum discount 13 per cent
Mailsort 3—economy class, target delivery within 7 working days. Maximum discount 32 per cent.

15. Using suitable envelopes

Another cost is that of envelopes, the size of which can be controlled by the format of printed enclosures. Large leaflets in large envelopes can arrive in a very battered state whereas smaller leaflets in smaller envelopes are more likely to arrive in the same condition as when packed. Senders of direct mail seldom seem to realise the rigours of the mail. Heavy catalogues need to be protected by stout manilla envelopes, yet they are often put in large thin envelopes which get torn round the edges so that the contents arrive in a very dog-eared condition. Mail is manhandled many times in bags which are flung in and out of vans and trains.

Another psychological factor occurs here. Most people will tend to open small or DL envelopes first, even putting aside large envelopes for the time being, unless a large envelope obviously contains something they are waiting for.

Mailing lists

16. Setting up mailing lists

The following are some of the ways in which mailing lists can be created or obtained.

(a) From sales bills bearing the names and addresses of purchasers.

(b) From the response to advertisements which either invite requests for literature and catalogues, or sell off-the-page, customers paying by cheque or credit card or being invoiced on delivery.

(c) From yearbooks, annuals, directories and membership lists. In the latter case some organisations sell addresses in the form of addressed envelopes or labels. Care has to be taken in using a recent edition of a directory, remembering that it probably took months to compile and could be partially out-of-date on publication. However, there are excellent directories which list the names of senior personnel so that mailings can be addressed personally. It is better to address people by name and not merely by job description such as Managing Director or Marketing Manager.

(d) By using a direct mail house, either to create and manage the whole mailing, selecting lists from their catalogue, or to address and post a mailing produced in-house.

(e) By hiring a list from list-brokers who specialise in this service. There are also firms which specialise in client's lists on computerised databases, adding and deleting names as requested, and so managing and maintaining a client's own list.

(f) By using the ACORN (A Classification Of Residential Neighbourhoods) marketing segmentation system to select people by residential classifications. This system, based on census figures, was evolved by CACI Market Analysis Division. Five hundred million items of 1981 census data were used by CACI in 1983 to revise the original ACORN system, and acknowledgement is made for reproducing Table 8.1 based on Crown and CACI figures.

In addition to ACORN there are rival systems based on similar geodemographic principles. MOSAIC defines 58 lifestyle categories, and differs from other systems by analysing Britain at postcode level rather than census enumeration district level. Super Profiles links postal geography with 10 lifestyles and 37 target markets. Monica is a CACI database which predicts age group of prospects by their first name, and claims this is true of 75 per cent of cases.

A sophistication of ACORN is the Post Office Consumer Location System (*see* 19).

Table 8.1 *The ACORN system*

		1981 Population	%
Acorn groups			
A	Agricultural areas	1,811,485	3.4
B	Modern family housing, higher incomes	8,667,137	16.2
C	Older housing of intermediate status	9,420,477	17.6
D	Poor quality older terraced housing	2,320,846	4.3
E	Better-off council estates	6,976,570	13.0
F	Less well-off council estates	5,032,657	9.4
G	Poorest council estates	4,048,658	7.6
H	Multi-racial areas	2,086,026	3.9
I	High status non-family areas	2,248,207	4.2
J	Affluent suburban housing	8,514,878	15.9
K	Better-off requirement areas	2,041,338	3.8
U	Unclassified	388,632	0.7

(*cont.*)

			1981 Population	%
Acorn types				
A	1	Agricultural villages	1,376,427	2.6
A	2	Areas of farms and smallholdings	435,058	0.8
B	3	Cheap modern private housing	2,209,759	4.1
B	4	Recent private housing, young families	1,648,534	3.1
B	5	Modern private housing, older children	3,121,453	5.8
B	6	New detached houses, young families	1,404,893	2.6
B	7	Military bases	282,498	0.5
C	8	Mixed owner-occupied and council estates	1,880,142	3.5
C	9	Small town centres and flats above shops	2,157,360	4.0
C	10	Villages with non-farm employment	2,463,246	4.6
C	11	Older private housing, skilled workers	2,919,729	5.5
D	12	Unimproved terraces with old people	1,351,877	2.5
D	13	Pre-1914 terraces, low income families	762,266	1.4
D	14	Tenement flats lacking amenities	206,703	0.4
E	15	Council estates, well-off older workers	1,916,242	3.6
E	16	Recent council estates	1,392,961	2.6
E	17	Council estates, well-off young workers	2,615,376	4.9
E	18	Small council houses, often Scottish	1,051,991	2.0
F	19	Low rise estates in industrial towns	2,538,119	4.7
F	20	Inter-war council estates, older people	1,667,994	3.1
F	21	Council housing for the elderly	826,544	1.5
G	22	New council estates in inner cities	1,079,351	2.0
G	23	Overspill estates, high unemployment	1,729,757	3.2
G	24	Council estates with overcrowding	868,141	1.6
G	25	Council estates with worst poverty	371,409	0.7
H	26	Multi-occupied terraces, poor Asians	204,493	0.4
H	27	Owner-occupied terraces with Asians	577,871	1.1
H	28	Multi-let housing with Afro-Caribbeans	387,169	0.7
H	29	Better-off multi-ethnic areas	916,493	1.7
I	30	High status areas, few children	1,129,079	2.1
I	31	Multi-let big old houses and flats	822,017	1.5
I	32	Furnished flats, mostly single people	297,111	0.6
J	33	Inter-war semis, white-collar workers	3,054,032	5.7
J	34	Spacious inter-war semis, big gardens	2,676,598	5.0
J	35	Villages with wealthy older commuters	1,533,756	2.9
J	36	Detached houses, exclusive suburbs	1,250,492	2.3
K	37	Private houses, well-off elderly	1,199,703	2.2
K	38	Private flats with single pensioners	841,635	1.6
U	39	Unclassified	388,632	0.7
Area total			53,556,911	100.0

17. Updating and culling

It is important to have an up-to-date mailing list, and it is bad policy to build a continuous mailing list which is never checked or revised. People do move, change their names or die. A mailing list of customers can be out-of-date after two years and in some cases in six months. Culling is important. Check mailings are sent out by some firms, enclosing request cards for their latest catalogue. It costs a lot of money to print catalogues so they should not be wasted.

Lists should not be added to indiscriminately, and sometimes it is better to compile a new list for each mailing if they are carried out at long intervals. Computerised lists can be attractive if they are used regularly, but if errors are entered wrong addresses will continue to be used because no complaints may be forthcoming, and if the same address is entered in varying styles it can be very difficult to trace all the alternative duplicates and eliminate them. Recipients can be irritated by repeat mailings of the same shot. This is a medium where it is easy to please or displease the recipient.

Because direct mail can annoy people it is sometimes, and often unfairly, denigrated as *junk mail*. True, it is unsolicited and people may object to receiving commercial offers, but it all depends on whether the mailing has been well targeted to those likely to respond to offers and propositions. Much of the criticism of junk mail has arisen because so many people's names and addresses have become available. One of the biggest users of direct mail are financial firms which exploit the availability of huge share registers of privatised companies. They mail shareholders with offers of other investments such as unit trusts, insurance schemes and pension schemes. Inevitably, there can be repetition.

18. The Mailing Preference Service

Not everyone wishes to receive promotional material in their homes, while some are willing enough to accept more. An interesting development is the Mailing Preference Service (MPS) sponsored by the four leading trade associations in the industry plus the Post Office. The object of the scheme is to permit any member of the public to have his or her name deleted from or added to a mailing list operated by a number of the sponsoring trade associations. It is, for instance, a condition of membership of the Association of Mail Order Publishers (AMOP) that the MPS service be operated.

For the public, the service acts as a safety valve for those who object to receiving mail-shots, and thus helps to maintain the good name of the medium. An inherent problem with direct mail is that the advertising is unsolicited, whereas with other media one expects to be exposed to advertising. It has been given a good deal of publicity in TV programmes like *That's Life* and *Checkout* which have been dealing with viewer's complaints about junk mail.

A similar scheme has been run in the USA for many years. When the MPS was launched in Britain in 1984, the majority of requests were for deletions, but in America it has been found that add-ons outnumber deletions. It will be interesting to see whether a similar pattern will emerge here, but it may be that in a small country like Britain with many large circulation national daily and Sunday newspapers the experience will differ from that in a very large country with no comparable national press media and therefore possibly greater acceptance of direct mail advertising. Members of the public who wish to take advantage of the MPS should write to 22 Eccleston Street, London SW1W 9PY, while trade enquiries should be sent to the managing agents of the scheme, the Association of Mail Order Publishers, 1 New Burlington Street, London W1X 1FD. The AMOP, incidentally, represents firms which sell books, magazines, records and cassettes by post.

19. Consumer Location System

A Classification Of Residential Neighbourhoods (ACORN, as devised by CACI and described in **16 (f)** above) is a system for classifying people according to the type of area in which they live. The Post Office's Consumer Location System (CLS) links ACORN with the Target Group Index (*see* 15:**22**) to provide a profile of potential consumers for a given product or service, and through the postcode system can enable more precise targeting of advertising campaigns, and in particular direct mail. The system makes it possible to specify mass consumer markets in much tighter terms; establishes a rational basis for inter-media cost comparisons (direct mail comes out well for many product fields); and gives access to accurate lists of names and addresses of potential purchasers within specific target markets.

Free booklets and general advice on the use of the Consumer Location System are available from Royal Mail Marketing (RMM2.3), Freepost, 33 Grosvenor Place, London SW1X 1EE.

20. Electronic post

Electronic post is a bulk-mail service which combines computing with laser printing and Post Office services. It can be used for mailings of from one thousand to a million or more. The client either supplies a computer tape carrying addresses and messages or sends them by direct data transmission. The Post Office prints the letters and envelopes then delivers them to an agreed timescale, which can be as quickly as the following day. It can be used for sales letters, news releases, reminders, invoices and statements. The text can be identical or individual and personalised, provided all the data is on the tape. If artwork is provided, graphics can be included, and 21 typefaces in various sizes are available. The system is operated by Postal Marketing, 22–25 Finsbury Square, London EC2A 1PH.

Mail drops

21. Door-to-door distribution

Not all direct advertising, or distribution of materials, is sent by post. A large volume is delivered door-to-door to houses, shops or offices. This can provide saturation coverage of chosen areas, although it need not be as haphazard or wasteful as might be thought. Computers can once again be of considerable use in advertising to provide selectivity by enumerating districts from computer tapes based on the statistics of the national census.

There are three types of mail-drop service, (*a*) by specialist door-to-door distributors; (*b*) by the Post Office; and (*c*) in conjunction with the delivery of free newspapers.

22. Typical mail-drop material

In the case of door-to-door distributors, teams, usually consisting of women employed part-time, are used to hand-deliver samples, leaflets and special promotional items such as money-off premium vouchers which can be redeemed at local shops. Envelopes for posting films to film processors are often hand-delivered, as are shopping magazines containing advertisers' offers which again contain cash vouchers. Bonusprint advertise on television and tell viewers an envelope will be delivered at their homes for sending films for processing. They also refer to their mail drops in their ads on the Post Office video service screens (*see* 5:15). This kind of direct advertising can be a sales promotion aid. Trade advertising can also be conducted in this way, mail drops being made to selected retailers.

23. Advantages and disadvantages
Mail drops are obviously cheaper than direct mail, requiring no envelopes, addressing or postage. Saturation coverage is possible, which is desirable with products and services used by the mass market. If it is desired to support retailers, or to boost sales in certain areas, it is a valuable medium. However, if a number of items are distributed simultaneously, as often happens, householders may resent a litter of leaflets, and perhaps pay less attention to them than they would if a single item was delivered with its solus or monopoly effect.

Direct response marketing

24. Reasons for growth
It is no accident that direct response marketing has had such a remarkable success in recent years. The history of distribution has come full circle for direct response rejects the impersonal nature of mass media advertising and supermarket-style shopping and has brought the manufacturer and the buyer closer together, resembling the original face-to-face situation of seller and buyer in the market-place or small shop. The reasons for the growth and success of direct marketing are as follows.

(a) Lack of personal services in self-service stores, supermarkets and hypermarkets.
(b) Problems of car-parking and road congestion near shopping centres.
(c) Popularity of credit and charge cards.
(d) High cost of using sales representatives, whether in consumer or business-to-business marketing.
(e) Arrival of new media such as magazines with weekend

newspapers and encouragement to use the telephone instead of the post in order to buy—even if the offer came by post.

The industry has its own monthly magazine, *Direct Response*.

25. Range of methods

Today the variety of means by which 'armchair' shopping can be conducted are only limited by the ability of modern mail order traders to conceive yet another technique of what is now called direct response marketing. We have moved a long way from the mail-order bargains of the popular press or the mail order club catalogues, although both still exist. It is now a sophisticated business extending rapidly into the realms of alternative television, micro-computers and videodisc catalogues. At the same time, traditional media continue to be used, but this does now include commercial television, as with recorded music producers. The largest single user of direct response is insurance, and Fig. 8.1 is an example of a coupon from an insurance advertisement.

26. Direct marketing agencies

Reference was made to direct response agencies in 3:22 (c), and this has become a very substantial area of agency business, conducted either by specialist agencies, or by specialist subsidiaries of well-known agencies. A major reason for the expansion of direct response marketing has been the demand from clients for 'accountable advertising' where they can measure the response in enquiries, sales leads or sales.

According to the *Campaign Report* of 25 May 1990, the top ten direct marketing agencies are as listed in Table 8.2. However, an interesting feature of this report (and its table of the top 50 agencies) was the way in which it separated *income* from *turnover*, whereas with other types of advertising agency *billings* are given. This is because in direct marketing, many costs are merely passed on to the client, a major difference between the original concepts of above-the-line and below-the-line advertising, the former being based on commission-paying media.

The varying amounts in the turnover column reflect the different types of campaign costs such as print, postage or advertisement space. This is a growth area in British advertising, many new agencies have appeared in recent years, and these are

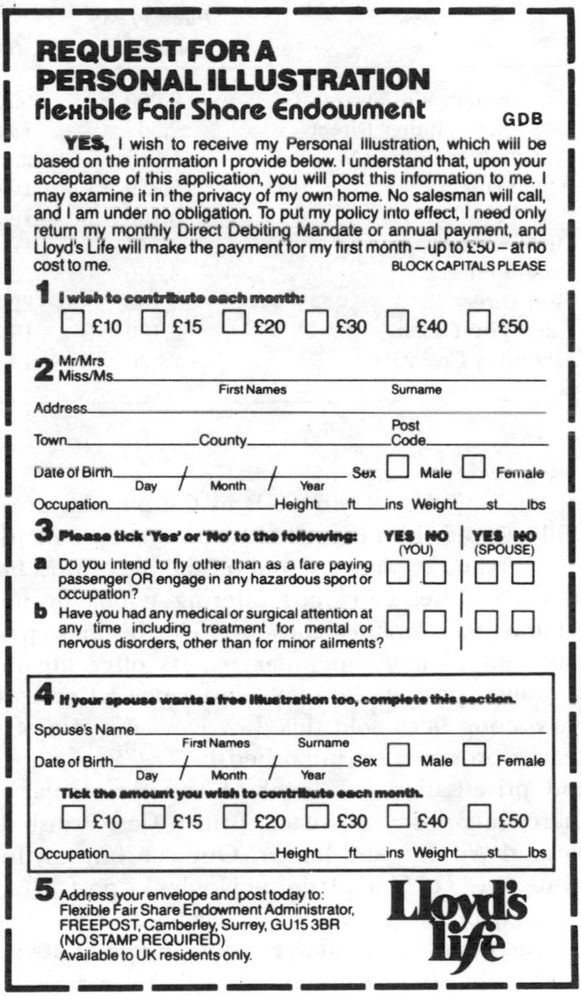

REQUEST FOR A PERSONAL ILLUSTRATION
Flexible Fair Share Endowment GDB

YES, I wish to receive my Personal Illustration, which will be based on the information I provide below. I understand that, upon your acceptance of this application, you will post this information to me. I may examine it in the privacy of my own home. No salesman will call, and I am under no obligation. To put my policy into effect, I need only return my monthly Direct Debiting Mandate or annual payment, and Lloyd's Life will make the payment for my first month – up to £50 – at no cost to me. BLOCK CAPITALS PLEASE

1 I wish to contribute each month:
☐ £10 ☐ £15 ☐ £20 ☐ £30 ☐ £40 ☐ £50

2 Mr/Mrs Miss/Ms ____ First Names ____ Surname ____
Address ____
Town ____ County ____ Post Code ____
Date of Birth ____ Day / Month / Year Sex ☐ Male ☐ Female
Occupation ____ Height ____ ft ____ ins Weight ____ st ____ lbs

3 Please tick 'Yes' or 'No' to the following: YES NO (YOU) | YES NO (SPOUSE)
a Do you intend to fly other than as a fare paying passenger OR engage in any hazardous sport or occupation? ☐ ☐ | ☐ ☐
b Have you had any medical or surgical attention at any time including treatment for mental or nervous disorders, other than for minor ailments? ☐ ☐ | ☐ ☐

4 If your spouse wants a free illustration too, complete this section.
Spouse's Name ____ First Names ____ Surname ____
Date of Birth ____ Day / Month / Year Sex ☐ Male ☐ Female
Tick the amount you wish to contribute each month.
☐ £10 ☐ £15 ☐ £20 ☐ £30 ☐ £40 ☐ £50
Occupation ____ Height ____ ft ____ ins Weight ____ st ____ lbs

5 Address your envelope and post today to:
Flexible Fair Share Endowment Administrator,
FREEPOST, Camberley, Surrey, GU15 3BR
(NO STAMP REQUIRED)
Available to UK residents only.

Lloyd's Life

Figure 8.1 *Coupon from an insurance advertisement.*

the power-houses behind the direct mail, catalogue selling, inserts and off-the-page ads which now flourish.

Table 8.2 *Top ten direct marketing agencies*

Rank	Agency	Income 1989 (£000)	Turnover 1989 (£000)
1	Wunderman Worldwide	9,000	55,500
2	Ogilvy and Mather Direct	7,367	18,263
3	Watson Ward Albert Varndell	6,910	25,574
4	Aspen Direct	5,439	10,490
5	Beard Hawkins Direct	5,150	10,240
6	DDM Advertising	4,114	12,160
7	Programmes	3,596	3,996
8	Grey Direct	3,162	22,000
9	Evans Hunt Scott	3,100	17,000
10	McCarthy Cosby Paul	2,830	13,900

27. Off-the-page

From small black and white ads in the popular press to full-colour, full-page ads in the weekend colour supplements, a huge variety of goods and services are sold off-the-page. Most hobby and enthusiasts magazines carry ads offering goods by post, from foreign stamps to computer software. The business pages offer unit trusts, and even the popular papers offer life insurance, motor-car and private hospital insurance. Correspondence courses have long been sold this way. Even the sale of shares is conducted by prospectuses published in *The Times* and *Financial Times*, and privatisation has involved the spectacular issues of public shares in British Aerospace, British Gas, British Telecom, BP, Cable and Wireless and Jaguar. One can buy anything from cases of wine to Isle of Man platinum Nobles by post.

The Linguaphone Institute (*see* Fig. 8.2) have made their entire advertisement a coupon to cut out, and good use is made of either a compact audio cassette or a plastic record to pursue further the direct response marketing effort (*see* also 5:**7**).

In addition to off-the-page press advertisements there has been a boom in *inserts* tipped into publications. Some readers find them a nuisance and tip them in the bin before reading the magazine, but it depends on their interest value to readers, that is, how well they are targeted. A good way to avoid having inserts

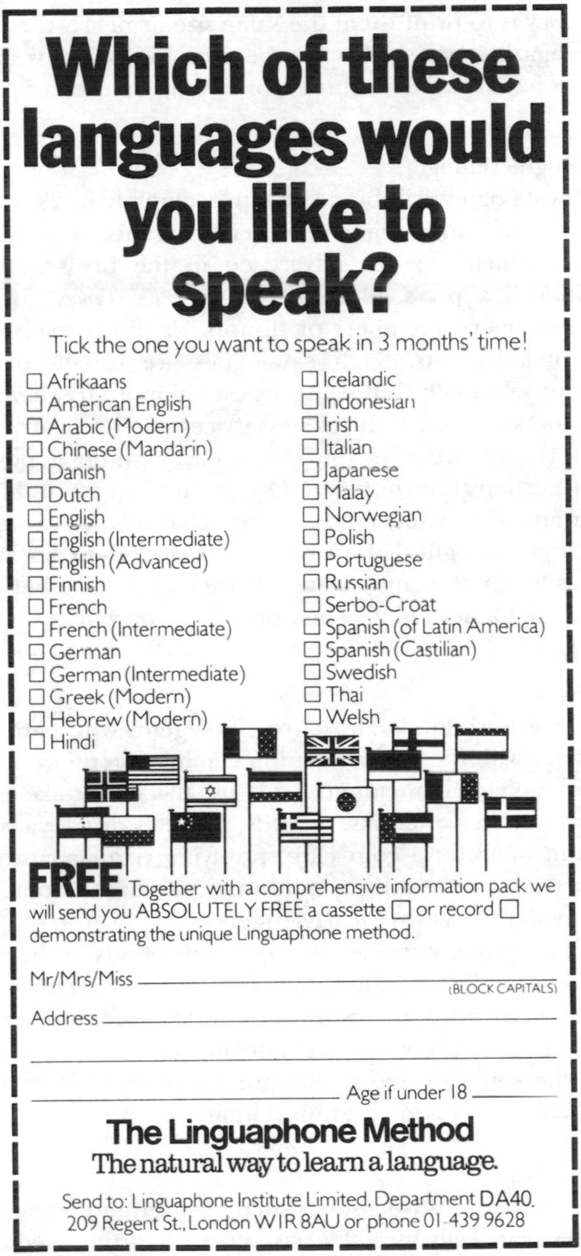

Figure 8.2 *A whole advertisement as a coupon.*

thrown away is to print them the same size or nearly the same size as the magazine page. This has become big business and large publishers have special machines for tipping in inserts.

28. Catalogue selling

Club catalogues will be dealt with separately in **29**. A number of commercial and non-commercial organisations sell from catalogues which may be advertised in the press and on TV (perhaps with a press ad tie-up in, say, *TV Times*), or sent to regular customers, members or donors, or direct mailed against selected mailing lists. Such catalogues are usually distributed annually or seasonally, but some are issued more frequently. They may be for specific products or services such as garden seeds, bulbs or roses; foreign stamps or coins; fashion goods; wines; pipes; or perhaps tour holidays. One of the biggest in this field is the Automobile Association. Many charities raise funds by distributing catalogues of Christmas cards, calendars and gifts, and occasionally they may issue gift catalogues at other times of the year. Catalogues can also be tipped into journals.

29. Clubs

There are two kinds, those for club agents who enrol a circle of members, with the agents earning commission on the sales; and clubs for individual members who usually undertake to buy a minimum number of books, records, cassettes or CDs a year. The Royal Mint operates a coin club, notifying regular customers of new issues but not requiring minimum purchases. Some airlines operate mail order clubs for passengers.

The first group enrol agents by means of ads in the women's press and in family magazines like *TV Times* and *Radio Times*. The reader should note the special wording of the application coupons in these ads. Particular information is requested such as whether the applicant has a telephone, and there is generally an age limit and perhaps geographical limits.

30. Television

With certain advertisers such as gramophone record companies (e.g. Tellydisc), TV has become a prime medium. The viewer telephones the order to a TV service number where it is entered on a computer, and the advertiser receives a print-out of orders within 24 hours.

31. Telephone selling

The telephone has become a medium in itself, and according to Lester Wunderman of Wunderman International, the two biggest media in the USA are the two direct media of direct mail and the telephone. The more compact urbanised conditions in Britain probably preclude this happening on the American scale, but there have been big developments in what is sometimes called telemarketing. In fact some advertising agencies now have a subsidiary engaged in telephone marketing.

Now British Telecom promises to revolutionise telephone selling with a TV-like screen beside the telephone to screen a picture of the person at the other end of the line. The possibilities of this development are obviously very great for telephone selling since merchandise can be shown to a caller.

However, like junk mail, telephone selling has its merits and demerits. It is an excellent way of selling advertisement space including classifieds. But a number of home improvement firms often annoy householders by ringing them in the evening, perhaps interrupting their favourite television programme.

32. Viewdata

The teletext systems of Ceefax (BBC) and Oracle (ITV) are one-way electronic TV transmissions, but Viewdata (Prestel) is an interactive system which is being taken up more and more for direct response marketing purposes. It was first introduced in 1979, and its growth has been limited only by the number of homes with sets equipped to enjoy the service, although owners of popular micro-computers such as the BBC Acorn, Sinclair or Commodore can enjoy a cheap entry into the Prestel system by purchase of a modem and software and payment of a weekly membership subscription to Micronet 800. This means that there are now thousands of members who have access to Prestel. The Micronet facility makes possible instant tele-shopping such as the purchase of software which can be despatched and charged to the caller's telephone account.

British Telecom operates a series of regional computers which hold pages of information, and more than 300,000 pages are available on a host of subjects. If a viewer requests a brochure it is received by the advertiser (or information provider as he is called) in seconds. Nothing can compete with such instant response.

Homelink is a joint venture service operated by the Nottingham Building Society, the Bank of Scotland and Thomas Cook, which makes cheques and correspondence unnecessary and enables funds to be transferred instantly from the member's account to pay for the purchase. The service is described in the Homelink advertisement reproduced in Fig. 8.3. This advertisement appeared in the *Daily Telegraph, Financial Times, Guardian, The Standard, The Times, Mail on Sunday, Observer, Sunday Express, Sunday Telegraph, Sunday Times* plus specialist professional, financial and management magazines.

Mail-order clubs such as Kays and Great Universal can be joined by the Tele-ordering method, and Tele-shopping makes possible the instant purchase of goods shown on Prestel pages, including books from W.H. Smith. Goods can be ordered from Debenhams and Harrods 'off the screen'. This is done by including a response frame ordering facility with the advertising pages. With Tele-booking it is possible to reserve hotel accommodation in the UK and 70 other countries. These last three services are included in Viewtel's Club 403 (produced by Viewtel 202), for which the viewer needs only a Prestel-fitted TV set and a credit card.

33. Teledata

Advertisers quote the Teledata (BHP) number 071-200-0200 to make enquiries or order goods. It is a 24-hour personalised telemarketing service, making it unnecessary for customers to mail coupons (as in off-the-page direct response), and for advertisers to handle them. All the sales information is held in a computer. For example, an advertisement for the Hyundai Stella 1.6 motor car, concluded with: 'phone Teledata 071-200-0200 for a brochure and the name and address of your nearest dealer'. Not only did the Teledata receptionist give the addresses of the nearest dealers, and note the caller's address in order to send the brochure, but she asked where the advertisement had been seen and the make and year of the caller's present car.

There are similar systems through which consumers can buy goods as varied as sports gear, foreign stamps and houses, while

HOMELINK 4448877e Op

∏BS STATEMENT OF ACCOUNT

Account No 11800999900
MR J S SMITH

Date	Code	Dr/Cr	Balance
12.03.84	CQ	45.65	12,375.79
19.03.84	CASH	124.21	12,500.00
22.03.84	CQ	14.65	12,485.35
28.03.84	EFT	56.78	12,428.57
30.03.84	CQ	12.63	12,415.94
03.04.84	CQ	789.23	11,626.71
05.04.84	CASH	873.29	12,500.00
08.04.84	CQ	100.32	12,399.68
12.04.84	UCQ	125.00	12,524.68
14.04.84	INT	226.45	12,751.13

— 10.00PM SUNDAY —

Watch your Interest grow

This is just one facet of Homelink's unique Homebanking and discount Teleshopping service.

After years of secret development we've harnessed "pie in the sky" science fiction and made it work in the home. Fact.

Check your bank statement 24 hours a day, pay all your bills and even book your holiday, 7 days a week.

All from your armchair, on your ordinary T.V. set.

No other Building Society can offer you Homelink or anything like it.

FREEFONE HOMELINK or Prestel *444#. Or simply fill in and return this coupon or call in at any Thomas Cook Travelshop.

DON'T WASTE A SECOND. Please send me full details of HOMELINK.

NAME _____

ADDRESS _____

POSTCODE _____ TEL _____

HOME●LINK
SIMPLY PRESS IT AND GET IT!

A UNIQUE PARTNERSHIP BETWEEN BRITISH TELECOM,
NOTTINGHAM BUILDING SOCIETY AND BANK OF SCOTLAND.

Nottingham Building Society incorporates London Commercial,
Grantham and Lincoln Building Societies.   BANK OF SCOTLAND
Prestel and the Prestel symbol are trademarks of British Telecommunications.

Post coupon to: Nottingham Building Society, 5-13 Upper Parliament Street, Nottingham NG1 2BX.
Or FREEFONE HOMELINK now!

Figure 8.3 *This Homelink advertisement demonstrates the use of Prestel Viewdata.*

Computerised car selling is an effective way of matching offers and requirements in the second-hand car market. Details of available cars are held in the computer, and when prospective buyers telephone a description of the kind of car they want the telephonist searches for suitable cars. If a car does not sell, the price can be reduced while if the customer does not offer enough he can offer more, and so a process of market price adjustment can take place until a sale or purchase is concluded.

34. Electronic mail

This is a system whereby mail is received on a Telex or non-Telex computer terminal with a modem which permits a print-out on a printer. There are several systems such as British Telecommunications Gold, Western Union Priority Mail, and the Cable and Wireless Easylink service which permits messages to be received by non-Telex users or Telex messages to be received on non-Telex terminals. Although limited to recipients who have the necessary receiving equipment, the growth of such office facilities is making electronic mail a viable direct response medium especially since there is the interaction facility to respond directly and quickly.

Consumer protection

35. Mail Order Protection Scheme

Direct marketing relies on trust. Customers have to send money in advance and do not see the goods until they arrive. That is why this form of trading is less common in developing countries.

In Britain, the Mail Order Protection Scheme means that customers are protected by the publishers who do not wish to receive complaints from readers (*see* Fig. 8.4).

36. Direct mail standards

Established with Post Office support, the Direct Mail Services Standards Board promotes improvements in the ethical and professional standards of the industry. (*See* also **16:43**.)

THE NATIONAL NEWSPAPER

MOPS

MAIL ORDER PROTECTION SCHEME

ORDER WITH CONFIDENCE

Mail order advertisements within this newspaper requiring payment to be sent in direct response are approved under the terms of the Mail Order Protection Scheme (MOPS).

This means that you are fully protected from financial loss should the advertiser default and cease to trade.

The scheme does not cover certain types of advertisements including classified announcements and purchases from catalogues and brochures.

Should you have an enquiry or need advice about mail order advertisements write to the MOPS office in London giving the following details: –

  i) date of the advertisement;

  ii) name and address of the advertiser;

  iii) nature of product and method of payment.

REMEMBER MOPS exists for your benefit.

Full details of the scheme and the excluded categories of advertising can be obtained by sending a S.A.E. to **The National Newspaper Mail Order Protection Scheme (MOPS),** 16 Tooks Court, London EC4A 1LB.

Figure 8.4 *Typical MOPS advertisement.*

37. Legal and voluntary protection

It is important to understand the difference between the self-regulatory requirements of voluntary codes, plus the house rules of the media owners, and the statutes which make certain practices illegal and liable to prosecution. The British Code of

Advertising Practice (*see* 16:**36**), among other things, stipulates what may be said about the investment value of collectables (coins, medals, plates, etc.). One of the problems which media owners seek to prevent is the advertising of products which are not stocked until orders are received, by which time the supplier's price may have risen, possibly leading to bankruptcy if the advertiser honours the orders at his quoted price. The law, on the other hand, may be concerned with the correct description of goods. For example, a one-time racket was to describe textiles as 'art. silk'. In small type, the full point between art and silk could be deceptive, and it was easy for readers to assume mistakenly that the garment was made of silk when in fact the words meant artificial silk, i.e. rayon.

There are many laws which could concern the direct response marketer, and some may be of general application wherever the goods are sold. Relevant statutes are explained in Chapter 16. To these may be added the common law of contract. Most of these laws apply to off-the-page direct response, some apply to all forms of direct response marketing, and the Broadcasting Act and its Code apply solely to commercial radio and television.

The question of legal versus voluntary control is discussed more fully in Chapter 16.

Progress test 8

1. Distinguish between *direct mail* and *mail order*. (**2**)
2. What are the special characteristics of direct mail? (**3–8**)
3. When can direct mail be a primary advertising medium? (**7**)
4. Describe the pattern of an effective sales letter. (**10**)
5. What is a one-piece mailer? (**12**)
6. When is a printed envelope important to a direct mail campaign? (**13**)
7. How may mailing lists be compiled? (**16**)
8. What do the letters ACORN stand for, and how can it be applied to direct mail? (**16**)
9. Describe the Mailing Preference Service. (**18**)
10. What is the Consumer Location System? (**19**
11. What is meant by 'electronic post'? (**20**)
12. How does a mail drop differ from direct mail? (**21**)

13. What is direct response marketing? **(24, 25)**

14. Explain the meaning of 'off-the-page'. **(27)**

15. Explain the direct response methods of catalogue selling and mail order clubs. **(28, 29)**

16. What are the latest techniques in direct response marketing? **(30–34)**

17. How do the media protect consumers from abuses of mail-order trading or direct response marketing? **(35)**

18. How are consumers given legal protection from abuses of mail order trading or direct response marketing? **(37)**

9
Exhibitions

Importance of exhibitions

1. History

Exhibitions are popular throughout the world and have a long history, originating with old trading markets such as the 'marts' in what are today Belgium and the Netherlands, where British merchants sold their wool and woollens in the fourteenth century. The exhibition developed into the show attended by either the trade or the general public. London for many years became a major exhibition centre, to mention only the Great Exhibition of 1851, the Wembley Exhibition of 1924, and the Festival of Britain in 1951. In recent years the National Exhibition Centre in Birmingham has rivalled London although many events are held at Olympia, Earls Court, the Horticultural Halls and the Barbican Centre in the City.

An insight into the British exhibition scene is given by the research report published by the Exhibition Industry Federation on its findings for 1989 when the number of exhibitions held in the UK increased by 8.6 per cent to 707, compared with the previous year. Key findings were:

1. 74 per cent of sales leads were new ones.
2. 29 per cent of leads were expected to be converted to sales.
3. 83 per cent of exhibitors said exhibitions were important for maintaining client contacts.
4. 90 per cent of exhibitors have a positive attitude and intend to exhibit again.
5. 10.6 million visitors attended UK exhibitions in 1989.
6. 8.27 per cent were overseas visitors.

These figures give an optimistic picture, showing expansion in the number of shows, in visitors, in expenditure and in attracting overseas participation.

2. International exhibitions

Throughout the world there are major exhibition centres, often government supported (unlike Britain!), the chief ones in Europe being Frankfurt, Basle and Milan. Many exhibitions are nowadays held in the Gulf states, an indication of the need to develop their emergent economies. Permanent trade exhibition centres exist in developing countries such as Malaysia and Nigeria. The Department of Trade and Industry supports exhibitors interested in exports by organising British exhibitions abroad, taking British pavilions at Expos and arranging Joint Venture schemes with subsidies for British participants.

Types of exhibition

3. Introduction

This is a versatile medium, and its many forms are described in **4–14** below.

4. Public indoor

Usually held in specially built halls, the public show is based on a theme of public interest such as food, the home, do-it-yourself, gardening or holidays and travel. The most famous is the *Daily Mail* Ideal Home Exhibition which has been held for more than 50 years.

5. Trade or business indoor

A more specialised type of exhibition, this will probably have a smaller attendance consisting of *bona fide* visitors who are invited, given tickets in their trade journal or admitted on presentation of their business card.

6. Joint trade and public indoor

Some events, such as motor shows, may have days allocated to trade or public visitors.

7.   Private indoor

These are usually confined to one sponsor, but occasionally consist of a few sponsors with associated but not rival interests. Venues are usually hotels, local halls, libraries, building centres or company premises if suitable.

8.   Outdoor

Certain subjects lend themselves to outdoor exhibitions, for instance aviation, farm equipment (at agricultural shows), camping and large construction equipment. Exhibition stands may also be available at outdoor or tented events like flower shows, gymkhanas and horse shows. In hotter countries, exhibitions normally held indoors in the northern hemisphere will be held out-of-doors.

9.   Travelling

Mobile exhibitions can be transported by caravan, specially built exhibition vehicles, converted double-decker buses, trains, aircraft and ships. British Rail has its special Ambassador exhibition train which can be used by a single client and taken to a choice of railway stations throughout the country where visitors can be received. It can also be taken to European countries. Mobile van shows are common in developing countries, travelling from town to town and village to village.

10.   Portable

This is the kind of knock-down exhibition which can be carried in an estate car or small van, and put up in hotels, shops, public halls and libraries. It can be supported by sales girls, demonstrations, seminars and slide, video or film shows. Some can be left unattended in public places if they are self-explanatory, like a book exhibition in a public library.

11.   In-store

These are popular with foreign sponsors who organise weeks in different towns to display foods, wines, fabrics, pottery, glassware or tourist attractions. Similarly, British Weeks are organised in foreign cities. The displays are usually in appropriate stores, but a special entertainment evening may be organised for the public in a theatre or hall, when singers, dancers and/or films may constitute the programme. In-store demonstrations and fashion shows may also be organised such as those for sewing machines, while Marks & Spencer have organised public fashion shows during the evening at their stores.

12. Permanent exhibitions

Some large organisations may hold exhibitions within their premises or in special halls or parks. A particularly attractive one is Legoland, a children's park at Billund, Denmark, which demonstrates Lego toys.

The following are well worth visiting, combining as they do well mounted exhibits with video shows:

The Thames Barrier Exhibition, near Woolwich.
The *Mary Rose* Exhibition, Portsmouth Dockyard.
The Eurotunnel Exhibition, Folkestone.

13. Conferences

In association with annual conferences there is often an exhibition supported by suppliers which delegates may visit between and after conference sessions. Some of them are quite small, perhaps arranged in an ante-room or in the foyer of the hotel, but others are as big as the conference itself. The larger exhibitions are usually held at venues like Brighton or Harrogate where there are combined conference and exhibition facilities.

14. Window

Here we have a special use of the portable exhibition, when the window of a business can be made more attractive by accepting the loan of a ready-made exhibit. This idea has been taken up by a great many building societies. Some exhibits, like those of Rentokil, may be relevant to property owners, but an astonishing array of subjects are shown in this way and they are certainly more attractive than the usual displays of interest rates which do not differ much from one building society to another whatever names they may give to similar investment schemes. Thus, both the exhibitor and the building society benefit from the attention gained.

Characteristics of exhibitions

15. Introduction
Exhibitions are unlike any other forms of advertising and can include selling direct off-the-stand to visitors. The special characteristics of exhibitions are summarised in **16–21**.

16. Focal point and magnet
The chief value of an exhibition is that it draws attention to its subject and so attracts people, often from great distances. Thus the exhibitor has the opportunity of meeting people he would never meet nor have time to contact. The message of the exhibition, and often that of individual exhibitors, spreads far beyond the event itself, and coverage is possible throughout the appropriate media at home and abroad. However, this last point depends on how far the exhibitor exploits the public relations opportunities, which often means collaborating with the exhibition press officer months in advance. One public relations opportunity is to *invite* the official opener to visit the stand since he or she usually has an itinerary arranged in advance for a short tour of the exhibition.

17. Time-consuming
An exhibition requires a lot of time for its preparation, and for manning the stand. It is essential that the stand is manned by knowledgeable people capable of answering visitors' questions.

18. Prototypes
Exhibitions provide opportunities to display prototypes of new products, and to receive visitors' comments and criticisms.

19. Face-to-face confrontation
Confidence, credibility and goodwill can be established by meeting potential customers face-to-face. This applies to both distributors and consumers.

In an article 'Exhibition UK—The Facts' in *Sales and Marketing Management* (July/August 1990), Bill Murray, marketing manager of British Telecom, was quoted as saying, 'At exhibitions we get the opportunity to discuss actual business issues with our customers and look at how British Telecom can help them achieve their business objectives, such as improved efficiency, better customer and staff relations and, most importantly, increased profitability'.

20. Demonstration and sampling

There are ideal opportunities actually to show the product which is more authentic than describing and illustrating it in advertisements, catalogues and sales literature. Similarly, sampling provides a good sales promotion opportunity.

21. Atmosphere

The atmosphere of an exhibition is very congenial, even though a long visit may be hard on the feet. For many people it is an outing to be enjoyed and there is an atmosphere of entertainment like going to the circus or the theatre.

Using exhibitions

22. Information about exhibitions

There are many trade papers which give forward dates of exhibitions, the most complete details appearing in *Exhibition Bulletin*. Other publications which announce some exhibition details are *British Rate and Data, Conferences and Exhibitions International* and *Sales and Marketing Management.*

23. A checklist for potential exhibitions

The following points should be borne in mind before booking space in an exhibition.

(a) *Organisers.* Is the event organised by a responsible firm? Are they members of the Association of Exhibition Organisers? Have they run this or other shows before?

(b) *Date.* What is the date, is it convenient and does it clash with any other event?

(c) *Venue.* Is it a good venue, that is one likely to attract a good attendance? Is it a convenient one for transporting exhibits to and from? Some foreign venues may impose transportation and customs problems. Does it have good transport links? Is there adequate car-parking? Are there nearby hotels?

(**d**) *Cost of sites.* What is the charge per square metre and are, perhaps, modestly priced shell schemes available?

(**e**) *Facilities.* Are all the necessary facilities available such as water, gas or electricity, if they are required?

(**f**) *Publicity.* How will visitors be attracted?

(**g**) *Build-up and knock-down.* Is there adequate time allowed before and after the show for erection and dismantling of stands?

(**h**) *Public relations.* What press office and press visit facilities will there be?

This is an aspect of exhibitions which is overlooked by many exhibitors. It pays to co-operate with the exhibition press officer months before the event. Valuable press, radio and television coverage can be gained from exhibitions, and this is a valuable bonus. Hundreds of journalists visit shows, looking for good stories and pictures. They do not carry suitcases and will shun clumsy press kits packed with irrelevant material.

(**i**) *Associated events.* Are there any associated events like a conference or film/video shows?

(**j**) *Is it justified?* Is the cost of designing and constructing a stand, renting space, printing sales literature, providing hospitality (especially at a trade show) and taking staff away from their regular work justified? Has the company something new to show, does it need to meet distributors and/or customers, must it compete with rival exhibitors? What value may be anticipated for the money spent—in goodwill or sales, including perhaps the finding and appointing of new agents or distributors?

In his very useful book, *Exhibitions and Conferences from A to Z,* (Modina Press, 1989) Sam Black makes the following comment:

'Exhibitions are visited by people expecting to see actual objects. Photographs, diagrams and illustrations play an important part in conveying technical or general information but they should be subsidiary to the three-dimensional exhibits. People will read quite detailed explanatory copy on an exhibition stand if it explains an exhibit which has attracted their curiosity, but isolated panels of text will rarely be read.'

To help choose an exhibition in which to participate there is the annual analysis of UK shows, *Which Exhibition,* published by Conference and Travel Publications of Forest Row.

Progress test 9

1. Describe the main types of public, trade and private exhibitions. (**4–14**)
2. What are the main characteristics of the exhibition as an advertising medium? (**16–21**)
3. Where would you find information about dates and venues of forthcoming exhibitions? (**22**)
4. If you were considering participation in an exhibition what points would you check before signing a contract for space? (**23**)
5. Why are press kits a waste of money? (**23**)

10
Copywriting

Writing copy that sells

1. The creative team

As the IPA definition states, advertising must present 'the most persuasive selling message'. Copywriting is the art of writing selling messages. It is salesmanship in print. If it fails to provoke the desired attention, interest, desire, conviction and action it has failed (*see* 11:2). Of course, it is likely to be assisted by other forms of creativity such as pictures, typography and perhaps colour, but the copywriter should think visually and direct these other elements to achieve his purpose.

The copywriter should work closely with the visualiser and typographer to obtain artistic and typographical interpretation of his copy. The copywriter cannot successfully work in isolation, merely writing the words, with artists working in similar isolation to create the physical appearance of the advertisement. Ideally, and for practical reasons, the complete advertisement should be a team effort. The design or layout should give effective presentation of the words, the illustrations should give emphasis and support, and the typography (choice of typefaces, and their size and weight) should make the copy legible and give emphasis where necessary. The copywriter should always try to write visually.

2. Special literary style

The writing of advertisement copy is a specially skilled kind of writing, and has a style utterly different from that of a book, poem, article, short story or news report. Advertising and public relations writing require two very distinct literary styles. Even the copy for a press advertisement, a sales letter and a piece of sales literature each require their own special treatment, although all three aim to sell.

3. Basic rules
The essential characteristics of copywriting are as follows.

(a) It must sell, even if it only reminds.
(b) The secret of successful advertising is repetition, whether by continuously advertising or by the use of repetition in the advertisement.
(c) People do not necessarily want to read the advertisement. Therefore the message must not waste words, and must convey its message quickly.
(d) If the reader hesitates at an unknown word, attention is lost. Therefore every word must be easily understood and there must be no ambiguity.
(e) Short words, short sentences, short paragraphs help to demonstrate the message and make it easy and quick to read and absorb.

Copy devices

4. Introduction
To achieve its special literary style, and its persuasiveness, the devices described in 5–11 can be used.

5. Clichés
There are certain simple, well-used and sometimes seemingly banal words which are actually highly successful in advertising. They are sometimes called *buzz words*. The most powerful word in advertising is 'free'. It can be applied in many ways, even in the address if Freepost or Freephone facilities can be offered. Even when there is not really a free gift or sample, it is more compelling to offer a free leaflet or a free catalogue. Few people can resist something for nothing!

Other effective advertising clichés are 'Now', 'New', 'Here', 'At Last' and 'Today'.

6. Action words

Verbs can be used to give the copy a sense of urgency and to help the copy to move along. These are almost all short words. Typical examples are:

Buy	Write	Taste	Look
Try	Phone	Watch	Take
Ask	Call	Smell	Drink
Get	Send	Hear	Let
See	Cut	Listen	Do
Ring	Post	Drive	Start
Come	Fill	Eat	Enjoy

Here are some examples of how these words can be used, together with the clichés mentioned earlier.

(a) 'Send today for your free sample, and try the new flavour.'
(b) 'Fill in and cut the coupon, and post it today.'
(c) 'Hear the surf, smell the flowers, taste the wine and enjoy yourself.'
(d) 'Call in and buy one now.'

While the action words above are all short there are, of course, longer ones which can have their positive effect too, such as:

Discover	Remember	Protect
Explore	Examine	Replace
Restore	Complete	Renovate
Repair	Donate	Present
Consider	Decide	Apply

Obviously, there are scores of verbs which can be used in copy but, by isolating the examples given, attention is drawn to the kind of words which help to enliven the sales message. As will be shown, however, there are many other devices which the copywriter can exploit.

7. Emotive or exciting words

These are adjectives, words which are descriptive and enhance the facts. For example, the caption to a picture in a tourist advertisement or brochure could read:

'View from bedroom window.'

However, that does not say very much. It is not very exciting. If the reader looks closely at the picture, the picture may seem to be very nice. The reader has to make an effort to arrive at this conclusion. Why should he bother? The copywriter can do it for him by saying:

'The magnificent view from the bedroom window.'

Even this is not very personal. It does not relate to the potential tourist who has not been convinced that the advertised holiday is for him or her. So why not say:

'You can enjoy this magnificent view from your bedroom window.'

Now we are getting somewhere, but what is the view *of*? The picture cannot speak for itself, so why not be explicit and say, using another descriptive word:

'You can enjoy this magnificient view of the mighty Matterhorn from your bedroom window.'

Now the reader is truly 'put in the picture', and we have added yet another device with the alliterative use of three 'Ms', magnificent, mighty and Matterhorn (*see* 8).

Some of the adjectives which can be used in copy include:

Splendid	Delightful	Wonderful
Amazing	Gorgeous	Beautiful

We can also use emotive generalities such as:

Economical	Money saving	Time saving
Labour saving	Mouth watering	Inexpensive
Value for money	Satisfying	Rewarding

They give no details yet these words help to create a mental image of the product or service, and to *create desire* and *inspire confidence*. The car is economical because it uses less petrol, the holiday is inexpensive and value for money because the price includes so much, the conference will prove to be a rewarding experience.

8. Alliteration

Alliteration results from repeating sounds, and is thus a form of repetition (*see* example in **7**). This repetition of sounds should be pleasing to the ear, not overdone and so obvious that it is irritating. All the devices suggested in this chapter should be accepted by the reader as the natural words to use, even though the effect is specially contrived. Copy may be cleverly written, but it should never appear to be clever, otherwise it will sound false and the reader will feel cheated. Nevertheless, if readers are considering holidays they expect them to be something exciting which can be looked forward to. They do not want them to sound like jail sentences. Below are some famous uses of alliteration and rhyme in advertisements which have appeared over the years.

Players please
Mars are marvellous
Let the train take the strain
Three Nuns, none nicer
Don't be vague, ask for Haig
Go well, go Shell

Alliteration lends itself very well to slogans, making them memorable, but it can be used discreetly and pleasantly in sentences in the text like this:

'Take a ride round the town in the new Crown roadster.'

9. Colloquialisms

Once upon a time the prestige ads in *The Times* and the serious ones in the technical and professional journals used impeccable English. Some of the prestige ads were even written by famous authors, just to give them literary flow. Not so today. They have short, sharp copy just like the ones for FMCGs.

They, like so many consumer ads today, use chatty, conversational colloquialisms such as 'don't', 'couldn't', 'wouldn't', 'won't', 'you'd', 'what's', 'that's' and other abbreviations. We also have snappy expressions like 'Pick 'n Choose', 'Fish 'n Chips'.

10. Punctuation and grammar

The modern copywriter would probably fail an English

examination, if only for abuse of punctuation to achieve effect. One-word sentences that cannot possibly be parsed may be used. Prepositions and conjunctions will be omitted and nouns, verbs, adverbs and adjectives will be linked with dashes or dots. The ellipsis is used freely. Sentences like this will be written:

'Now—special offer!—only 50p if you rush today—biggest value you've ever seen.'

or:

'Now. Special offer! Only 50p if you rush today. Biggest value you've ever seen.'

Much use may be made of the *screamer*, as the exclamation mark is called. In contrast and in contradiction, apparently pedantic use is made of the full point or full stop at the end of some headlines. This is deliberate, giving impact to the headline, and it is known as the *emphatic full point*. Here is an example:

'Write his name in gold.' (Remy Martin)

And here is one from a few years ago which made a charity appeal ad extra compelling:

'Save the children. Now.'

11. Repetition
Finally, there is the use of repetition which may occur in the following ways.

(a) Using the same word to open each paragraph of the text.
(b) Plugging the company or brand name throughout the text.
(c) Repeating the name throughout the headline, pictures, captions, subheadings, text, signature slogan and logo.
(d) Repetition of the ad itself or repeating the same style in a series, or maintaining the same style of layout and typography whenever ads appear. Use of the same position in a publication is also a useful form of repetition, although that is a matter for the space buyer.

Copy elements

12. Seven elements

Now that we have considered the various literary devices which the copywriter can use, let us look at the whole advertisement by analysing the seven elements which may constitute a hard-selling advertisement. In addition to these copy elements there will be the visual creative elements of layout, illustrations, typography and perhaps colour, but in this chapter we are concerned only with the wording.

The seven copy elements are the *headline, subheadings, text, price, name and address, coupon* (if there is one) and the *signature slogan* or *strapline.*

13. Headline

In the past headlines were usually short, and they were often slogans. Today they are more often statements extending to one or two sentences, and displayed so boldly that they are virtually seen rather than read. This visual change in headline writing is probably a result of television with its emphasis on looking. There are also many different kinds of headline so that the copywriter can choose the most original and attention-getting kind of headline for the purpose, and also so that one can be used which is different from that used to advertise rival products. Here are 25 kinds of headline, with an invented example of each.

(a) *Declarative.* The world's toughest tyre.
(b) *Interrogative.* Do you want more interest?
(c) *Commanding.* Buy your books at Brown's.
(d) *Challenging.* Why put up with higher prices?
(e) *Testimonial.* ' I always use Washo', says Millicent Day.
(f) *Association of ideas.* Even Roger Bacon liked eggs.
(g) *News.* The new Royal cooker.
(h) *Emotional.* No one knows she's crying.
(i) *Incongruous.* The fat to make you thin.
(j) *Identification.* Bullman's Brown Ale.
(k) *Curiosity.* Ever heard of a pig cleaning a pipe?
(l) *Bargain.* Now only 99p.
(m) *Humorous.* Josephine's Restaurant is open every night!

(n) *Picture and caption.* She's enjoying an indoor tan (below picture of girl with sun lamp).

(o) *Topical.* The sherry to cheer your Christmas guests.

(p) *Slogan.* Crookes the cleanest cleaners.

(q) *Play on words.* Who's for Denis?

(r) *Alliterative.* The wonderful watches by Waterman.

(s) *Gimmick.* z-z-z-z-Buzz-z-z-z-z-Bar.

(t) *Negative.* Don't spend it, bank it.

(u) *Displayed copy.*

> This is the lawnmower
> which takes you for a
> ride round your lawn.

(v) *TV-tie up.* Perfect picture control (repeating TV commercial jingle).

(w) *Quotation.* 'My kingdom for a horse'—play it safe with Bronco Brakes.

(x) *Split.* An armchair in the sky (picture of passenger on airline) with Pacific Airlines.

(y) *Intriguing.* What's square about a round hole?

14. Subheadings

It is in the writing of subheadings that the copywriter is encouraged to write visually for they contribute very much to the design and typography of the advertisement. They introduce contrast and emphasis since subheadings can be printed in a different typeface, or in larger and bolder type, or possibly in a different colour. The purpose of subheadings can be to:

(a) maintain a sense of movement so that the eye is carried progressively through the copy;

(b) provide typographical contrast as stated above;

(c) emphasise selling points;

(d) divide the ad into sections if there are different ideas or items;

(e) absorb the interest of glancers who take in only the display lines;

(f) make the ad more interesting, more readable, more legible and not a mass of dull, grey type.

15. The text

The text consists of the body matter or the main wording of

the advertisement which is printed in smaller type than the display lines. The display lines consist of the headline, subheadings, prices, name and address and the strapline or signature slogan. Thus, when writing the main copy for an advertisement the copywriter should use his imagination to think how he can use display or bold lines of type to highlight the text and encourage people to read it.

Just as there are many kinds of headline to choose from so there are different ways in which the text can be written. Twelve kinds of text copy are described below.

(a) *Emotive.* Within this kind of copy the emotions can be appealed to. The principal emotional needs are self-assertion, sex and love, companionship, self-preservation, acquisitiveness, curiosity, comfort and security.

An insurance ad may appeal to the emotional need for security from the hazards of fire, burglary, injury or family responsibilities. A gift advertisement may appeal to the emotion of love, and one for collectables such as stamps, coins or antiques to the emotion of acquisitiveness. Ads for health products appeal to the emotional need for self-preservation. Many charity ads appeal to the emotions in different ways.

(b) *Factual—hard-selling.* This is the typical ad which follows the five-point AIDCA formula (*see* 11:2). It is very competitive, persuasive and action promoting. The action may be provoked by a free offer or price cut, and there may be addresses to write to or call at and phone numbers to ring, or response may be sought by means of a coupon.

(c) *Factual—educational.* This is still a hard-selling ad, but it will be more informative, like the ads for the latest-model motor-car.

(d) *Narrative.* Here we have a more literary and leisurely written text, but this style is not limited to prestige ads. The copy is more like a story, and it might be used to promote a holiday cruise. Such copy is also used in the business press to tell the story of a bank or insurance company, and it has been used to recruit nurses and police.

(e) *Prestige.* Again, the copy may be in the narrative style, but being used mainly for public relations purposes the modern prestige or institutional ad has taken on a more vigorous character, setting out facts and arguments in no-nonsense terms.

(f) *Picture and caption.* In this kind of ad there is usually a series of pictures or cartoons with captions underneath, perhaps explaining how to use the product.

(g) *Monologue or dialogue.* Real or fictitious characters may be used to present the sales message. This could be a testimonial advertisment with well-known personalities expounding the merits of the product or the service.

(h) *Gimmick.* Difficult to put over effectively because there is usually need for concentrated reading, this style is sometimes used when a very original presentation is required. It is more likely to be used in magazines, which are read less hurriedly than newspapers, and addressed to sophisticated readerships.

(i) *Reader.* Such advertisements are usually headed by a statement that it is an advertiser's announcement because editors do not like advertisements which pretend to be editorial. However, there are shopping features in which a series of reader ads (usually illustrated) are assembled.

(j) *Testimonial.* This may be in the form of a monologue, but it could be a testimonial statement linked to normal text copy. Here is an example from an advertisement for Fotopost Express:

'I never trust my colour films to anyone else.' Wendy Craig.

Although this was virtually a headline (accompanied by a portrait of the actress) it occupied half the space, the rest of the copy being details of the service, special offers and order coupon.

(k) *Quotation.* It is possible at times to find a statement in a book, play or speech which is relevant to the subject, such as a famous person's description of a place. The following was used in a tourist ad for Botswana: 'Said Frederick Courtney Selous in 1870, "*I never enjoyed any part of my wanderings so much*".'

(l) *Back-selling.* This sort of copy is used to tell readers about a material, ingredient or component which is contained in a finished product, the object being to encourage its continued usage and especially to encourage buyers of the finished product to insist that it includes this item. It could also be applied to equipment in a new house such as the central heating system.

16. Price

People are very price conscious, and can be annoyed by an advertisement which does not state at least a minimum price. If one looks through a newspaper or magazine it will be seen that a very large number of ads make a major selling point of price, and that it is often displayed boldly. There can be a psychological appeal to price: it can be a bargain not to be missed, it may be exceptional value for money, while a high price can suggest quality and possibly even greater desirability. There can also be allusions to price ranging from 'hundreds of bargains' to 'It's not the cheapest' according to the class of product or service.

17. Name and address

It may be sufficient merely to identify the name of the product or company, supported by the logo, but other advertisers—in order to identify themselves clearly, and to attract response—feature their name and address boldly. Usually, this is featured at the end of the ad, and if there is a coupon it should be included in both the main part of the ad and in the coupon, otherwise the address will disappear with the coupon and the reader will have lost the identity of the advertiser should further reference be necessary.

18. Coupon

The writing of coupons is more serious than may be thought, and it is seldom sufficient to ask for no more than a name and address. It is essential that the coupon makes the offer clear, and sets out very clearly any choice of offers, so that the reader understands what he or she is requesting (or ordering), and so that the advertiser can supply satisfactorily. The name and address must be fully given, and this may require a declaration regarding, 'Mr, Mrs or Miss', or 'First name', and the reader should be asked to clarify the address by stating town, county, country, postcode or zip code. This is very important because the same towns occur in both different parts of a country and different parts of the world. Postcodes help immensely in securing safe delivery. A telephone number may also be desirable.

When readers are asked to send money the instructions regarding payments should be clear and specific, and there are requirements under the Advertisements (Hire Purchase) Act that when payment may be made by instalments the number and cost of instalments shall be stated together with the full price so that the consumer is aware of any higher price as a result of paying by instalments.

Advertisers have to be careful, if enquiries are to be used as leads for salesmen, to give the reader the opportunity to refuse a salesman's call. This requirement is specified in the British Code of Advertising Practice. Readers should not be pestered by uninvited salesmen.

19. Signature slogan or strapline

This is the pay-off line, and it can be used as a device to create a corporate image. It has become a common practice to conclude ads with a signature slogan, and the following are some examples:

We always go one better (Texas Homecare)
It's Daft Not to (Littlewoods Pools)
You Get a Smarter Investor at the Alliance and Leicester
A Smarter Way to Save (Superdrug)
Japanese Technology Malaysian Style (Proton)
Bringing You The Latest Technology (Dixons)
Giving Children A Future (UNICEF)
You're Better Off Talking to Barclays
None Bigger None Better (Anglian window centres)
Daring to be different (Suzuki)
Where Children Learn to Love Books (The Red House)
Someday all watches will be made this way (Seiko)
We're Flying Better Than Ever (Pan Am)
We've Got It Right Across the Channel (Sally Ferries)
Bringing out the best in the world (RTZ)
Once driven, forever smitten (Vauxhall)
Because today isn't yesterday (Bankers Trust Company)
Solutions for Business (Coopers & Lybrand)
Engineered Like No Other Car In The World (Mercedes-Benz)
For all our tomorrows (BP)
Technology that works for all of us (Samsung)
The world's leading international airport group (BAA)
For the *best* of America (TWA)
The small team with big resources (Deutsche Girozentrale Deutsche Kummunalbank)
Building peoples dreams (ITT)
The *global* computer & communications company (Fujitsu)
In Touch with Tomorrow (Toshiba)

Guaranteed to Get to Her (Interflora)
Top breeders recommend it (Pedigree Chum)
We're all you need to know (AA)
The building society you can bank on (Halifax Building
    Society)
A Friend For Life (Bank of Scotland)
Energy is our business (British Gas)
Better things for better living (Du Pont)
All you need (Visa)
The World Telephone Company (Cable and Wireless)
You can tell when it's Shell

Progress test 10

1. What is meant by the section of the IPA definition which reads 'the most persuasive selling message'? (**1**)
2. Why should advertisement copy never contain words which potential readers are unlikely to understand? (**3**)
3. Give an example of a 'buzz word'. (**5**)
4. Give five examples of action words. (**6**)
5. What is alliteration? Give an example of a slogan which uses alliteration. (**8**)
6. Name the seven copy elements. (**12**)
7. Invent examples of declarative, curiosity, topical and play on words headlines. (**13**)
8. What are the six purposes of subheadings? (**14**)
9. What is a reader advertisement? (**15**)
10. Why can price be an important part of the copy? (**16**)
11. Write the wording for a coupon so that readers may apply for a free holiday brochure. (**18**)
12. Give two examples of actual signature slogans or strap-lines. (**19**)

11
Layout and typography

Planning the advertisement

1. Teamwork

Advertisements are usually produced separately by the visualiser, who designs them, and the copywriter, who writes the message and creates the basic idea and theme known as the copy platform. As has already been emphasised in 10:1 these two creative experts should work as a team. The copywriter should think visually, that is consider *how* the words should be seen as well as read. It is a bad system for the two to work in isolation, and for the visualiser merely to fit words to a design. If there is no teamwork, and no discussion between visualiser and copywriter, the result could be an advertisement crammed with too much copy printed too small to be legible. Similarly, the copywriter could suggest how the advertisements should be illustrated, while the visualiser could suggest how many words are required for the available space.

2. AIDCA (Attention, Interest, Desire, Conviction, Action) formula

This is a well-used formula which helps in the overall planning of an advertisement, and it is particularly applicable to the hard-selling advertisement. It applies not only to the copy, layout and typography but also to the choice of medium, the space size and its position in the publication. An analysis of the five elements of the formula will explain this more precisely.

3. Attention

Unless an advertisement wins *attention*, diverting the reader from either the editorial or other advertisements, it will not even be noticed. Attention may be achieved by position in the publication (either which page or on which part of a page), or by the size or shape of the advertisement. Even a tiny advertisement will attract attention if it is in the right position (e.g. a house for sale classified or a holiday resort ad in a section on holidays). Generally, a top right-hand position on a right-hand page gains the most attention when the advertisement does not fill the whole or half the page. Creative devices can be used to attract attention, e.g. colour, headline, illustration together with the general layout and choice of typeface. Thus, attention-getting may depend on a blend of factors, not forgetting the subject of the advertisement itself.

4. Interest

There is no point in using these devices to make people look at the advertisement unless it also gains their *interest*. It may do so selectively, and certain readers will be interested in advertisements for, say, cosmetics, foods, clothing, houses, motor-cars or computers. Interest may be achieved by the offer, the pictures, or the copy, and these will in turn be strengthened by the originality of the wording and presentation.

5. Desire

Readers must be more than attracted and interested, they must be encouraged to *desire* the product or service. How, creatively, can it be made desirable? What benefits are offered? There is an exchange situation: what will the reader gain by paying the price?

6. Conviction

It is all very well creating the wish to buy, own or enjoy the product or service, but it is also necessary to inspire *conviction* that it really is worth buying and that it will give satisfaction. This may require convincing facts, proof of performance, testimonials and so on. Readers are likely to lose interest if essential information is missing from an advertisement.

Such information could include the *price*, which can be one way of judging a product or service. Is it good value for money? Some advertisers are very foolish about omitting prices, as if they are afraid this will put people off, or feel that, in the case of a luxury item, it does not matter. Price can be a very convincing factor, whether it be low or high. People do tend to believe that they get what they pay for. Consequently, price is often a major factor in the majority of advertisements, and may even be one of the methods of attracting attention in the first place.

7. Action

How can the advertisement induce response? A press advertisement is static, and it is not easy to provoke the reader into taking some desired action. Of course, there may be an immediate appeal to action in the headline, or it may be implicit in the entire advertisement. However, certain devices may be used, such as a coupon, invitation to sample or test, exhortation to visit a dealer or showroom, or a list of stockists which make it easy to find a supplier. Some advertisements merely remind, others build up interest and desire against some future time when a purchase may be made, but others seek immediate action. This is especially true of direct response advertising which seeks orders by post or telephone, and one way of making this easy for the customers is to illustrate acceptable credit cards.

Design and layout

8. Stages in design

The design of a press advertisement goes through a number of stages. First, rough scribbles, scamps or *visuals* will be sketched in pencil, and numerous experimental versions will be produced by the visualiser, until he arrives at either two or three alternatives or the final one. Final ideas will be worked up in a form which is sufficiently intelligible and can be shown to the client for approval. As a provisional layout, it will have no final artwork, photography, lettering, typesetting or type mark-up. Illustrations will be represented by sketches or maybe Polaroid photographs or stock pictures, and the wording will be shown in a 'Greek' jumble of characters.

When this layout is approved, artwork is commissioned, and the layout artist produces finished layouts with typographical mark-ups regarding typefaces and sizes. For letterpress printed advertisements, the production department will buy halftone blocks and typesetting and produce stereotypes of the entire advertisements. For litho and photogravure printed advertisements, camera-ready copy will be produced for photography and platemaking by the printer. Printing processes are explained in Chapter 12.

9. Example

This is demonstrated in Fig. 11.1, the visual for the eventual advertisement in Fig. 11.2.

In the LCCI Advertising examination there is usually a compulsory first question requiring copy and layout which should be produced separately. The copy should be capable of being typed (although handwritten in the examination). It should contain every word which is to appear in the advertisement—headline, subheadings, text, name and address and the wording of the coupon if one is to be included. The layout should be rather like Fig. 11.1, the only wording being the display lines.

10. The eight laws of design

The basic principles of design, which can be applied to advertisements, are: law of unity; law of variety; law of balance; law of rhythm; law of harmony; law of proportion; law of scale; and law of emphasis. These will now be discussed in detail.

11. Law of unity

All parts of a layout should unite to make a whole. This unity can be disturbed by an irritating border, too many different and conflicting typefaces, badly distributed colour, disproportionate elements, or 'busy' layouts containing a confusion of parts.

12. Law of variety

Nevertheless, there should be change and contrast as with bold and medium weight of type, or good use of white space. The advertisement should not be monotonous, and grey masses of small print need to be relieved by subheadings. Variety can also be introduced by the use of pictures.

Figure 11.1 *Visual of press advertisement.*

Living like rats, cooped up like chickens, slaughtered like cattle. What kind of animal was the British soldier of 1916?

What moved a GERMAN *General* to say that the BRITISH *"fought like lions but were led by donkeys"*?

What's it like to spend days ankle deep in *freezing mud,* weeks infested with *lice* and months surrounded by the stench of *putrefying corpses?*

 What bravery must it take to go *'over the top'* into NO MAN'S LAND to almost certain death at the hands of the enemy?

The answers to these questions don't just lie deep in the heart of *some foreign field.* They also lie deep in the heart of CHELSEA.

Though no one can *simulate the full horror of* trench warfare, at the NATIONAL ARMY MUSEUM we can promise to *stimulate the mind.*

Using models, videos, reconstructions ~ even a trench called *Suicide Corner* ~ we can bring the FIRST WORLD WAR to life for you.

We can also bring to life many other aspects of the military man through the ages.

In fact, after a visit to our displays of *weapons, uniforms, paintings* and regular *special exhibitions,* it's possible to get a unique insight into the FIVE HUNDRED YEAR HISTORY of the British soldier. *Warts and all.*

You'll find the NATIONAL ARMY MUSEUM near SLOANE SQUARE *tube,* in *Royal Hospital Road, Chelsea.* We're open 10am to 5pm Mondays to Saturdays, 2pm to 5:30pm Sundays. ADMISSION is FREE.

And don't worry, you don't have to bring your own *rations.* We've even got a *café.*

National Army Museum

NO POMP. JUST THE CIRCUMSTANCE.

Figure 11.2 *The finished advertisement as it appeared in the press.*

13. Law of balance

It is essential that an advertisement should be well balanced. The *optical* balance is one-third down a space, not half- way. A picture or headline may occupy one-third, and the text copy two-thirds, so achieving an optical balance. The *symmetrical* balance falls mid-way so that a design can be divided into equal halves, quarters and so on, but care should be taken not to divide an advertisement into halves which look like separate advertisements.

14. Law of rhythm

Even though a printed advertisement is static it is still possible to obtain a sense of movement so that the eye is carried down and through the advertisement. A simple device is to indent paragraphs of text (as in a book or newspaper report) so that the eye is led from paragraph to paragraph. But the general flow of the overall design should be pleasantly rhythmic.

15. Law of harmony

There should be no sharp, annoying and jerky contrasts —unless perhaps that is the deliberate intention as in some kinds of store or direct response ads which use bombastic shock tactics. Normally, all the elements should harmonise, helping to create units.

16. Law of proportion

This applies particularly to the type sizes used for different widths of copy: the wider the width (or *measure*) the larger the type size, and vice versa. A narrow advertisement needs small text type, but a wide advertisement needs larger text type, unless the type is set in columns.

17. Law of scale

Visibility depends on the scale of tones and colours, some appearing to recede, others appearing to advance. Pale, pastel colours recede while bold, primary colours advance. Black looks closer to the eye than grey, and red is the most dominant colour. Black on either yellow or orange is very bold whereas white on yellow is weak. The law of scale can be used with typographical design when headlines and subheadings are made to contrast with grey areas of text type. Where colours are concerned, this principle can be applied whenever full colour is used in press advertisements, TV commercials, posters and packaging.

18. Law of emphasis

The rule here is that *all emphasis is no emphasis* as occurs if too much bold type is used, or there are too many capital letters. A sentence in upper and lower case lettering reads more easily than one wholly in capital letters. Yet emphasis is essential, and this links up with the other laws of variety and scale. An advertisement can be made to *look* interesting if there is emphasis such as bold type or if certain words are emphasised in a second colour.

White space—daylight!—can also be an effective way of creating emphasis. Every inch of space does not have to be filled with words just because it has been paid for! One wonders how many people bother to read the pages of small print in the prospectuses for new share issues which appear in the *Financial Times*, or the tedious whole page advertisements crammed with small print which are sometimes placed by foreign governments.

Another form of contrast is to reverse white on black, a method often used with logotypes and name-plates. Reverse colour should not be overdone for it tends to reduce legibility. A bad mistake is to print a lot of text in white on a black or coloured background.

19. Other forms of white space

Apart from providing emphasis, white space can also give clarity and legibility to the message. This can be done in two ways: by indenting paragraphs (i.e. book style, unlike the block paragraph of business letters), and by spacing between lines of type. The latter is known as leading (pronounced 'ledding' because with hot metal setting it consists of strips of lead which are not type-high), but it can be set by using a type size such as '10 on 11' meaning that a 10 point type has 1 point leading, this separating the lines of type with one point (1/72 in.) of white space.

20. Arrangement of headlines

The headline can be made more legible, meaningful and attention-getting or impactive if care is taken in its layout. To achieve this it may be necessary to select words of suitable length, or the best number of words for effect. A long headline may be broken up or stepped so that it achieves these design effects. This also depends on the shape of the space—is it a wide half page or a narrow column?

Below is an example of a headline set as one line to suit a wide space, and then stepped to suit a narrower or a narrow one.

You may not like hot dogs

You may not
like hot dogs

You may
not like
hot dogs

Sometimes the designer has to make *adaptations* to suit different space sizes and shapes.

21. Illustrations

Pictures used to illustrate advertisements may be tonal photographs and wash drawings, or line drawings. Before deciding on the art medium it is wise to know the printing process and the kind of paper used by the newspapers and magazines in which the advertisement is to appear. A picture may reproduce well on the super calendered or similar paper used for magazines, but be disappointing on the poor quality newsprint used for newspapers.

However, reasonably good pictures can be printed in newspapers, especially now that so many newspapers are printed by offset-litho or even flexography.

Typography

22. Definitions

Typography is the art of selecting typefaces, of which there are hundreds of designs; blending different typefaces; casting off the number of words to fit spaces; and marking up copy for typesetting, using different sizes and weights.

A *fount* of type is a whole alphabet complete with signs and punctuation marks, and a *family* is a set of different weights, widths, sizes and varieties of a particular typeface. There are two main groups of typefaces, *display* (*see* Fig. 11.3) and *book* or *text*, although the larger sizes of text types can be used for display purposes. A typical mix of display and text faces might be a *sans serif* type for display and a *serif* type for the small print. The serif is the thin line drawn across the ends of stems and arms of letters. A serif face is easier to read in small size type, and especially on shiny paper, than a sans serif type. Books and newspapers are generally set in serif type.

Good typography leads to legibility, and attractiveness, and certain designs of type can create style and character or be characteristic of the advertised subject.

Companies with corporate identity schemes specify a particular typeface for all print including advertisements, thus establishing a house style. However, it is important that the particular typeface is universally available from all printers and publishers, unless this problem can be overcome by providing camera-ready copy. One national estate agent adopted a type-face which was not available from all local newspapers in which the agent's property ads appeared. This problem can exist with modern computerised photo-typesetting when printers may have a limited range of typefaces.

23. Typesetting

Originally, type was set by hand. The expressions 'upper case' and 'lower case' for capital letters and small letters respectively were derived from the cases or drawers in the type cabinet in which individual characters were located. Hot metal mechanical setting is still used in some print shops and may consist of linotype typesetting machines which set slugs of type the width of the column, or monotype typesetting machines which set individual characters.

24. Photo-typesetting

Today, however, most copy is produced on photo-typesetting machines, and no metal is used. The alphabet is on a disc and the characters are photographed to the required size, the setting being produced on film or paper. Nowadays, such machines are also computerised with visual display unit screens so that corrections can be made by running the original and correcting it. A writer can even produce copy on a word-processor and transmit it by telephone line direct to the computerised photo- typesetting machine at the printers.

GOUDY EXTRA BOLD
abcdefghijklmnopqrstuvwxyz
ABCDEFGHIJKLMNOPQRSTUVWXYZ
1234567890 ß &?!£$(.,;:)

HORATIO MEDIUM
abcdefghijklmnopqrstuvwxyz
ABCDEFGHIJKLMNOPQRSTUVWXYZ
1234567890 ß &?!£$(.,;:)

FUTURA DEMI BOLD
abcdefghijklmnopqrstuvwxyz
ABCDEFGHIJKLMNOPQRSTUVWXYZ
1234567890 ß &?!£$(.,;:)

ROCKWELL BOLD
abcdefghijklmnopqrstuvwxyz
ABCDEFGHIJKLMNOPQRSTUVWXYZ
1234567890 æøßÆØ &?!£$(.,;:)

PROTEUS BOLD
abcdefghijklmnopqrstuvwxyz
ABCDEFGHIJKLMNOPQRSTUVWXYZ
1234567890 æøßÆØ &?!£$%(.,;:)

MICROGRAMMA MEDIUM EXTENDED
abcdefghijklmnopqrstuvwxyz
ABCDEFGHIJKLMNOPQRSTU
VWXYZ
1234567890 &?!£$(.,;:)

Figure 11.3 *Examples of display faces.*

Figure 11.4 *Part of the storyboard for a TV commercial produced by Alliance International for Woolwich Equitable Building Society. The theme music was* **We've Got To Get Out of Here** *(The Animals).*

Television commercials

25. Storyboard

The 'visual' for a TV commercial is a set of cartoon drawings set in TV-screen shapes which tell the story of the proposed commercial. This is known as the *storyboard* as shown in Fig. 11.4.

26. Special effects

The agency's TV producer is responsible for the conception of the TV commercial. The actual commercial is then made by an outside film director and film unit (*see* 3:46). Most commercials are first made on film, but can be transferred to video for post-production treatments such as computer graphics. Others are videotaped in the first instance. Other special effects can be used such as stop-motion as when packages unwrap themselves, or animation using a series of cartoon drawings which are filmed as movies.

The married print, combining picture and sound, is usually made after the commercial has been approved by the television authorities. This enables corrections to be made if necessary to the sound track.

Progress test 11

1. Why should the visualiser and the copywriter work together as a team? (1)
2. What are the five elements of the AIDCA formula? (2–7)
3. Explain the difference between a rough visual and a finished layout. (8)
4. Name and explain the eight laws of design. (10–18)
5. Explain what is meant by 'all emphasis is no emphasis'. (18)
6. How can white space be used as an effective part of the design of an advertisement? (18, 19)
7. What is meant by indenting paragraphs and leading? (19)
8. How can a tonal picture be converted into a line drawing for good reproduction on newsprint? (21)

9.   Explain the terms 'fount', 'family', 'display typeface' and 'text typeface', 'sans serif' and 'serif'. (**22**)

10.   What effects can be achieved by good typography? (**22**)

11.   What is a storyboard? (**25**)

12.   Explain the terms 'stop-motion' and 'animation'. (**26**)

12
Printing processes

The five main processes

1. Introduction

While it is not necessary for the advertising student to understand the technical intricacies of printing processes and machines, it is important to have a general knowledge of printing processes, and especially the particular classes of work which can be produced by them. This chapter discusses the five main processes: letterpress, lithography, photogravure, flexography and silk screen.

2. Letterpress

This is a relief printing system, which may be likened to a date stamp or a typewriter character in that printing is achieved by pressing an inked raised surface to the paper. The machine may be flat-bed or rotary, and it may use single sheets of paper or, in the case of rotary machines, a continuous reel or web of paper.

For letterpress printing all printing areas must be raised above the surface as dots (halftone), lines or type. The non-raised or non-type high areas will leave white or un-inked space.

This is a very versatile process and one of its advantages is that every kind of paper can be used. Where tonal pictures are required halftone screens from very coarse to very fine can be used to suit the paper. Literally anything from a business card to high quality full-colour catalogues or books can be produced by letterpress, and there are special machines which can print on delicate materials such as foil.

The disadvantages of the letterpress process are usually that rotary machines are big, and they require a large number of operatives, while it is not very economical for very large runs unless plates are stereotyped and perhaps replaced, or several machines are used.

Moreover, the production of metal type and printing plates requires a whole department—literally a foundry floor in the old Fleet Street newspaper plants. This required a large and costly work-force. This whole department has disappeared in the change-over to offset-litho which is not only less labour intensive and cheaper to operate but produces better quality print. Nevertheless, a number of small jobbing printers still use letterpress.

3. Lithography

This is a very old process, and very popular with German printers. Originally, lithographic printing required a large slab of porous stone, and litho stone came from the Jura mountains in Germany. The process is a 'planographic' one, in that the printing image is laid flat on the 'stone' or plate. Printing from it works on the principle that grease and water will not mix. Thus, if the image (the printing area) is greasy or greased, and it is inked, the application of water will remove the excess ink and leave ink only on the greasy area. Hence the original porous stone. Today, lithography uses metal plates, and there are rotary as well as flat-bed machines, and printing can be made from webs of paper as well as from flat sheets.

4. Offset-lithography

The expression *offset* is commonly used for lithography. It means that there are in effect three cylinders in the offset-litho machine. The plate, curved round the *plate cylinder* with the image in positive form, first prints on to a second *blanket cylinder* so that the image becomes negative or reversed. The blanket cylinder then offsets the image on to the paper which is conveyed through the machine by a third *impression* cylinder.

5. Advantages of lithography

The process has become universally adopted in many forms including small office machines. It has the following advantages.

(a) Machines are compact.

(b) Special papers have been produced for the process.

(c) A fine screen can be used for halftones (even for newspaper printing).

(d) Illustrations are less expensive to reproduce because special halftone plates are unnecessary.

(e) Photo-typesetting can be used.

(f) High quality inks with extra pigment and glossy effects can be used.

(g) The preparation of the printing plate is cleaner and simpler since there is no hot metal. The print shop resembles a hospital rather than the hot, noisy and dirty letterpress print-shop.

(h) Copy is pasted down and photographed for plate-making. Customers can supply camera-ready artwork instead of the metal blocks, typesettings or stereos used for letterpress printing.

(i) Litho machines are very suitable for multi-colour work. Figure 12.1 is an outline drawing of a typical four-colour litho machine.

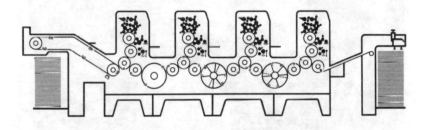

Figure 12.1 *Four-colour litho machine. Courtesy, Heidleberg*

6. Photogravure

The chief merit of photogravure is the long life of the printing plate or *sleeve*, and its ability to print on comparatively cheap and apparently good quality shiny super-calendered paper as used by women's magazines. In a better quality version, photogravure can also be used for printing postage stamps and reproductions of works of art. The system was introduced into the UK to print long runs of popular magazines, and has subsequently been used to print weekend colour magazines. However, the newer women's magazines and the TV magazines have turned to

Figure 12.2 *Webs of newsprint being loaded on to a Metroliner offset-litho press at the News Centre, Portsmouth.*

web-offset litho as this process has been able to use webs of super-calendered paper.

Originally, photogravure was the opposite to letterpress and lithography in being an 'intaglio' process with the printing surface recessed in square cells of different depths to accept quantities of ink to produce depths of colour. The ink is literally sucked out of the cells and on to the paper. This resembles the copper etching in which the design is etched or cut into the surface.

7. Hard-dot system

A newer version of photogravure, which produces print comparable in quality to offset-litho, is the German electronic Klischograph hard-dot cylinder gravure system which is a surface instead of a recessed process. It has surface areas of various sizes according to the lightness or darkness of tone, instead of having recessed cells of different depths according to the depth of tone.

8. Flexography

Originally used in Britain for printing on delicate materials, such as foil for confectionery wrappings, flexography was developed in the USA for newspaper production. The process is now used by the *Daily Mail* and its sister publications at its new plant in SE London.

It is a rotary web letterpress process but one which uses flexible rubber plates, and rapid drying solvent or water-based inks. By applying improved photopolymer plates and special inks flexography has been adapted for newspaper production, rivalling offset-litho. Flexo inks are brighter than offset inks and, as the *Daily Mail* has advertised, they do not rub off on the reader's fingers. There is also very good picture and colour reproduction.

9. Silk screen

This was originally an ancient Chinese printing process using a screen or mesh made of human hair. The basic principle is the stencil, ink being pushed or rolled through a cut-out design placed over a screen of silk, nylon, organdie or metal mesh. From very simple cut-out designs to photographic ones, silk screen presses are capable of printing on both a variety of materials and on non-flat surfaces such as bottles. It is therefore a very versatile process which can print on paper, board, plastic, glass, wood, textiles, rubber and so on. Typical examples are posters (e.g.

those seen on shop windows); book jackets; clock faces and instrument panels; ashtrays; advertising pens; milk, soft drink and beer bottles; T-shirts; balloons; and ties.

Choice of process

10. Availability of processes

The print-buyer should be aware of both the processes available, and the process which is most suitable for the job. All five main processes are used in Britain, but this is not true of every country. In fact, in many developing countries where new newspapers were launched, offset-litho machines were installed many years before Britain's national newspapers adopted the process. The various kinds of lithography are most universally available.

11. Consulting the printer

It is wise to discuss print jobs with different printers, in order to understand the process being used and the quality of work that can be undertaken. Quotations should be requested, and if the reasons for different prices are not readily understood printers should be asked why the quotation is either so high or so low. A very simple explanation may be the speed of the printer's machine. Price may depend on the paper sheet size which a machine can accept. This can affect either the number of copies which can be cut from a sheet, or the extent of waste if trimming is necessary. It is always best to discuss print work with printers rather than simply present them with a design and copy. A print job involves technicalities such as typefaces, kind of paper, use of colours, size of the finished job, binding and especially folding. Given the opportunity, the printer can give advice which can result in a better-looking, more practical and perhaps more economical job.

Progress test 12

1. What is the principle of the letterpress printing process? (**2**)
2. What is the principle of the lithographic printing process? (**3**)
3. Explain the term 'offset'. (**4**)

4. What is the principle of the photogravure printing process? **(6)**

5. How does the Klischograph system differ from traditional photogravure? **(7)**

6. What is flexography? **(8)**

7. What is the principle of the silk screen process? **(9)**

8. In what ways does silk screen differ regarding items which can be printed by this process? **(9)**

9. Why is it important to obtain quotations from different printers, and to question why prices for the same job may differ considerably? **(11)**

13
Public relations

Differences between public relations and advertising

1. Introduction

Public relations is often confused with advertising, and sometimes wrongly termed 'publicity' and placed in the promotional mix as in the fourth P of the Four Ps concept of the marketing mix. Worse still, public relations is wrongly regarded as a form of advertising, even as 'free advertising'. It is therefore essential, especially in books on advertising, to understand the nature of public relations and how it differs from advertising. The two are very different forms of communication, but advertising is likely to be more effective if public relations is well carried out.

Briefly, public relations aims to create understanding through knowledge (*see* 13) and, if it is to be successful in educating the market, it must be factual, credible and impartial. Advertising, as already demonstrated in previous chapters, has to be persuasive in order to sell and it may be emotional, dramatic and certainly partial. Thus, a basic difference is that in order to succeed public relations must be unbiased while advertising has to be biased.

Public relations may be thought to consist only of press relations, or rather media relations since radio and television are also involved. Modern public relations extends into all the functions of commercial and non-commercial, public and private organisations. It deals with matters far removed from marketing and advertising, to mention only community, employee, shareholder and political relations. A major area of public relations in recent years has been the handling of crisis situations such as strikes, disasters and take-over bids. For a fuller account of public relations the reader is advised to read the author's companion handbook *Public Relations.*

2. Definitions of public relations

Here are two well-known definitions, the first being that of the (British) Institute of Public Relations, and the second resulting from an international conference of public relations institutions held in Mexico City in 1978.

(a) *IPR definition.* 'Public relations practice is the planned and sustained effort to establish and maintain goodwill and mutual understanding between an organisation and its publics.'

The importance of this definition lies in its emphasis on *planning* public relations—just like an advertising campaign—and on *mutual* (or two-way) communication. Inflow of information and feedback is just as valuable in public relations as outflow of information. Public relations can be likened to the eyes and ears as well as the voice of an organisation. It is a kind of intelligence system.

(b) *The Mexican statement.* 'Public relations practice is the art and social science of analysing trends, predicting their consequences, counselling organisation leaders, and implementing planned programmes of action which will serve both the organisation and the public interest.'

This very interesting definition emphasises three aspects of public relations: the need to carry out research in order to appreciate the situation before planning a public relations programme; the giving of advice to management; and the need for public relations to be in the public interest. The latter also implies the need for public relations messages to be authentic, truthful and credible.

3. Differences

The principal differences between public relations and advertising are outlined below.

(a) Public relations writing (and other creative communications such as films and video) must be factual and informative, and free of 'puffery' (*see* **20**). To achieve credibility it needs to be educational rather than persuasive, giving factual information rather than making emotional or dramatic claims (unlike copywriting) and should avoid self-praise.

(b) Public relations applies to many organisations which may not engage in advertising. A fire brigade does not advertise for fires.

(c) Public relations deals with the editors and producers of the media, but advertising with the sellers of advertisement space or airtime.

(d) Whereas advertising is usually addressed to particular market segments and certain social grades, public relations may be addressed to the numerous publics or groups of people with whom an organisation has to communicate. They may not be buyers of the company's goods or services, e.g. shareholders or employees. (*See* also 4)

(e) The costs of public relations are different. In advertising, major costs are space, airtime and production. In public relations they are time since public relations is labour-intensive, plus production costs such as printing house journals or making videos.

(f) In each case the media are different. Advertising will mostly use existing commercial media such as press, radio and TV, plus direct mail and exhibitions. Public relations will use a much bigger variety of commercial media, plus the created media of house journals, films, slides, video, audio tapes, private exhibitions, educational print, seminars and sponsorship. The latter has become an increasingly important public relations tool. (*See* also **16**).

(g) Advertising agencies and public relations consultancies may be remunerated differently, the former receiving commissions from the media and discounts on supplies (or charging percentages), although some charge fees, while the latter depend mainly on fees based on time, and do not ususally receive commission or discounts.

(h) While the majority of advertising personnel work in agencies, the majority of public relations personnel do not work in consultancies but in companies and other organisations. A survey conducted by Cranfield School of Management on behalf of the Institute of Public Relations showed that 60 per cent of public relations staff worked in-house. It is therefore a fallacy that the public relations world is dominated by consultancies, however glamorous they may seem to the outsider.

(i) Advertising aims to persuade people to take some desired action such as visit a shop, respond by post or telephone, or simply remember, in order to buy. Public relations aims to create mutual understanding, which may be of the organisation itself (the corporate image), or of products or services. However, it may extend to other things as will be seen when *publics* are discussed in **4**.

From the above comparisons it will be seen that public relations and advertising are entirely different worlds, and that even in a business organisation public relations may enter into many more facets than advertising. Many in-house public relations managers have nothing to do with advertising, report direct to top management, and service the total organisation and not merely marketing. Advertising should not be regarded as the more important simply because it costs more. Forms of communication which result from training, such as behaviour towards customers, are expressions of public relations, since they may affect goodwill, confidence and reputation.

Some dictionaries have misleading definitions of public relations of which one of the silliest is the following from *The New Collins Concise Dictionary of the English Language* : 'The practice of creating, promoting, or maintaining goodwill and a favourable image among the public towards an institution, public body, etc.'

First, public relations is not concerned with 'the public' (or the 'general public') but with numerous groups or publics. *See* **4** below.

Second, public relations does not seek to create a favourable image. An image cannot be created: it can be only what it is. It may be necessary to establish a *correct image* but it may not be a favourable one. How does one create a *favourable* image of the prison service, HM Customs and Excise, The Inland Revenue or even, sometimes, the police, the Post Office or British Rail? But unpleasant or bad things can be explained so that they are understood. The word 'favourable' is best forgotten in public relations for the world is a mixture of good and bad.

4. Who are the publics?

The plural word 'publics' is generally used in public relations. The eight basic publics are as follows.

(a) *The community.* In the vicinity of the company premises or location there are usually people who are its neighbours. Good relations with the community can be very important to the success of an organisation.

(b) *Potential employees.* They may exist in the community, schools, colleges, universities, other companies or even overseas.

(c) *Employees.* Every category of employee is included here.

(d) *Suppliers.* They will range from public services to suppliers of business services, components and raw materials.

(e) *The money market.* The local bank manager, shareholders, investment analysts, the financial institutions and the Stock Exchange make up the money market.

(f) *Distributors.* Everyone concerned with transferring the product or service to the customers or users are distributors. They may be wholesalers, brokers, retailers, importers or exporters.

(g) *Customers and users.* The current buyers, actual or potential, form this important public which may embrace many groups (e.g. children) who are not necessarily addressed by advertising.

(h) *Opinion formers or leaders.* These are people who express opinions which may help or harm an organisation according to the extent or correctness of their knowledge. They could be parents, teachers, politicians, newspaper columnists or TV personalities.

Public relations consultancy services

5. Consultancies in the UK

There are some 1200 public relations consultancies in the UK, and about 100 of those handling the major volume of consultancy business are members of the Public Relations Consultants Association. There has been an upsurge in consultancy business in recent years and some of the leading firms have annual incomes of £4 million or more. The increase in consultancy business has been largely because they offer a greater variety of services today, or specialise in particular ones.

6. Types of consultancy

Consultancies range from very big ones of which Shandwick, Hill & Knowlton, Burson-Marsteller, and Daniel J. Edelman are among the biggest, down to one-person businesses. In addition, there are those which specialise in certain areas of public relations such as corporate and financial (mostly located in the City), sponsorship, parliamentary liaison (giving advice on parliamentary matters and procedures affecting clients) and house journal production. Others offer special knowledge of certain industries like food, fashion, motor-cars or travel.

The financial consultancies have grown with the need to service privatisation share offers and to deal with take-over bids. There has also been demand to train clients in crisis situations, it being recognised nowadays that any organisation can suffer any kind of crisis.

A form of crisis which has become prevalent in recent years has been the contamination of food products in supermarkets, although fortunately most of them have proved to be hoaxes. Nevertheless, firms like Heinz and Mars have suffered the double handicap of loss of public faith in their products, and removal of their products from supermarket shelves to protect the good name of retailers. Such events, perpetrated by activist groups, gain maximum media cover which has to be counteracted.

7. Use of consultancies

There are at least five special uses of consultancies.

(a) When there is no in-house public relations department a public relations consultancy may be employed to conduct a public relations programme.

(b) When the public relations department is exceptionally busy, an outside unit can augment its activities.

(c) When an outside advisory service is required.

(d) When a special *ad hoc* service is required like those mentioned above in **6**, a consultancy may be employed because, for instance, there is to be a new share issue, sponsorship is contemplated, or legislation is passing through the House of Commons which concerns a company and it is necessary to know what is going on.

(e) When a company is located at a distance from media centres like London, a consultancy may be employed because it is better located to deal with the media. However, this has become less vital and consultancies are located throughout the UK.

8. Cost

A consultancy is paid for the work it performs, and it is essential that the fee is adequate to cover the volume of work involved. Consultancy services are carefully budgeted, but whereas many advertising agency services cost the client nothing if media purchases provide sufficient commission income, the consultancy client does have to pay for everything including the time of the account executive. This is perfectly fair and professional, and it is not necessarily true that consultancies are expensive and that it is cheaper to have one's own staff public relations officer. Sometimes consultancy fees and public relations officer salaries are falsely compared: the in-house public relations officer costs more than just his salary for he or she has operational expenses beginning with an office and secretary. The in-house public relations job is usually a full-time one, thus costing more than part-time or *ad hoc* consultancy services.

9. Advantages of consultancies

The special merits of consultancies (which may be compared with those of the company public relations department, *see* **11** below) are as follows.

(a) Experience based on handling a variety of accounts.
(b) Knowledge of and contact with the media.
(c) An independent outside point-of-view which is valuable when performing the important advisory role of public relations.
(d) Buying ability and knowledge of sources of supply such as printers, photographers, video producers and so on.
(e) Well-trained professional staff.
(f) Special skills which can be shared with other clients, and which would be uneconomic to employ full-time.
(g) International contacts such as overseas associates or offices in other countries which can be useful if the company exports or operates internationally.

In-house public relations departments

10. Position in company

Ideally, the public relations department should be independent, servicing production, finance and marketing, but directly answerable to the chief executive (*see* Fig. 13.1). In many large companies the public relations officer (whatever his title and there are many variations) is a board director. This ideal situation does not always occur, and the public relations officer may be positioned in the marketing department which suggests limited public relations duties and status. In other companies the responsibility for public relations may fall on the shoulders of various executives such as marketing, advertising, product or sales promotion managers, but again this suggests a very limited use of public relations. In some developing countries where management has not yet accepted the importance to them of public relations, the in-house public relations officer may occupy a less senior or well-defined position, perhaps being concerned more with personnel and protocol matters.

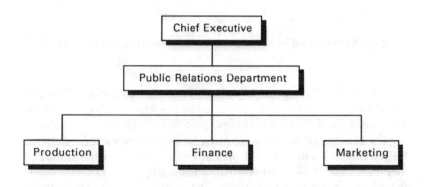

Figure 13.1 *Ideal positioning of a public relations department.*

Figure 13.2 illustrates how a public relations department might be staffed.

11. Advantages of in-house public relations officer

The advantages of an in-house public relations officer as compared with a public relations consultancy, are as follows.

(a) The staff public relations officer works full-time for the company, unlike the consultant whose time is controlled by the

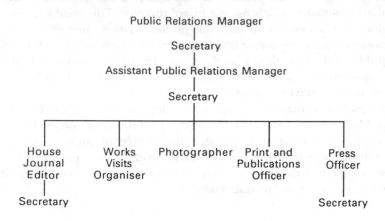

Figure 13.2 *Possible staffing of a public relations department in a large manufacturing company.*

size of the fee. This is an important point to remember. Fees are based on time. If the consultant gives the client more time than he is paid for, one of two things must occur. Either, the value of the fee is reduced or the time must be taken from another client. Either way, the client could go bankrupt which is why he has to maintain strict time-sheet control of his work.

(b) Working inside the company, the staff public relations officer has the opportunity to be familiar with the whole business. Indeed, the public relations officers should know more about the company than anyone else in it if he or she is really to advise the chief executive. This demands good internal lines of communication, which is often helped if the public relations officer edits the staff newspaper and so has to meet people throughout the organisation.

(c) The public relations officer may be a product of the company or industry and have technical knowledge, although this is not absolutely vital. A good public relations officer, if well trained, qualified and experienced, should be able to apply expertise to any communication problem. For instance, it used to be the case that banking public relations officers were bankers first, but many outsiders have now come into banking public relations.

(d) Because of the public relations officer's close links within the organisation, he or she could have ready access to information, and especially the ability to check the accuracy of information, whereas the consultant may be more remote from such sources.

Public relations and advertising

12. Value of public relations to advertising

From what has been described so far it will be seen that public relations concerns the total communications of the total organisation. It is not confined to marketing, nor is it a form of advertising. Public relations is not a 'soft sell'. Nevertheless, advertising can benefit from public relations activity. In fact, advertising may well fail because of lack of public relations. This does not mean that public relations is superior to advertising, but that it is different and because of its own communication techniques it can contribute to the success of advertising just as it can contribute to good management–employee relations or good financial relations. The chief benefit lies in the creation of understanding.

13. Public relations transfer process

The creation of understanding is best explained by reference to the 'public relations transfer process' as demonstrated by the model in Fig. 13.3.

A company, product or service may be subject to one or more of the four negative states in the left-hand box of the public relations transfer process model. Here are some examples.

(a) *Hostility.* There may be hostility towards a company because company behaviour has been criticised, a product has performed badly, a company personality has received bad publicity, the company is of foreign origin, or simply because it is very big! There may also be hostility towards the industry because it is believed to be hazardous, or endangers the environment. Hostility may be undeserved or quite irrational. There are people who

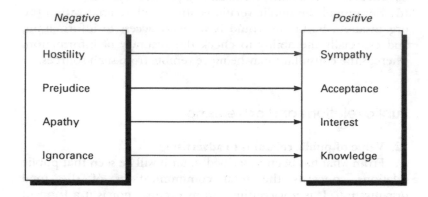

Figure 13.3 *The public relations transfer process: knowledge leads to understanding.*

dislike nationalised industries, multinationals, chemical companies and those which create noise, smell or other inconveniences.

(b) *Prejudice.* This is a more difficult obstacle to overcome, and is usually long-standing and derived from family, educational, ethnic or even geographical influences. Many people are still prejudiced about flying, holidays abroad, foreign foods, computers or both advertising and public relations.

(c) *Apathy.* Disinterest is very hard to overcome. People tend to be conservative, set in their ways and unwilling to try new things. They may be so satisfied with their closest interests—family, home, job, hobbies—that they do not wish to extend their interests further. They may be apathetic about things that could benefit them such as banking, insurance, savings, diet, holidays or different kinds of clothes.

(d) *Ignorance.* In a complex world everyone is ignorant about many things. It is inevitable. There was a time when most people were ignorant about detergents, television, central heating or air conditioning, woodworm, convenience foods, video-cassettes, show-jumping or hovercraft, all of which large numbers of people take for granted today.

These are all negative attitudes with which advertisers have to contend, and which public relations is concerned with changing into positive attitudes. It is no use advertising something if sales will be impossible because of sales resistance based on hostility, prejudice, apathy or ignorance. Vast expenditures on advertising will not demolish that sales resistance, or at best unnecessarily heavy expenditures on advertising may be necessary because public relations methods have not been used to create a receptive marketing situation in which advertising can work economically and effectively.

14. Pre-advertising public relations

In some cases, especially with new inventions and technical products, or new services, an advertising campaign is more likely to succeed if people understand what is being advertised. In other words, the market has to be educated or developed. Depending on the kind of product or service, this could take a few months or two to three years. The market has to be familiarised with the new idea.

A good example at the time of writing is Eurotunnel which has not yet reached the stage when its services can be advertised. The Eurotunnel project, one of the world's all-time technical marvels, is also a classic example of public relations having to battle with the four negative states of hostility, prejudice, apathy and ignorance. Instead of being regarded as a national triumph it is a victim of unprecedented misunderstanding and abuse. This is not so in France where the French have eagerly bought up Eurotunnel shares. The scaremonger British media have exploited fears of rabies, water leakage, fire hazard and terrorist attack on the basis that bad news is good news and that is what sells newspapers. You do not sell newspapers by lauding the feats of tunnel engineers. Only the death of one makes news.

All this has not been helped by the indifference of a private enterprise oriented government, the indecisiveness of British Rail, the unpredictable fate of Kent property owners, and the introduction of a giant catamaran Channel ferry, plus squabbles between the tunnel owners and the contractors over escalating costs and the need for new bank loans and a further public share issue with the likely date of profits receding further into the future.

It is a public relations nightmare. The one objective media treatment was the excellent TV programme, *Tomorrow's World,* which did portray the tunnel as an admirable technical achievement. At Folkestone there is the splendid purpose-built Eurotunnel exhibition, packed with visitors, which is a practical proactive effort to present the facts and enlighten the public.

Sixty years ago people scoffed at the idea of flying passengers across the Atlantic, although the German airship *Graf Zeppelin* was doing so weekly, until the Americans flew their bombers to Britain during the Second World War. They thought Thomas Cook was mad when he launched holidays in Switzerland, but now you can have a package tour to Beijing. In the 1930s they laughed at Baird's television, and now we have instant world television news by satellite. London was always depicted as 'foggy London town', until coal fires were banned. Video cameras were clumsy pieces of twin equipment, but Sony has produced one you can palm in the hand. Things change, and public relations is very much to do with helping to effect change by spreading knowledge and creating understanding.

Over the years, non-drip paint, central heating, double-glazing, woodworm treatment, winter weekends in Russia, colour television, video-cassette recorders, home computers, and various investment and savings schemes have benefited from public relations to prepare the market. A product which failed and cost the advertisers a fortune because of the lack of public relations build-up was New Smoking Mixture cigarettes made of a substitute for tobacco.

15. Coincidental public relations

For security reasons, it may not be possible or sensible to give prior announcement of a new product or service because of the intensity of competition. This applies to many FMCGs such as foods and confectionery, and also new models of motor-cars. The public relations has to coincide with the launch, and coverage will be sought in the mass media.

16. Post-advertising public relations

A new development has been that for some products, especially those using commercial TV, a point may be reached when media advertising becomes decreasingly cost-effective. The alternative may be some form of public relations, sponsorship being a typical example. While sponsorship may be used for advertising or marketing purposes, it is becoming increasingly popular as a public relations technique when it is necessary to familiarise the market and to establish a corporate image (*see* 7:9). Canon's costly sponsorship of the Football League was an effort to do what advertising could not do economically in creating market awareness (the company was shocked to find how it had been eclipsed by Olympus in the British market). Canon estimate that to have used advertising would have cost five times more than the sponsorship.

17. Continuous public relations
Now let us consider another contrast between advertising and public relations. Most advertising campaigns are seasonal or of short duration, except those that remind us repeatedly of well-known products, mail-order clubs which are constantly seeking members, and direct response firms which promote a regular series of offers. There are two reasons for this. Certain goods sell either only or mostly at certain times of the year. For example, summer holidays are promoted at the beginning of the year, clocks at Easter and Christmas, sherry and toys at Christmas, central heating in the autumn, garden aids in the spring and early summer, and motor-cars in February–March–April. Advertising money is spent when sales are heaviest, or at least the heaviest expenditure is at such times.

Public relations, however, is a continuous process, and it occurs irrespective of advertising and quite often in entirely different media. It is wrong to assume, or even to expect, that because certain media are used for advertising purposes public relations coverage should be gained, or will be automatically provided, in the same media. There is no relationship between the two. Advertisements may be placed in publications which do not use, or rarely use, public relations material and vice versa, e.g. Sunday newspaper colour supplements and the *Radio Times*. A food firm may advertise mostly in national newspapers and on TV, but public relations coverage may be largely in women's magazines which do not appear on the media schedule.

The continuity of public relations activity, and its independence from advertising, results in the company or its products being in the news throughout the year. A holiday resort can be newsworthy at any time, but holiday advertising has to be pitched when people are planning holidays and perhaps have Christmas bonuses with which to pay for a deposit on a package tour.

Press relations

18. Definition

Press relations aims to achieve maximum publication or broadcasting of public relations information in order to create knowledge and understanding. While the old expression 'press release' has given way to 'news release', 'press relations' and 'press officer' have tended to remain although 'media relations' would be more accurate and 'media manager' is a job title sometimes used. Whatever the terms used, press relations means servicing the media with news, pictures and feature articles, arranging interviews and organising news events.

19. News and advertising compared

There is a very big distinction between the nature of news and advertising. The only reasons why an editor will print public relations material is because it is of interest and value to readers. If he published material which failed to meet this criteria readers would be lost, the paper would fold and the editor would be fired. The public relations officer therefore has to make sure that everything supplied to the media is newsworthy and publishable, although there is no guarantee that it will be published since space is limited and the inflow of competing materials may be enormous.

The situation is different with advertising. Once the space has been bought in whatever quantity permitted by the appropriation, the advertiser can say anything within the limits of the law and the British Code of Advertising Practice. The actual appearance can be controlled by booking dates, and the position and size of the space by booking accordingly.

With public relations material, no such control exists for the editor will decide if, when, where, and how to use the information or pictures supplied. In fact, the editor could rewrite a news release, add good or bad comments, or put it in the waste-paper basket. About 70 per cent of news releases are rejected because they are unpublishable. A news release should resemble a report published in the news columns of a newspaper. Releases rarely do. They are usually what someone wants printed, not what readers are likely to want to read. A primary reason for rejection is that they are really 'puffs' or advertisements.

There are two simple rules about writing publishable news releases. The subject should be in the first three words. The opening paragraph should summarise the whole story, and be capable of telling the story in a nutshell if only the first paragraph is printed.

20. What is a puff?

A puff is a piece of writing which proclaims the virtues of a company, product or service, praising it and urging readers to favour it, e.g. by making a purchase. In other words, it is an advertisement. It is a piece of copywriting, not journalism. It is a good description of 80 per cent of the news releases which infuriate editors.

Unfortunately, many people engaged in advertising, marketing or sales do not understand the difference between the writing of news and the writing of advertisements. They insist on clever headlines, and try to make the story lively by inserting adjectives. They turn it into an advertisement and kill it. But public relations is not about advertising or selling anything: its job is to provide the media with information of *interest and value* to readers, viewers or listeners. If it is used, valuable publicity will result—but only if it satisfies the editor and pleases the editor's audience.

21. Conclusion

In this chapter some comparisons have been made between public relations and advertising techniques. This is deliberate. Much misunderstanding occurs between those engaged in advertising, marketing, public relations and journalism because these differences are not realised let alone understood or practised. On the one hand advertising and marketing people tend to expect public relations material to be a kind of advertising while editors complain about receiving public relations material which is really advertising. The simple distinction has to be remembered: public relations educates and informs and is impartial, but advertising persuades and sells and is partial.

Case study: The Ever Ready Derby

22. Introduction

The Derby, a horse-race for three-year-olds and run over one-and-a-half miles at Epsom in June, is Britain's premier classic horse-racing event. Its bi-centenary was celebrated in 1979. Until 1984, it had never been sponsored. On 6 June 1984 the Derby was sponsored by Ever Ready Ltd, and in an exciting finish the odds-on favourite El San Greco was beaten by Secreto.

In succeeding years Ever Ready have continued to sponsor this famous horse-race which attracts punters who may never place a bet on any other race. Millions of people watch the Derby on TV, but it is preceded by some two hours of Derby Day programme which usually includes the arrival of the Royal Family.

23. Background

The company was emerging from a difficult five-year period, which can be analysed in six stages. The growth of the Alkaline Long Life Sector was slow but steady, but Ever Ready Ltd had a poor market share of only 5.7 per cent in 1982–83. Before this period the management had considered a product name change from Ever Ready, a famous name in batteries, to Berec (representing British Ever Ready Electrical Company) in order to further development of a world brand name. In December 1981 the company was taken over by the Hanson Trust, resulting in reorganisation. The Ever Ready image, which had been a strong one, had deteriorated by 1982. The new management set up in 1982 was determined to re-establish pre-eminence of the name and by the end of that year there was a large increase in the advertising spend. In October 1983 there was a very heavy spend on the launch of Gold Seal, the new Alkaline Long Life range of batteries.

24. Hanson Trust

The new owners of Ever Ready are a very successful industrial management company with important holdings in the UK (Ever

Ready, Allders, London Brick, Crabtree) and are of a similar size in the USA.

25. United Racecourses Ltd

This company owns the racecourses at Epsom, Sandown and Kempton Park. The Derby is a costly event needing significant funds to remain competitive in world terms. The winner of the Derby usually goes on eventually to earn substantial stud fees. However, the economics of racing demand that there is an increasing need for supplementary funds for the Derby.

26. Timing/the deal

Sponsorship has not been favoured for the main classics, but in 1983 this opposition was dropped and United Racecourses, for economic reasons, actively sought sponsors for the Derby and also for the Oaks, the fillies classic which follows the Derby three days later. Modern sports sponsorships often come about in this way, sports promoters seeking sponsors and potential sponsors seeking events to support. Several companies expressed interest, but these were mainly foreign. This was the year when Japanese companies came to dominate sports sponsorship, not only in Britain but in many parts of the world.

An approach was made to Hanson Trust, specifically to Sir Gordon White, chairman of the US end of the business. This was in December 1983. Rapid negotiations were concluded and a deal was struck on 13 January 1984. The base cost of the sponsorship is £600,000 a year with a three-year contract totalling £1.8 million. To this must be added the extra costs of the press conference Derby Luncheon, and hospitality for company guests on the day. Ever Ready also ran trade promotions, sales incentives and advertising relating to the Ever Ready Derby in the months running up to the event.

27. Special rights

The sponsorship fee entitles the company to the following privileges with their consequent advertising or publicity value.

(a) Rights to the names *Ever Ready Derby* and *Gold Seal Oaks*.
(b) Rights to all racecourse advertising.

(c) Special privileged places and positions for the company's trade guests.

(d) Rights to advertising in the racecard.

(e) Free advertising for TV monitors round the course.

(f) The Ever Ready name on the winning post.

28. Organisation

The specialist consultancy responsible for organising the sponsorship is British Equestrian Promotions whose managing director is well-known show-jumping commentator Raymond Brooks-Ward.

29. Development of the event

This was conducted in 1984 by a committee consisting of P. J. Bonner, marketing director, D. Westwood, advertising and promotions manager, and A. J. Maskens, senior product manager (for Ever Ready Ltd); Raymond Brooks-Ward and Neil Fairley (for British Equestrian Promotions); Tim Neligan, managing director, and Robert Browse (for United Racecourses Ltd); Andy Bryant (for Allen Brady and Marsh, advertising agents); and Stuart Rose (for Jones-Rose (PR), public relations consultants).

30. Main functions

There were four main functions, the press conference for press and TV journalists at the Grosvenor House Hotel on 13 January 1984 when the sponsorship was announced; the Derby Luncheon for all trainers, owners, jockeys and the media; the Ever Ready Derby at Epsom on 6 June 1984 and the Gold Seal Oaks at Epsom on 9 June 1984.

31. Coverage

The Derby is the biggest event in the British racing calendar and consequently during the spring and early summer there are constant references to the Ever Ready Derby. There is a bonus even in the fact that there are many earlier races when Derby hopefuls are on trial, and speculation occurs about both horses and riders, culminating in the actual event. The race is not only televised and broadcast, but there are repeats during the evening. There is usually a magnificent TV shot when the saddle cloth boldly named Ever Ready is placed on the winning horse in the winner's enclosure. The story persists after the event with interviews and commentaries.

Progress test 13

1. Define public relations. (2)
2. Describe some of the main differences between public relations and advertising. (3)
3. Name the eight basic publics. (4)
4. What is parliamentary liaison? (6)
5. Name five special uses of public relations consultancies. (7)
6. How does a public relations consultancy obtain payment from its clients, and how does this differ from the advertising agency commission system? (8)
7. How should the in-house public relations officer be positioned in the management structure of an organisation? (10)
8. What are the special advantages of employing an in-house public relations officer? (11)
9. Draw a chart to demonstrate the public relations transfer process. (13)
10. What is meant by pre-advertising, coincidental and post-advertising public relations? (14, 15, 16)
11. For what reasons would an editor print a news release? (19)
12. What is 'puffery', and why should it be avoided when writing public relations material? (20)

14

Corporate advertising

Introduction

1. Definition

In this chapter we are not concerned with advertising which is addressed to consumers to buy goods or services, or to distributors to buy stock for resale. Instead, we shall now consider some uses of advertising on the company's own behalf. The broad expression 'corporate advertising' refers to special advertising to promote the business or financial interests of a company. It includes prestige (or institutional), advocacy or issue, take-over bid and financial advertising.

2. Target audiences

Mostly such advertisements will appear in the business and financial press, and will be aimed at an AB but largely A (upper middle class) readership. Very occasionally, commercial television may be used. In the event of a crisis, such as a strike, disaster or the recall of a defective product, advertisements may be addressed to the public, or sections of it.

Prestige or institutional advertising

3. Public relations

Prestige advertising includes the image-building ads which are really a form of public relations, advertising space being bought to present controlled messages where, when and how the company wishes. Instead of issuing news in a broadcast fashion and hoping that editors will print it somewhere, some day, and reasonably accurately, the company takes space and is responsible for what is said in selected media on specified dates.

4. Style

Prestige advertisements may be produced in a very literary and artistic form in order to enhance the corporate image, but the modern tendency is to adopt the crisper, more precise style of persuasive copywriting, and to present the company's story, merits and achievements in a pungent and positive way. Figure 14.1 is an

---

Sadaichi Gassan
transforms metal into masterpiece

From a raw piece of iron weighing around 10 kg, Sadaichi Gassan and his apprentices forge one of the finest swords in Japan.

Gassan today practises the refined art of the swordsmith that has been passed down through his family for over 800 years.

Such is Gassan's skill, knowledge and feeling for the work, that he has been declared a Living National Treasure. A title bestowed on only the finest craftsmen dedicated to preserving the traditional culture of Japan. Gassan believes that it is his duty to create swords as beautiful and high in quality as the magnificent swords of the ancient past, and to hand down his own techniques to future generations.

His determination is evident in the care and precise attention to detail he maintains throughout the many stages of producing a sword.

He works only in ground metal made of the best iron sand called "tamahagane" steel from Okuizumo and his own home-made steel.

These two are then carefully tempered together using Gassan's unique tempering secret to create a beautifully smooth texture.

Gassan is a rare craftsman who seeks, and achieves, perfection.

The watch he wears is made in a way Gassan can readily appreciate.

A gold Rolex Day-Date Oyster, transformed from precious metal to masterpiece by Rolex craftsmen. A high-precision timepiece which bears the coveted title of "Officially Certified Swiss Chronometer".

A fitting choice for a Living National Treasure.

ROLEX of Geneva.

Only a select group of jewellers sell Rolex watches. For the address of your nearest Rolex jeweller, and for further information on the complete range of Rolex watches, write to: The Rolex Watch Company Limited, 1 Green Street, London W1Y 4JY or telephone 071-629 5071.

Figure 14.1 *Example of the copy from a prestige advertisement.*

interesting example from *The Economist,* perhaps ironic in view of the success of Japanese watches!

Advocacy or issue advertising

5. Propaganda

This kind of corporate advertising is common in the United States, but it is used in the UK occasionally. In contrast to prestige or corporate image advertising with its public relations characteristics, advocacy advertising is more often propaganda. It either presents a case for a business, or states its position in relation to a political issue. We are now in the realms of business politics, a company attacking policies or proposed legislation, or defending itself from antagonistic governments, political parties or pressure groups, or perhaps showing how it is being socially responsible by adhering to official policy and recommendations. The examples in **6** and **7** will demonstrate the use of such advertising.

6. Defence

A company may have been criticised by the media or by politicians or other opinion leaders, and advertisements will be published to state the company's side of the story. It will present facts about itself to disprove the criticisms. For example, it may state the volume of employment it provides, the prosperity it has brought to a region, the taxes it pays, or the contribution it makes to exports and to the country's balance of trade. In TV commercials, British Airways has announced the millions of pounds its international services bring to the British economy. Some American multinationals, such as ITT and IBM, have used advertising to show that they, too, are contributing to the British economy when they have been accused of milking it on behalf of their American parent companies.

According to the opposing policies of Labour and Conservative governments, we have seen advertisements for companies threatened by either nationalisation or privatisation. This is very confusing when each of the two governments has contrary policies on these big issues, and the advertisement becomes little more than propaganda for opposing views, however justified it may seem to be to the opposing parties. 'Hands off' advertising was published by sugar, banking and insurance interests under Labour governments, and there was opposition to the privatisation of the highly profitable British Telecom. British Airways issued prestige advertising which could be read to mean either 'Why sell us off?' or 'Why not buy our shares when they are offered?' just as much as 'Aren't we successful?'

7. Positioning

The government may have declared its policy, with or without special legislation, on issues which affect the company. It may therefore be politic to announce publicly that the company respects this policy, and how it is complying with the requirements. There are many issues of this kind which concern companies either liable to, or deemed liable to, present a social problem. These can include:

(a) harm to the environment such as pollution;

(b) harm to the ecology, such as destruction of wildlife;

(c) waste of energy resources when conservation is required;

(d) health hazards, as with the use of certain ingredients in foods, cosmetics or medicines;

(e) safety hazards, as with the design or use of certain materials in the manufacture of toys;

(f) road safety, and the design of motor-cars to minimise fatalities in accidents;

(g) loss of money which can occur with investments, mail-order trading, or guarantees which are not supported by a trust fund in case a company goes out of business.

In recent years we have seen a number of 'green' campaigns ranging from the openly propagandist ones of organisations such as Greenpeace to attempts by commercial companies to jump on the 'green' bandwagon. Some of the latter have been sincere, other campaigns doubtful exploitation of a fashionable or topical theme.

Diversification and take-over

8. Diversification

Some companies are believed to be monopolistic, or engaged in only one industry, and advertising may be used to correct this image and to show the true breadth of its activites. This sort of advertising may also be directed at the share market since investors are likely to have greater confidence in a company which has a healthy spread of interests, and can sustain downturns in certain markets. Tobacco firms are nowadays involved in many businesses such as beer, foods and hotels and catering. Tate and Lyle are not confined to sugar. Chemical firms like ICI make insecticides, paints and plastics. These broader images are presented through corporate advertising.

9. Take-over bids

In the event of a take-over bid, when an apparently stronger company buys up a large number of shares of a weaker company, and then tries to make the remaining shareholders a favourable offer, the two companies may become caught up in a battle of competing claims and offers. This is usually done by means of advertisements in the business press as well as in letters to shareholders. These financial struggles can be seen from time to time in newspapers like *The Times, Financial Times, International Herald Tribune* and *Wall Street Journal.*

Crisis advertising

10. Crisis situations

Crises of various kinds can strike companies, and urgent advertising may be necessary. The following are possible crisis situations requiring the use of special advertising that is different from the normal uses of trade or consumer advertising.

(a) A strike may require advertisements stating the employer's side of the dispute.

(b) An accident may need advertisements which state when normal services will be resumed.

(c) A product defect may require advertisements which identify the problem and ask customers to return the product for modification or replacement.

11. Example

Figure 14.2 reproduces a typical product recall advertisement.

IMPORTANT ANNOUNCEMENT

TO OWNERS OF ELECTRIC COOKERS

TRICITY SOVEREIGN 4638
(from serial numbers 185 00001 to 1286 02000)

ONYX 100M
(from serial numbers 986 00001 to 1086 00100)

KENWOOD SL101
(from serial numbers 586 00001 to 786 00100)

In the interest of customer care Tricity Domestic Appliances would like to ensure that all the above products have an additional fail-safe device installed free of charge. There exists a remote possibility that under certain circumstances the top oven could overheat while the cooker is unattended.

Only the models above are affected. We would therefore like to arrange for one of our service engineers to call to inspect your cooker and if necessary carry out a modification.

How do you know if your cooker is involved?
● Check the model number against those mentioned above.
● Check the serial number. This information can be found below the main oven door on the front of the cooker.

-------**WHAT ACTION SHOULD I TAKE?**-------
● **Dial freephone 0800 400418 to notify us.**
● **Please be ready to quote your name, address and daytime telephone number. Also your model and serial number.**
● **Alternatively write to: Sovereign Desk Freepost, P.O. Box 14, Newton Aycliffe, Co Durham, DL5 6BZ.** No stamp required

Your request for a service call will be immediately forwarded to your local service centre to arrange an appointment at no charge.

You can continue to use your cooker provided that until an engineer has called, you ensure that it is always switched off at the cooker point when not in use.

**Tricity Domestic Appliances apologise
for any inconvenience caused.**

Figure 14.2 *A typical product recall advertisement.*

Financial advertising

12. Share issues

When a private company becomes a public company, and its shares are to be sold on the Stock Exchange, when a nationalised undertaking is privatised and shares are offered to the public, or when a public company wishes to borrow money and offers debentures, a special form of advertising is required under the share issue regulations.

It takes the form of a *prospectus* which usually appears in full in *The Times* and the *Financial Times*, occupying two or more pages with background information on the company and an application form for the purchase of shares. Condensed versions may also appear in other newspapers. In the case of large share issues such as those for privatised national enterprises the prospectus is usually published throughout the national press. Millions of shares are offered on an instalment or tranche basis.

13. Annual report

Another form of financial advertising which can be regarded as 'corporate' (as distinct from the normal trading advertisements of financial houses described in Chapter 1) is that used to announce the annual report and accounts, sometimes with an offer to interested persons of a copy of the printed report, and usually with a digest of the chairman's report.

14. Others

There are also those rather dull advertisements which appear in the business press, headed 'This advertisement appears as a matter of record only', which list the holdings held by various financial partners in an enterprise, and are a necessary public announcement so that there is no secrecy about the participations, or as a brief token announcement about a new share issue.

Progress test 14

1. Define corporate advertising. (1)
2. How can advertising be used for public relations purposes? (3)
3. What is advocacy or issue advertising? (5)
4. Give examples of the use of corporate advertising to 'position' a company. (7)
5. How is corporate advertising used to explain diversification? (8)

6. Explain the use of corporate advertising in the course of take-over bids. **(9)**

7. What sort of crisis situations require corporate advertising? What is meant by product recall? **(10, 11)**

8. How is corporate advertising used to announce a new share issue? **(12)**

15
Advertising research

Value of research

1. Scope of advertising research

Advertising research is a branch of marketing research, and it is both a sort of insurance to avoid wasting money on ineffective advertising and a means of monitoring the effectiveness of a campaign while it is running and after the campaign has ended. It is also possible and advantageous to link advertising research with other forms of marketing research which the company is undertaking. Today, the advertiser has the benefits of many sorts of research, and they are usually recommended and commissioned by an advertising agency. In fact, in its own interests a good advertising agency may insist on the use of research to ensure that it produces and conducts successful advertising. This applies particularly to copy-testing to establish the best idea, theme, selling points or presentation before entering into costly artwork or production of commercials and the buying of space and airtime.

Research is not confined to testing creativity. There is a wealth of independently researched statistical information on sales, readership and audience figures so that the most economic media can be used. In addition to this it is possible to control the duration of appearance of an advertisement by assessing when enough people have had the opportunity to see the advertisement a sufficient number of times.

This is in line with the IPA definition of advertising which refers to presenting 'the most persuasive selling message to the right prospects for the product or service at the lowest possible cost'. Advertising research can help to achieve this effectively and economically.

2. Reliability of research

How reliable is marketing research? The answer to this is that while it is better than crystal ball gazing or astrology, marketing research does not produce facts but only tendencies and indications which are open to interpretation. For example, the opinion poll technique is often applied to political surveys, but the accuracy of the figures tends to depend on how near to an election the poll was conducted, the final voting being the only true result.

Research in developing countries

3. Limitations

From this chapter's survey of the techniques and statistics available in the UK to advertisers, and especially to their advertising agencies, it will be appreciated that methods and information can be applied to the planning and creation of advertising campaigns which are both economic and effective. However, such a wealth of intelligence rarely exists in developing countries. Media may be expensive simply because of the costs of producing newspapers, magazines or television programmes for small readerships or audiences. Field research may be difficult or costly to conduct, although a number of surveys have been conducted which have produced otherwise unknown data.

For instance, a media survey in Kenya revealed the number of people who 'listen to newspapers' which are read to them by literate members of the family. It has also been found in Nigeria and Zambia that radio may be less penetrating than is often believed, and that people living in remote areas use radio (and especially pop or 'high life' music) purely as a companionable background sound, and pay little heed to news from distant cities of which they have little knowledge. Major world events may not be of much concern to a villager whose interests are limited to his local community. On the other hand, the travelling film show and product demonstration will be more significant, and in Malawi the textile firm of David Whitehead has taken fashion shows to villagers to promote dress-making materials (*see* 4:**33**).

4. Social grades

The British system of social grades, also used in advertising research, especially readership and audience surveys, has been described in 2:7. It was seen that the three largest (C^1, C^2 and D) total 74 per cent or nearly three-quarters of the adult male and female population. They form the mass market for FMCGs, the readers of the popular press (e.g. the *Sun, Daily Mirror, Daily Star, Today, Daily Mail* and *Daily Express*) and the watchers of prime-time evening television.

Elsewhere in the world, other methods may be used to represent the different classes in a society, e.g. the socio-economic way of grading by income, or the educational status method. Some typical tables for developing and less developed countries are given in the author's companion M & E HANDBOOK, *Modern Marketing*. In a developing country, where most people are rural dwellers, 70 per cent may be classed as lower class, quite the opposite of the British experience.

Research before, during and after the campaign

5. Pre-campaign research

The aim of research before advertising appears is to:

(a) define the copy platform or theme;
(b) pre-test proposed advertisements; and
(c) plan the media schedule.

The marketing department will have researched other matters concerning the market, the product and the package, and it will continue to research (or subscribe to surveys) regarding what, how and where consumers purchase (e.g. by means of consumer panels), and the movement of stocks and the brand share held (e.g. dealer audit research). Some of this general marketing research may also assist in the creation of advertisements and the choice of media.

6. Defining the copy platform

What will make the most effective appeal—price, quality,

something new, a special offer? Should the advertisement be serious or humorous? Should there be a lot of copy or mostly pictures? It is no use plumping for the first idea. When the presentation is made to the client there must be sound justification for the proposed advertisement or series of advertisements. The following kinds of research may be used.

(a) *Motivational research.* In this type of research, a number of clinical tests are used to discover the hidden motives for buying. If questioned by normal research techniques respondents may say they buy because, for instance, they like the new design of the motor-car, but motivational research will probe deeper and produce the underlying motive that, for example, it is believed to be the safest car for family motoring, and will therefore satisfy the buyer's wife. It uses clinical tests and a small sample of people, and was pioneered in the USA by Dr Ernst Dichter. Motivational research was popular in the 1960s but has given way to more simple techniques such as the discussion group.

(b) *Discussion group.* Motivational research can be expensive, and a much less expensive method is to set up a discussion group controlled by a chairman who poses questions, listens to the discussion which sparks off spontaneous ideas and comments, and summarises the answer. A report is then written presenting the answers to the questions. These answers can indicate the copy theme which should be adopted by the creative department of the advertising agency.

7. Copy-testing

When the theme has been worked up creatively as a press advertisement, radio script or preliminary mock-up of a TV commercial, it will be tested on a sample of people representative of the market. One idea may be tested at a time, or different versions will be tested simultaneously. Press advertisements can be shown to respondents, then withdrawn and questions asked to test what is remembered. Commercials may be broadcast or screened to an invited audience in a hall or private theatre. Reactions can be tested by recording which commercial would most encourage purchase.

A number of techniques are practised such as interspersing the commercial under test among others and comparing the responses obtained. Does the new one achieve a greater willingness to buy than the others?

In some campaigns it may be necessary to go on testing until a version achieves the desired response rate. In one well-known press advertising campaign five versions were rejected before the agency was satisfied that the sixth was the one which could be presented to the client with confidence. The campaign, with annual refinements, ran successfully for three years.

8. Reading and noting

Another method is to place the advertisement in a limited regional edition of a national newspaper, and then to question a sample of readers of the newspaper next day. The sample is found by asking people in the street whether or not they read the previous day's paper, and whether or not they saw the advertisement. Those who did are then taken through every part of the advertisement and questioned to test what percentage of these readers remembered each item. Once the weaknesses and the strengths of the advertisement are established, the final advertisement is produced for the campaign proper in the full national edition of that paper and in the other publications on the media schedule.

9. Research during the campaign

When the advertising campaign is running, further reading and noting tests may be held, but probably a more simple next-day recall test can be used to measure what percentage of readers or viewers saw and remembered details of the advertisement when it appeared the previous day.

If the company is subscribing to a monthly dealer audit report, this information can indicate how the campaign is influencing sales. Other data such as the number of enquiries received or orders taken will also test the effectiveness of a campaign. If the advertisement contains a keyed coupon, that is one with a code such as STI for the first insertion in the *Sunday Times*, the response can be counted. If the cost of the space is divided by the number of enquiries, a cost-per-reply figure can be calculated, and this can be done to arrive at a cost-per-conversion-into-sale figure.

10. Testing the final result

When the campaign has finished some of the methods already described can be used again, especially in assessing the total number of enquiries or orders obtained (and the relative cost for each publication), while dealer audit—being a continuous study—can produce a graphical representation of the effect of the campaign over the period of its run. A target may have been set such as a given percentage increase in the volume of sales, or an improvement in the share of the market held by the product in relation to rival brands. For instance, has the brand moved up from third position to second or first position? Or has the brand retained its previous position in spite of the efforts made by competitors? If it is a new product, what share of the market has the advertising campaign achieved? To be fair, any other influences must be considered too. The sales force may have been strengthened or there could have been a coincidental sales promotion scheme such as a money-off offer.

11. Continuous research

Two forms of continuous research need explanation here. 'Continuous' does not mean every day but regularly, say every month. The advantage of continuous over single or *ad hoc* surveys is that they record trends over time. They show how sales of a brand vary and compete with other brands, influenced perhaps by advertising or sales promotion campaigns.

The two main kinds of continuous research are the consumer panel and dealer (retail or shop) audit. Consumer panels are carefully recruited and consist of housewives or householders who agree to keep a diary of their purchases. The diaries are posted to the research company for tabulation. The final report will show what social grades buy which brands in which quantities, how often and where. Dealer audit requires a recruited cross-section of retailers who are visited regularly and their invoices and stocks checked to record the movement of brands and the shares of the market held by each brand.

Media research: sources of statistics

12. Independent media surveys

A number of research organisations produce regular

independent media studies. They are 'independent' in the sense that they have tripartite sponsorship representing the three sides of advertising through bodies serving the advertisers (e.g. Incorporated Society of British Advertisers), advertising agencies (e.g. Institute of Practitioners in Advertising) and the relevant media bodies (e.g. Press Research Council, Outdoor Advertising Association, Association of Independent Radio Contractors or the Independent Television Association). Some surveys are conducted continuously, as with press and television, or periodically as with radio, or occasionally as with outdoor.

In addition, individual media owners such as publishing houses, television contractors and London Underground conduct their own surveys. There is, therefore, a wealth of statistical information concerning readerships and audiences.

13. 'Readership' and 'circulation'

These two terms are sometimes misunderstood or even wrongly used to mean the same thing. They describe entirely different press media data. 'Readership' is an estimate of the number of people who *read* newspapers and magazines, and the figures result from surveying a sample of the reading public. 'Circulation' is the average audited net sale, or the number of copies actually *sold* at the full cover price, other copies being deducted from the total number printed.

Readership is estimated by means of extensive readership surveys (*see also* **16**). Readership is *not* found by multiplying the circulation figure by a given number. This would be nonsense if only that journals read in waiting rooms and hairdressing salons have readership figures far in excess of newspapers.

Circulation figures are based on audited net sales, *not* field research. In their absence there are sometimes 'publishers' statements' which have been likened to 'publishers' lies'.

14. Audit Bureau of Circulations

The ABC was founded in 1931 (and there are today similar bureaux in other countries) to inform advertisers and advertising agencies of true numbers of newspapers or magazines which are sold or, in the case of controlled circulations, have reliable distribution against requests. It was created because publishers were selling advertisement space on the basis of spurious circulation figures which were often total print orders irrespective of the actual number of copies sold. Today the ABC works closely with *British Rate and Data*, and no ABC figure can be claimed unless it has been certified by the ABC. The procedure is for the publisher's own accountants to complete audit forms showing the net circulation figures, and after scrutiny the ABC issues an audited net sale figure based on an average number of copies sold per day, week or month as the case may be over the preceding six-monthly period prior to 30 June and 31 December. (The figures in 4:7 are rounded-up approximations based on ABC figures). Nearly 3,000 British publications quote ABC figures. Exhibition attendances are also certified.

Thus, ABC figures are actual figures and are not based on interviews as in the case of readership figures. Readership figures, however, take into account secondary readership and are therefore much larger. A problem with ABC figures is that when copies are lost as a result of strikes, a publication can suffer a loss of sales through no fault of its own, that is, not because sales have fallen. It also has to be realised that at certain times of the year, and on certain days of the year, the circulation may be greater or smaller than the average ABC figure.

At one time sales fell for Saturday editions of dailies, mainly because those not working on a Saturday, and who normally bought their paper on the way to work, did not do so. However, recent ABC figures show that those papers which have Saturday magazines, actually sell more copies on a Saturday. The Saturday magazine has induced people to buy a copy of the Saturday edition, or to place a regular home delivery order with a newsagent.

The comparative costs of different publications can be calculated on the basis of a cost-per-thousand net sale. In the competition for sale of advertisement space, ABC figures become a major sales argument.

15. Verified Free Distribution

This development in the auditing of circulation figures was made necessary by the rapid growth of free newspapers. (*See* 4:7(c).) Again, advertisers are entitled to know reliable figures, which is not easy when copies are delivered door-to-door, handed out to passers-by in the street, or delivered in bulk to distribution centres. Verified Free Distribution is a subsidiary company launched by the ABC in 1981, resulting in credible data in this difficult field.

Delivered newspapers, magazines and directories can qualify for VFD certification, while bulk supplies (e.g. copies distributed by hotels, shops and airlines) receive BVS (Bulk Verification Services) certification. Vast numbers of copies are involved, and the first 200 free newspaper titles to be registered with VFD represented 10 million copies distributed of each issue.

The Croydon Post carries the VFD symbol beside its title and for one six-month period its VFD figure of free copies was 107,463 copies. This free newspaper has an interesting history. Originally it was sold as the *Mid-Week Post,* sister paper of the long-established *Croydon Advertiser.* When it failed to sell it was converted into a free newspaper and with saturation house-to-house circulation it was able to command profitable advertisement revenue. Free newspapers are rather like controlled circulations: guaranteed distribution on a big scale plus market penetration are big attractions for advertisers.

16. Joint Industry Committee for National Readership Surveys

Known as JICNARS (the reader should note the oddity that the 'NA' in the initials stand for 'national'), this body took over the National Readership Survey from the Institute of Practitioners in Advertising in 1968. The constituent bodies of this tripartite independent research organisation are the Press Research Council (representing newspapers and magazines), the IPA and the Incorporated Society of British Advertisers. Some 200 national newspapers and magazines are included in the readership survey, plus certain other specialist journals from time to time, and a sample of 30,000 people are interviewed. During the continuous survey, questions are asked about ITV viewing, listening to ILR, and cinema-going, in addition to many questions relating to readership. Using the A, B, C^1, C^2, D, E social grades which were devised specifically for JICNARS, demographic profiles are produced of the readership of each publication. As with ABC figures, JICNARS figures are issued every six months for the periods January–June and July–December.

These figures may be to the advantage or disadvantage of particular journals, but for advertisers and their advertising agencies JICNARS data provides revealing information about how many people of what kind read the 200 or so leading publications. Two papers with similar titles and circulations may appear to attract similar readers, but this may not be the case. Some journals may have large readerships because (like the *Financial Times* which has a small circulation) it is essential reading in business offices. Some magazines may enjoy large readerships because they are frequently passed on to other people, or they are read in doctors' or dentists' waiting-rooms or in hairdressing salons. These publications just go on being read and have long lives.

In selling space, JICNARS data can produce valuable support, and the following from an advertisement in the trade press for *Reader's Digest* is typical: 'Our readership is up by 60,000 to a massive 6,928,000. It's nice to know that the world's biggest magazine is still getting bigger.'

17. Joint Industry Committee for Poster Audience Research

In 1983 JICPAR took over from JICPAS which had become moribund. The new body, representing the Outdoor Advertising Association of Great Britain, the Incorporated Society of British Advertisers, the Institute of Practitioners in Advertising and the Council of Outdoor Specialists, has revived poster audience research. A poster size classification and audience measurement project, funded by the OAA, was instigated in 1984. A central data bank was also set up, a User Subcommittee now looks into JICPAR functions, and there is a Publishing Subcommittee to publicise JICPAR activities.

OSCAR offers target audience demographics for 175 groups nationally, and is based on nett likelihood to see posters. Data is continuously updated through ongoing audit and it is possible to give physical proximity details of panels to particular retailers.

Outdoor advertising is not only one of the oldest but it remains one of the most important advertising media. In a country like Britain, with its huge urban audiences, the poster industry needs to market its product with proper statistics, and its clients need similar information in order to evaluate the cost and value of outdoor advertising.

Over the years there have been many effective surveys which have demonstrated the size of the poster audience and the extent to which outdoor advertising reaches the majority of people. With such information it has been possible to plan campaigns using the minimum number of posters necessary to reach the maximum number of people in regional or national campaigns. The new-look JICPAR is probably encouraged by the demand from advertisers for cost-effective advertising and their complaint that press and TV advertisement rates are excessive. It is significant that many of the campaigns to launch new motor-cars have used posters to the extent that nowadays it is possible to see a row of hoardings bearing posters exclusively advertising a variety of rival motor-cars!

In addition to JICPAR studies there have been those of the transport advertising contractors for buses and London Underground. One worth noting was the *See You In Barking* tracking study into awareness of bus advertising, carried out by the British Market Research Bureau for London Transport Advertising in 1987. About 70 different bus side campaigns were measured. Some 500 adults were interviewed at 40 sampling points and during home interviews. A test campaign was devised by London Transport Advertising consisting of a poster of barking dogs and a caption 'See You in Barking' which was placed on 750 T-sides for a month. After two weeks, the interviews revealed that 32 per cent recalled the poster, and after four weeks 37 per cent. Other campaigns scored from 8 per cent to 63 per cent awareness, but the majority scored 32–37 per cent awareness.

London Underground has its Tube Research Audience Classification (TRAC) research which bases its reports on information given by 5000 Underground travellers who filled 28-day travel diaries. The TRAC database provides gross audience coverage and frequency for Underground advertisements. The data is reweighted to the latest Target Group Index (*see* also **23**).

18. Joint Industry Committee for Radio Audience Research
An annual radio audience report is produced by JICRAR, and this is commissioned and paid for by the individual ILR stations in membership of the Association of Independent Radio Contractors. The three members of JICRAR are the Institute of Practitioners in Advertising, and Incorporated Society of British Advertisers and the Association of Independent Radio Contractors. A sample of listeners are asked to complete diaries giving audience ratings at half-hourly periods for seven days and

reports are published quarterly. The reports are sold to subscribers by the AIRC. The AIRC also publishes comprehensive volumes for subscribers.

While commercial radio continues to grow both in number of local stations and number of listeners, it is still the poor relation of commercial television. Whereas television audiences are researched weekly it is perhaps indicative of the modest role of the medium that it can afford only a single annual survey which cannot be truly representative of radio audiences throughout the year. By its very nature, being more localised than television, radio does not attract the big national advertisers, but this could change if and when the proposed national commercial radio system comes about under the new Radio Authority.

19. Joint Industry Committee for Cable Audience Research

This is the newest of the tripartite research committees, and Survey Research Associates were appointed to prepare the first research report in 1984 and publishes quarterly data.

20. Broadcasters' Audience Research Board

Replacing JICTAR in 1981, and better known as BARB, it has an unfortunate title which is not easy to remember, and which encourages people to think that the 'B' stands for 'British' as in British Market Research Bureau (BMRB). The change came about with the combination of the television audience surveys of non-commercial BBC and commercial ITV. Previously, controversy had raged because the two services were subject to separate and very different weekly surveys resulting in conflicting figures.

For audience measurement, electronic meters are attached to a representative sample of television sets, and members of the household complete diaries to record their personal viewing, although this original JICTAR method has been modernised and developed to meet changed circumstances. There are now electronic methods of recording personal viewing, viewing on second sets in homes is now monitored, and there have been technical adjustments to cover the different viewing habits of viewers as between alternative channels (*see* also 4:**17**).

Table 15.1 *BARB area top ten: Individuals viewing*

London	Originating programme company	Screened by	TVR
1. EastEnders (Thu./Sun.)	BBC	BBC 1	28
2. EastEnders (Tue./Sun.)	BBC	BBC 1	27
3. Coronation Street (Wed./Sat.)	Granada	Thames	25
3. Neighbours (Tue. 1330/1736)	BBC	BBC 1	25
5. Neighbours (Wed. 1330/1736)	BBC	BBC 1	24
5. Neighbours (Fri. 1330/1736)	BBC	BBC 1	24
7. Neighbours (Mon. 1330/1736)	BBC	BBC 1	23
8. Neighbours (Thu. 1330/1736)	BBC	BBC 1	22
8. Coronation Street (Mon./Wed.)	Granada	Thames	22
10. The Bill	Thames	Thames	21
10. Coronation Street (Fri./Sat.)	Granada	LWT	21

Area Top Tens are also published weekly for the NW, Central Scotland, S and SE, East, Ulster, N. Scotland, Midlands, E and W, Yorkshire, Wales and the West, NE, SE and Border. The soaps won top places, but *EastEnders* naturally led in London and S and SE whereas *Coronation Street* (being a Manchester-based story) led almost everywhere else except for the SW where the first three were *Neighbours, Coronation Street* and *EastEnders*. These figures were for the week ending 29 July 1990, and are copyright BARB.

The TVR figure in the right-hand column of Table 15.1 is the percentage of individuals viewing the programme out of all those individuals in homes with sets capable of receiving ITV transmission from that area. The calculation is the average audience through the programme.

The Week's Viewing In Summary (from which the above is extracted) is produced for BARB by AGB, and copies are available weekly from BARB, Glenthorne House, Hammersmith Grove, London W6.

In February 1990 BARB appointed AGB Research and RSMB Television Research as joint contractors for television audience measurement with effect from 1 August 1991 for a period of seven years. The new method was tested alongside the previous panel for three months prior to August 1991. A larger panel is used under the new contract, monitoring more TV sets and more channels, isolating timeshift viewing programme by programme from the playback statistics, and registering the age and sex of guest viewers instead of estimating them. The timeshift calculation takes into account the playing at a later date of videotaped programmes. Results are available, if required, on a daily basis, the basic method of receiving results being electronic instead of on paper as in the past.

Since the end of 1989, RSMB (on a three-year contract) conducted a metered operation to monitor television viewing on homes receiving the Astra channels which carry four Sky channels, MTV Europe, WH Smith's Screensport and Lifestyle and Children's Channel, all satellite transmissions. BSB transmissions began on 25 March 1990, and the two research companies set up a separate BSB panel similar to the Astra Panel.

At the time of writing viewing figures for satellite television are uncertain as BSB was a new arrival, but figures released during the summer of 1990 implied that Sky Movies had more viewers than the traditional UK stations, which was not surprising since there were so many repeats of old shows. This was an open invitation to buy a dish, rent cable or hire videos. From the advertiser's point of view, a worrying factor was that satellite stations appeared to be watched by social grades with the least spending power, e.g. the elderly, pensioners and those on low incomes. However, Sky absorbed BSB in November 1990.

21. Media Expenditure Analysis Ltd

Estimates of media expenditure in the press and on television by advertisers are published by MEAL in their *MEAL Quarterly Digest*. It is very useful to know at least approximately what rival firms are spending. More than 150,000 advertisements are monitored by MEAL each month, half of them being on ITV, and 360 product groups are included. Each week in *Marketing* there appears MEAL's list of new advertisers for the previous week. This list: 'includes new brands; extensions to product ranges which previously have been advertised only as part of a range; brands which have not appeared over the past 18 months in the media which are regularly monitored. The brands have been taken from the six product categories which are usually associated with fast moving packaged goods.'

22. MEAL top advertisers

See also references to MEAL figures in Chapter 4.

23. Target Group Index

This service run by the British Market Research Bureau takes a different approach to TV audience research, and the TGI panel of 24,000 adults questioned annually exceeds the number of homes in the BARB sample. It records the sample's demographic characteristics and media exposure and provides data covering 400 product fields. Questions on TV viewing are by hourly segments whereas BARB correspondents record quarter-hour segments.

24. Advertising Statistics Yearbook

First published in 1983 under the auspices of the Advertising Association, this annual publication is a comprehensive collection of advertising statistics.

The *Yearbook* covers advertising and the economy; cinema, direct mail, poster, national newspapers, regional newspapers, business and professional magazines, directories, radio and television advertising; advertising expenditure by product sector; top advertiser and agency statistics; and many other topics.

Tracking studies

25. Measuring the effect of advertising

Far more comprehensive than a next-day recall study is the system of tracking studies to measure the effect advertising has on target audiences rather than the incidence of impact or recall. This service is provided by TABS Ltd (Tracking, Advertising and Brand Strength), an independent market research company formed in 1976 to supply a national *continuous* weekly syndicated monitor to track 'brand health' and advertising effectiveness across all major media. The information aims to refine and optimise the advertising's creative execution and media planning and buying. With the growth of highly critical media independents whose services depend on media planning and buying skills, tracking studies can be a valuable means of increasing their efficiency.

26. Essential difference

Media planners and buyers seek to achieve maximum 'share of voice' for their clients. Traditional media research estimates 'opportunities to see' (OTS) or exposure to a campaign, but this is based on hypothetical analyses of what **might** have been achieved rather than what really happened. Because a certain volume of people of different categories saw or remembered an advertisement does not mean that they ultimately did anything about it. The reach of an advertisement may say something about which medium produced the highest numbers or percentages, and this may lead to the calculation of cost-per-thousand figures, but no more. It treats 'share of voice' in terms of share of *shouting*, whereas tracking studies go further and test the share of *hearing*. Measurement of OTS and cost-per-thousand remain important, but measurement of influence goes a long way further in testing the cost-effectiveness of advertising, and that is what advertisers (the agency clients) really need to know.

27. The TABS method

By combining computer technology and a very efficient self-completion questionnaire (*see* Fig. 15.1), TABS monitors the *strengths* of reactions about advertised brands. The respondents place pencil ticks on scaled and other questions covering brand buying, brand usage, brand awareness, advertising awareness, brand goodwill, price image and detailed brand image. These pencil marks are read by an Optical Mark Reading computer, which converts them into scores and percentages among the target market for each of the various products or services covered. Responses are derived from a representative sample in each of the ten main TV areas. The sample size is 500 adults each week, made up of 250 each of housewives and men, totally 24,000 different adults a year.

28. TABS reports

Throughout the year subscribers receive 13 four-weekly reports. They cover FMCGs such as confectionery, drinks and toiletries, retailing, financial services, holidays and travel, durables (e.g. domestic appliances), clothing and do-it-yourself goods (e.g. decorating materials). This is an excellent example of continuous research. Moreover, the TABS measure is not a simple percentage awareness figure but is shown on a 10-point scaled score which is indexed 0–100. This picks up the different levels of a campaign's real impact on members of the target market which can range from very strong, clear and detailed recall through the many shades of grey to somebody who can scarcely remember a given campaign and may be confused about what they read, saw or heard and are not even sure about the brand.

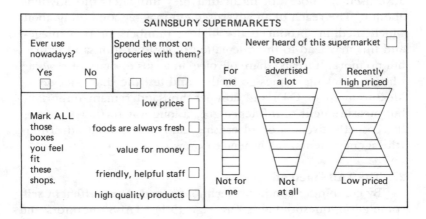

Figure 15.1 *Specimen page from a TABS questionnaire.*

29. Media covered

TABS scores for any given campaign are analysed not only among relevant subdivisions of the target market such as social class, age or with or without children but also according to the following *media consumption* criteria:

(a) readership of every named individual national daily newspaper;

(b) readership of every named individual national Sunday newspaper;

(c) weight of newspaper reading;

(d) readership of TV magazines (e.g. *Radio Times, TV Times*);

(e) readership of colour magazine supplements (e.g. *Sunday Times, Observer, Daily Telegraph, Mail on Sunday*);

(f) weight of ITV viewing (i.e. commercial television);

(g) Channel 4 TV viewing;

(h) breakfast ITV viewing (i.e. TV-am);
(i) listening to each of the 32 or more named ILR stations;
(j) by all the different interlaced combinations of weight of ITV viewing, newspaper reading and radio listening.

30. Decay

The impact of advertising is subject to a deterioration or decay factor after advertising campaigns have ended, something which justifies sustained advertising and refutes the old argument about why advertise something with which everyone is familiar! Some campaigns are deliberately rested and it is important to know when advertising should be resumed. Brooke Bond PG Tips television chimp commercials are a case in point. TABS reports can reveal rates of decay and heritage effects where there is a halo effect from the company's other or earlier advertising. Associated with all this are media implications in terms of pattern and frequency when allocating the appropriation, whether to adopt regular 'drip' or sudden 'burst' tactics, and the best time to advertise cost-effectively.

31. Relation to media

When the information provided is married to data on media exposure, it is possible to separate the contribution made by the creative execution from that of the media spend and mix. TABS analyses then pin-points weaknesses in both creative and media aspects of the campaign by measuring real effects such as improved awareness, image or buying attitudes. The result is a £ for £ assessment of the quantitative contribution made by the press, TV and other media.

32. Cost

There is a set-up charge to prepare the study, and a rate is charged per brand per annum for either all adults or men or housewives only (some products may be bought mainly by only one sex.) There are volume discounts for surveying 11 or more brands, which is an advantage to an agency handling many brands or a company with many brands. Typical costs per brand per annum are approximately £2,500 for either women or men, or about £3,000 for all adults.

NOTE: The expression 'tracking' tends to be used very loosely to include various forms of recall and awareness testing, but the TABS example makes a very precise use of the term.

Progress test 15

1. Describe some of the reasons for applying marketing research techniques to advertising. (1)
2. How reliable is research, and why should the resulting statistics be interpreted carefully? (2)
3. What problems or weaknesses are there concerning the evaluation of media in developing countries? (3)
4. How do social grades differ between Britain and developing countries? (4)
5. Name the three objectives of pre-advertising campaign research. (5)
6. What is motivational research, and how does it differ from other forms of research? (6)
7. How is a discussion group conducted? (6)
8. Describe the methods of pre-testing press advertisements and TV commercials. (7)
9. What is a keyed coupon and how can it be used to measure response? (9)
10. What are cost-per-reply and cost-per-conversion-into-sales figures? (9)
11. What is continuous research? (11)
12. Distinguish between 'readership' and 'circulation'. (13)
13. How are the circulations of free newspapers verified? (15)
14. Why are poster advertising statistics necessary? (17)
15. How does BARB measure television audiences? (20)
16. How can MEAL assist the advertiser? (21, 22)
17. What is a TABS tracking study, and how does this technique provide data different from other advertising research? (25–32)
18. Explain the expression 'decay'. (30)

16
Law and ethics of advertising

Legal and voluntary controls

1. Criticisms of advertising

This book opens with the economic justification for advertising, and although the extent of advertising tends to reflect the prosperity and standard of living of a country, there are many critics of advertising. It is often accused by representatives of the intellectual left (including school teachers!) of being an immoral and parasitical force which exalts false values and induces people to buy things they either do not need or cannot afford. It is said to create expectations that cannot be satisfied. In fact, in Indonesia TV commercials are banned because they are thought to increase the expectations of poorer people! What these critics mean is that they would prefer to live in a primitive society, or at best the sort of medieval one which existed before the industrial revolution began to pioneer modern society.

Critics of advertising tend to make one very big fundamental mistake: they blame the *tool* and not the *user*. There is nothing wrong with *advertising*, but there are *advertisers* who abuse or misuse advertising, deliberately or unintentionally. Consequently, there are consumerist organisations, consumer protection laws, and representatives of the advertising industry who seek to control abuses of advertising. Note that we refer to abuses *of* and not *by* advertising. The distinction is vital to a proper understanding of this chapter.

2.   Legal versus voluntary controls

Since the setting up of the National Vigilance Committee in 1926, the British advertising business has in its own interests sought to regulate advertising voluntarily. Various governments, but mostly Labour ones, have also sought to control advertising by imposing legislation. There are more than 100 statutes and regulations which are in some way relevant to advertising.

Some confusion exists over the merits and demerits of the two forms of control. Which is the more effective? Are both kinds of control necessary? These two questions invite very serious consideration for the answers are not simple beyond saying that both can be effective for different reasons, and both are valuable.

3.   Characteristics of legislation

The main characteristics of legal control are as follows:

(a) There are written regulations which the advertiser should obey in the public interest, under penalty of fine or imprisonment if proved guilty of an offence.

(b) The law can be preventive in making known what is illegal.

(c) Some laws depend on interpretation by the courts, and may not be effective until a test case has occurred to set precedents.

(d) The law has to be invoked either by the plaintiff suing, or by the Crown deciding to prosecute, according to whether it is common or statute law. This can be costly and time-consuming, and it can take a long time for the case to come to court. By the time the case has been heard (and this might take three to five years) the original offence will have been committed, causing whatever harm it may, while the issue will have become history.

4.   Characteristics of voluntary controls

These are different from those which apply to legal controls, and may be summarised as follows.

(a) There are written recommendations which the advertiser should obey in the public interest. An offending advertising agent risks losing his recognition status and right to commission, while the client risks damaging his reputation if a complaint is made to the Advertising Standards Authority (ASA) who publish their decisions in monthly reports which are widely quoted (*see* **38**).

(b) There are no penalties other than the above and the necessity to amend or withdraw an offending advertisement. The ASA has no power to impose fines.

(c) Voluntary controls are *self-regulatory* and are likely to prevent unethical advertising from appearing. The media act as censors, and advertising agents act as bulwarks, should an advertiser wish to advertise in a way likely to offend against the BCAP. The media do not want complaints from readers and they have their own reputations to safeguard, while the agent does not wish to lose income by imperilling his right to commission. Once again, we see that responsibility for reputable or disreputable advertising rests with the advertiser, not with advertising.

(d) If there is a written complaint from any member of the public, and it is upheld by the ASA, action can be swift. The ad can be modified or withdrawn. In a very serious and urgent case, as when a complaint is made direct to the media, action can be instantaneous. This occurred on one occasion when an advertisement quite unintentionally caused offence by making a statement which coincided with a tragic event in the news—which was unanticipated when the ad was created—and the advertisement was withdrawn in a matter of hours. The offence was totally innocent but unfortunately the ad appeared to be in very poor taste to readers who did not appreciate that it had been produced many weeks in advance in order to be printed in a colour supplement.

There have been two instances where humorous ads have upset Islamic sensibilities, and the threat of trade sanctions brought about immediate apologies and withdrawal of the unintentionally offensive ads. One which implied that a sheikh had run out of oil for his motor-car was intended to be funny, but it was regarded as being insulting by Muslims. A problem with many ads which provoke complaints is that the advertiser did not intend to cause offence. For instance, liquor ads provoke complaints from teetotallers!

(e) Generally, voluntary self-regulatory control can be more effective than legislation. It is interesting that in the past when the Advertising Association had its advertisement investigation department and administered voluntary controls, there was always the risk of incurring a libel action if an advertiser was criticised openly. The Advertising Standards Authority, however, was set up on a 'publish and be damned' basis to appease a Labour government which had accused the voluntary system of having no teeth, and wanted to introduce legislation which would be more effective.

(f) There is one exception where a code of practice is written into the law, and this is the ITC Code of Practice which was part of the Independent Broadcasting Authority Act 1973 and again forms part of the Broadcasting Act 1990. Although there are no prosecutions or penalties, the ITC does have the power of law in that certain categories of advertising are banned from commercial television and radio altogether, and all TV commercials have to be vetted before transmission. They can be rejected, or amendments may be required. The ITC Code is more far-reaching in its restrictions (which are not mere recommendations) and the viewer is well protected.

(g) There are certain aspects of advertising which are bad practice rather than anti-social or criminal, and the law cannot deal with them. Advertising is competitive, but there are limits. It does the industry no good if advertisers become too aggressive towards each other, and 'knocking copy' is a case in point. To denigrate a rival product is bad, but fair comparison is acceptable. Figure 16.1 is an interesting example of an advertisement which some people might consider derogatory, while others would accept it as making acceptable comparisons. It echoes the first Datsun ad in 1969 which made comparisons with the current model Cortina, and that caused a furore. *Marketing* (7 June 1984) referred to 'a provocative "new Cortina" platform', and said that 'the ads set a new standard in knocking copy'.

Doubtless the responsible advertising agents and the media found this copy acceptable, and doubtless Ford and Vauxhall were entitled to take a different view. The Advertising Standards Authority considered the Hyundai advertisement to be typical of the comparative ads which used to be common. Providing that substantiation for the claims is available and correct, the ASA would not question the ad. There would have been a question mark over the Hyundai ad if there had been any performance claims, but the copy was carefully phrased and there was no implication on performance. Readers may have been amused by the ad's audacity, but got the message, and the extent of the response received by Teledata would record the effectiveness of the ad.

We saw the successor to the Cortina in a different mould.
Many people mourned the passing of the much loved Cortina.
And, alas, they were not overjoyed with the replacement, the Sierra.
"A jelly mould" some have even been heard to say.
Now at last a serious successor has arrived.
The new Stellar 1.6 from Hyundai, the company that built Cortinas in
the Far East. A car that makes other 1.6 saloons pale in comparison.
At almost 2 inches longer and wider it makes a Cortina look small.
With 5 speed gearbox, central locking, electric windows, headlamp
washers, alloy wheels, and stereo radio-cassette the 1.6 GSL makes the
nearest priced Sierra look rather basic.
At £4,500 on the road the 1.6L even makes an Escort look expensive.
'Phone Teledata 081-200-0200 for a brochure and the name and
address of your nearest dealer. HYUNDAI.
The new Stellar 1.6. £4,500 to £5,500 on the road.

Figure 16.1 *Example of 'knocking copy'.*

Nevertheless, it was not as harsh as the one that appeared
some years ago in the colour supplements, showing a rival make of
motor-car as a wreck on a scrap merchant's cart! We call this
'knocking copy', but the Americans have an even more apt
expression—'ashcanning'! If such advertising becomes too
cut-throat, it does advertising no good, but occasionally the more
piratical advertising can be ironically amusing and very impactive.

5. Common and statute law

There are two kinds of law. First, there is common law which
is unwritten and largely based on precedent or what has been
decided previously, and which requires the plaintiff to sue the
defendant, the issue being decided on its merits by the judge.
Aspects of common law relevant to advertising are discussed in
6–13 below. Second, there is statute law in which the rules and the
penalties are set out in an Act (i.e. a Bill passed by Parliament and
so placed on the Statute Book), and since an offence will be
against the Crown, action can be taken by the public prosecutor
against the accused. Examples of legislation which affect
advertising are given in **14–29**.

Law of contract

6. Contracts

There are numerous occasions when advertisers, their advertising agents or their various suppliers are involved in contracts. To be legally binding a contract must have three elements, namely, an offer, an unconditional acceptance of the offer, and consideration in the form of some exchange or sacrifice. If the original offer is amended by the person to whom it was made it becomes a conditional acceptance which is now a new offer. This new offer has to be accepted by the other side. Thus, there could be an original offer to supply a brown bag for £5. If the offer is accepted, the £5 is paid, and the bag is supplied, the contract is complete. But if the customer says he or she will pay £5 only if the bag is a blue one a new offer has been made, and the contract will be concluded only if the supplier now agrees to supply a blue bag, £5 is paid for it, and it is duly supplied.

A contract does not have to be in writing, provided the three elements described above are adhered to, and verbal contracts often occur when orders are given on the telephone. If the order is completed in good faith the contract is valid, although should there be a dispute, written evidence is stronger and easier to prove than a conversation even if the work or service was carried out. Verbal contracts are therefore best confirmed in writing so that both sides are certain about their responsibilities. Advertisement space is often sold by telephone, especially classifieds with special telesales staff to either promote or receive orders.

7. Definitions

It may be found useful to define the following terms:

(a) *Simple contract.* A simple contract is one that is not under seal, and as already stated above it can be made orally, in writing or implied.

(b) *Express contract.* This is one in which the terms are set out in words, either orally or in writing, by the partners.

(c) *Implied contract.* Here, circumstances tend to create the contract as when one takes a meal in a restaurant or occupies a room in a hotel, and the provision of the meal or room and its payment constitutes a contract although nothing is in writing.

(**d**) *Executed contract.* In this case, the contract is performed by one or both parties. Smith may agree to erect a fence if Jones pays the bill. If the fence is built and the payment is made the contract is executed. Usually dates are agreed for performance of the work and payment for it.

8. Contracts in advertising

An understanding of the law of contract is important to those engaged in all aspects of advertising. Contracts will arise in:

(**a**) the purchase of advertisement space and airtime;

(**b**) the hiring of outdoor advertisement sites and exhibition stand space;

(**c**) service agreements with advertising agents, public relations consultants and other professional consultants;

(**d**) the purchase of print, display material, photography and artwork.

The law of contract will also apply to many aspects of customer relations, and contractual obligations must be absolutely clear in coupons and literature which offer goods and expect payment.

9. Invitations to treat

If an advertisement (including a window display) merely offers goods for sale there is no obligation on the part of the seller actually to supply these on demand. Legally, there is only an *invitation to treat* and not an *offer*. An invitation can be withdrawn, and has no resemblance to an offer which is a *single* action to a *certain* person, otherwise the supplier would have to supply everyone who accepted the invitation irrespective of whether or not there was sufficient stock.

10. Void and voidable contracts

There are certain situations and conditions which can make a contract void or voidable, and these include the legal capacity of the parties.

(**a**) *Mistake.* This is not easy to prove, but if there is a genuine mistake a contract may be held to be void. A mistake could occur in the wording, or even the setting of the wording, of an advertisement. Usually advertisers are responsible for their own mistakes, but if the mistake applies to both parties, the contract is more likely to be void, as might happen if both sides held the same belief which proved to be wrong.

(b) *Misrepresentation.* A representation is a statement which, while not a term of the contract, nevertheless has an important influence upon acceptance. If this fact is proved to be untrue it becomes a misrepresentation, and the contract is void. A deceitful misrepresentation is a fraud.

(c) *Privity.* Only the parties privy to a contract, that is, aware of it and participating knowingly in the agreement, are affected or bound by it.

(d) *Minors.* Under the Family Law Reform Act 1969, the age of majority is 18 (instead of 21 as previously). Anyone below the age of 18 is, in law, a minor who has no capacity to enter into a legal contract.

(e) *Persons of unsound mind and drunken persons.* Contracts made by such people are void at their option if it can be shown that they were incapable of knowing what they were doing, and this condition was known to the other party, at the time of contracting.

Defamation

11. Definitions

Damages may be sought if a person, organisation or product is intentionally or unintentionally brought into disrepute. Defamation takes two legal forms, spoken and transitory which is *slander* or *slander of goods* (which could occur in a derogatory advertisement), and *libel* which may be published or broadcast and can be permanent.

A libellous or scandalous statement must be:

(a) defamatory;

(b) false, unless the contrary is proved;

(c) understood to refer to the plaintiff;

(d) made known to at least one person other than the plaintiff.

12. Slander of goods

It is not often that the legal and voluntary controls coincide, but there are similarities between derogatory and therefore slanderous statements and knocking copy as prohibited by the BCAP. While the puffery of one product is obviously to the disadvantage of another, it is quite a different matter to savagely denigrate rival goods. Care has to be taken that comparisons are true, but it would be slanderous to publish, say, the results of tests which showed that named products were inferior. Comparisons have to confine themselves to indisputable facts such as brand A is available in five colours, brand B in ten colours, and not declare that the colours of brand A will fade but those of brand B will not.

13. Passing off

This occurs when a product is packed in a deceptive package or 'get-up' which suggests it is a well-known brand, and it is bought on this misunderstanding. The injured party may sue for damages representing loss of business if:

(a) the trade name or get-up is associated with his goods in the public mind;
(b) the acts objected to have interfered with or are calculated to interfere with the conduct of business or sale of goods in the sense that there is confusion in the public mind.

Passing off has become a malpractice in a number of developing countries like Nigeria where famous imported brands have been impersonated in such a way that unsophisticated people have been misled by the similar-looking packs. The deceptions can be achieved by using the same colour, and by using a name which is spelt almost the same way as the original, e.g. Coka-Kola.

Statute law

14. Typical statutes

There are far too many laws related to advertising to quote them all in a book of this size. Some statutes refer to particular trades, e.g. Pharmacy and Poisons Act, Fabrics (Misdescription) Act and the Fertilisers and Feeding Stuffs Act. In this book the reader will find it sufficient to be familiar with a selection of laws which are very much concerned with advertising.

15. Advertisements (Hire Purchase) Act 1967

This Act regulates advertisements giving hire-purchase terms which, for instance, must be correctly set out in a direct response advertisement so that the customer understands whether or not payment of instalments will incur payment higher than the cash price.

16. Consumer Credit Act 1974

Further regulations on the same theme are contained in this Act which also gives consumers the right to cancel a contract if 'oral representations were made in the presence of the debtor or hirer' in the discussion before the contract was undertaken. This usually refers to direct selling, and permits a 'cooling off' period of five days after the day when the customer received his copy of the agreement, e.g. an insurance policy sold by a visiting salesman.

17. Consumer Protection Act 1987

This is one of the most important pieces of consumer legislation, and should be noted carefully by the student of advertising. It implemented in the UK the EC Product Liability Directive. Earlier Acts are amended by this Act. There are parts on Product Liability, Consumer Safety and Misleading Price Indications. All previous legislation on prices is repealed, and there are stringent controls on bogus prices. A general duty is imposed on producers and suppliers to sell safe products. Producers, importers and own labellers are liable for unlimited damages for defects which cause injury or death. No proof of negligence or contractual relationship is needed. Retailers must be careful not to sell dubious foreign products, e.g. dangerous Christmas tree lights or toys, but such products can be recalled urgently to avoid an offence.

18. Control of Misleading Advertisements Regulations 1988

This piece of consumer legislation implements a Council Directive of the EC and is an example of the harmonising of Common Market legislation under the European Communities Act 1972. The Director-General of Fair Trading gives powers to institute a High Court action for injunction prohibiting misleading advertising, always provided that the complainant has failed to obtain satisfaction from a voluntary body such as the

Advertising Standards Authority. The regulations are not intended to compete with the British Code of Advertising Practice, but do provide a legal last resort if a complainant to the ASA has a complaint dismissed.

19. Copyright, Designs and Patents Act 1988

The Act restates the law of copyright as set out in the Copyright Act 1956; makes new provisions as to the rights of performers and others in performances; confers a design right in original designs; amends the Registered Designs Act 1949; makes provisions with respect to patent agents and trade mark agents; confers patents and designs jurisdiction in certain county courts; amends law of patents; makes provisions with respect of devices designed to circumvent copy protection of works in electronic form; makes new provisions penalising the fraudulent reception of transmissions; and makes the fraudulent application or use of a trade mark an offence.

Copyright subsists in original literacy, dramatic, musical or artistic works; sound recordings, films, broadcasts or cable programmes; typographical arrangements of published editions. Copyright does not subsist in a work unless the qualification requirements are satisfied as regards the author, the country in which the work was first published or, in the case of a broadcast or cable programme, the country from which the broadcast was sent. Copyright does not subsist in literary, dramatic or musical work unless and until it is recorded, in writing or otherwise. Usually, the duration of copyright is for 50 years from the calendar year in which the author dies, film is released, broadcast is made or is included in a cable programme.

The first owner of copyright is the author of a work unless where a literary, dramatic, musical or artistic work is made by an employee in the course of his employment, when the employer is the first owner subject to any agreement to the contrary. Thus, an advertising agency will own copyright of advertising material produced for a client, unless in the service contract it is agreed to assign the copyright to the client.

20. Data Protection Act 1986

This is an Act of some importance regarding databases and mailing lists as used for direct mail and direct response purposes.

Holders of computerised data have to register with the Data Protection Register. Copies of the Register are held in public libraries. Members of the public are entitled to apply for print-outs of data held about themselves, provided they know who holds the information and on which of their files it is held.

21. Fair Trading Act 1973

This Act has had a very significant effect on monopolistic practices in the advertising business. The Act provided for the appointment of a Director-General of Fair Trading and staff to study the effect upon consumers' interests of trading practices and commercial activities, and to advise on any necessary or desirable action. It is called the 'Consumers' Charter'. In November 1976 the Office of Fair Trading ruled that the traditional advertising agency recognition and commission system was an illegal monopoly under the Restrictive Trade Practices Act 1976 (*see* 3:9).

Under its new concept of *consumer trade practices*, that is, any method of undertaking the supply of goods or services, the Act refers to:

(a) the terms or conditions (whether as to price or otherwise) on or subject to which goods or services are or are sought to be supplied, or

(b) the manner in which these terms or conditions are communicated to persons to whom goods are or are sought to be supplied or for whom services are or are sought to be supplied, or

(c) promotion (by advertising, labelling or marking of goods, canvassing or otherwise) of the supply of goods or of the supply of services;

(d) methods of salesmanship employed in dealing with customers, or

(e) the way in which goods are packed or otherwise got up for the purpose of being supplied, or

(f) methods of demanding or securing payment for goods or services supplied.

The Director-General, if he considers a trade practice offensive, may propose an order for the control of the practice for consideration by the Consumer Protection Advisory Committee, and upon their recommendation the Director-General can ask the

Secretary of State to place the proposed legislation before Parliament.

22. Lotteries and Amusements Act 1976

Advertisements relating to competitions or sales promotion schemes in the form of prize contests have to comply with this Act, the chief point being that a competition must contain an element of skill, otherwise it is a lottery. A lottery is a distribution of prizes by lot or chance.

However, matching numbers (as used in petrol promotions) are excluded because customers do not literally compete with each other or buy a scratch card. Two examples have been the Woolworth £1 million Family Game, store visitors receiving a free ticket or scratch card each time they visited a Woolworth/Woolco store irrespective of whether they made a purchase. Similarly, Esso had their Find the Tiger game, free scratch cards being given to drivers calling at Esso dealers, again with the proviso that no purchase was required. Although no skill was involved, there was no lottery since the players were virtually offered a gift which they might or might not be lucky enough to win. The two schemes sought to get people to visit the store or petrol station, but they were not obliged to buy anything and, in effect, purchase a lottery ticket. However, such promotions may be loosely termed 'lotteries' although they do not come within the provisions of the Act. A lottery requires an entry payment.

23. Restrictive Trade Practices Act 1976

This could apply if a manufacturer tried to restrict supplies of goods because they were being offered as gifts. The Act also resulted in changes in the recognition and commission system (*see* 3:9).

24. Supply of Goods (Implied Terms) Act 1973

This Act amends the Sale of Goods Act 1893 to guarantee consumers' rights under the old Act, and combats unfair guarantees which claim to exclude consumer rights under the 1893 Act.

25. Trade Descriptions Act 1968

This Act is very important and its provisions must be observed when writing descriptions of goods in advertisements and catalogues and on labels, packaging or other descriptive or promotional material. It replaced the unworkable Merchandise Marks Act 1953 which required private legal action, and enforcement is now made through Weights and Measures and other officials. The three main offences are:

(a) false or misleading trade descriptions;
(b) false or misleading indications as to the price of goods;
(c) false or misleading statements as to services, accommodation or facilities.

It was announced in mid-1990 that the DTI proposed to amend the Act regarding estate agency claims, and to extend the scope of the Act to cover descriptions of real property, and to require strict liability for mis-statements about services, accommodation and facilities as if they were goods.

26. Definition of trade description
The 1968 Act defines a *trade description* as an indication, direct or indirect, and by whatever means given, as to the:

(a) quantity, size or gauge;
(b) method of manufacture, production, processing or reconditioning;
(c) composition;
(d) fitness for purpose, strength, performance, behaviour or accuracy;
(e) any physical characteristics not included above;
(f) testing by any person and results thereof;
(g) approval by any person or conformity with a type approved by any person;
(h) place or date of manufacture, production, processing or reconditioning;
(i) person by whom manufactured, produced, processed or reconditioned;
(j) other history, including previous ownership or use.

27. Implications
An important effect of the Act is the ban on false sale prices in retail stores, and under the '28-day clause' goods advertised at a reduced price must have been on sale at the full price over a

period of 28 days during the previous six months. There have, however, been certain abuses which the Office of Fair Trading has been powerless to control, when advertisements have offered goods at reduced prices although the higher price occurred at only one branch of a chain of shops. This seems to be a mockery of the Act.

The copywriter has to be very careful that the descriptions he writes are correct, and it is very easy to accept given information from merchandise buyers or suppliers. A number of prosecutions have occurred because of false or misleading descriptions which were in fact written in good faith and with no intention to mislead. Examples have been mail order catalogues and package holiday brochures. The copywriter really has to be suspicious of claims that bedrooms have particular views, or that the hotel is only so many minutes from the sea. The Act imposes serious responsibilities on those making claims in promotional copy, and it is no excuse in law that another party's information was relied upon. People can make very optimistic generalisations, and some very famous companies have been heavily fined for their carelessness.

28. Imported goods

The Trade Descriptions Act 1972 concerned imported goods bearing UK names or marks, and names or marks which resembled UK ones. This Act was repealed under the Consumer Protection Act 1989 which took over the 1972 Act's provisions. However, the Trade Descriptions Act 1968 remains valid regarding, say, deceitful labelling and advertising of wines which have a recognised source of supply. One must say 'Cyprus' or 'South African' sherry, and not just sherry. The champagne shippers have prosecuted those misrepresenting champagne.

29. Trade Marks Act 1938

A trade mark includes 'a device, brand, heading, label, ticket, name, signature, word, letter, numeral or combination thereof'. It is 'a mark used or proposed to be used in relation to goods for the purpose of indicating or so as to indicate a connection in the course of trade between the goods and some person having the right either as a proprietor or registered user to use the mark, whether with or without any indication of the identity of that person'. Sometimes, trade marks may be logotypes, but not necessarily, and a company may use both a registered trade mark and a separate logo. Briefly, a trade mark must have one at least of the following characteristics.

(a) Name of a company, individual or firm represented in a special or particular manner.
(b) Signature of the applicant for registration or some predecessor in his business.
(c) An invented word or words.
(d) A word or words having no direct reference to the character or quality of the goods, and not being according to its ordinary signification a geographical name or a surname.
(e) Any other distinctive mark, but a name, signature or word other than such as fall within (a)–(d) above is not registrable, except upon evidence of its distinctiveness.

30. Unfair Contract Terms Act 1977

This Act is important where guarantees and hire purchase agreements are concerned. When a consumer suffers loss or damage because goods are defective, no guarantee can limit or exclude liability if the manufacturer or supplier was negligent. The Act also protects the consumer from exclusion clauses in guarantees, as originally introduced in the Supply of Goods (Implied Terms) Act 1973.

31. Unsolicited Goods and Services Acts 1971 and 1975

The object of these Acts is to protect the consumer from *inertia selling*, that is the sending of goods which were not ordered but for which the recipient feels responsible. Such goods become the recipient's property if, during a six-month period starting with the day of receipt, the sender fails to regain possession, and the recipient does not unreasonably prevent repossession. However, this six-month period may be shortened if the recipient requests repossession by the sender within 30 days of expiration of the six-month period. If the sender does not repossess the goods by the end of the six-month period, the goods become the property of the recipient.

There are also other provisions. If a person is charged for unauthorised directory entries, he is not obliged to pay for them. The distribution of advertisements of a sexual nature are prohibited.

32. Wireless Telegraphy Act 1984

This Act aims to combat pirate radio, that is the operation of commercial radio stations outside the authority of the Radio Authority and competing with the authorised independent local radio stations. The Act gives officers of the British Telecom Radio Interference Services the power to seize offending equipment. In 1983, for instance, there were 97 raids on pirates resulting in 40 people being convicted. Some broadcast copyright material such as Independent Radio News bulletins. Radio Jackie attempted to pay a fee to the Mechanised Copyright Protection Society, but it was not accepted. However, pirate stations do not normally make copyright payments for records played, nor pay trade union rates, and they exploit transmitter power and even usurp frequencies intended for authorised stations. The maximum fine for broadcasting without a licence is £2,000. While it is not illegal for advertisers to buy airtime on pirate radio, the medium is obviously a precarious one.

Voluntary controls

33. Codes of Practice

There are several codes dealing with advertising in general (except radio and TV which are covered by the codes of practice of the Independent Television Commission and the Radio Authority), and certain specialised fields such as sales promotion, direct mail and transportation advertising. There are also the codes of conduct of the Institute of Public Relations and the Public Relations Consultants Association. The advertising control system is set out in Fig. 16.2.

34. Historical development

The British advertising business has a long and creditable history of voluntary control beginning with the creation of the National Vigilance Committee in 1926, the pioneer efforts of the

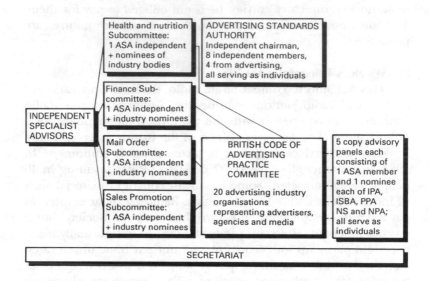

Figure 16.2 *Organisation of the advertising control system.*

Advertising Association in the 1930s, the first joint industry code of 1948 known as the British Code of Standards in Relation to the Advertising of Medicines and Treatments, and today's comprehensive British Code of Advertising Practice first introduced in 1962.

35. Revisions to codes

Codes of practice are constantly under review, and changing conditions often require new appendices, new clauses or revised wording. A fifth edition of the *British Code of Sales Promotion Practice* was published in July 1990, and an eighth edition of the *British Code of Advertising Practice* in December 1988, while an important amendment to the 'payments by results', clause 9, was made to the IPR Code of Professional Conduct in April 1990. The following are therefore general descriptions and the latest edition of each code should be obtained from the addresses given in Appendix 1.

36. British Code of Advertising Practice

The basis of the BCAP is that all advertisements should be legal, decent, honest and truthful; all advertisements should be prepared with a sense of responsibility both to the consumer and to society; and all advertisements should conform to the principles of fair competition as generally accepted in business.

It does *not* cover:

(a) TV and radio advertisements;

(b) advertisements in media published abroad and British media whose circulation is predominantly overseas (e.g. Arab and African magazines);

(c) advertisements for medicines which are promoted and advertised to the medical and allied professions (i.e. 'ethical' medicines);

(d) contents of catalogues issued by major national mail-order warehouses which use part-time agents as distinct from direct response advertising (except for advertisements seeking to recruit agents).

It is a self-regulating system of control, and its strength lies in its preventive influence, although complaints do arise and they are adjudicated on by the Advertising Standards Authority.

37. Contents of the BCAP

The Code is very extensive and covers many areas which are not covered by statute law. These include knocking copy and comparative advertising, the false use of the words 'free' if a direct cost is actually involved, and misleading testimonials. It also covers unacceptable practices connected with advertising and health claims. In particular the Code deals with products or services for which misleading claims may be made such as collectables, slimming products, advertisements relating to children, credit and investment advertising, mail-order advertising, and advertising for cigarettes, alcoholic drinks and vitamins.

38. Complaints by the public

Advertisements appear in the media inviting members of the public to submit advertisements which they believe offend against the Code. The Advertising Standards Authority, which administers the Code, investigates complaints which are justified (some are frivolous, outside the Code or concerning media such as TV/radio which do not come within its jurisdiction). Every month an *ASA Case Report* is published on free circulation to anyone interested (including the press), and the following is quoted from an editorial in *ASA Case Report 177* (January 1990), headed *A Shade Less Green* which discussed the exploitation of green issues by advertisers:

'Six months has passed since the Authority last commented on "green" advertising. A lot has happened in that time. The environment is still clearly the concern of the moment for many consumers and they continue to use the power of discretionary buying to make this known. In these circumstances the developing green tint of much advertising is not surprising. It is however reassuring that advertisers seem to be taking much greater care to ensure that "green" claims neither mislead nor confuse.

While we continue to receive public complaints about environmental claims an increasing number of businesses are presenting their "green" claims in a comparative rather than absolute manner. "Green" has given way to "greener" and "environmentally friendlier" has taken over from the much criticised blanket claim of "environmentally friendly" (which only a few months ago headed many a misleading green advertisement).

Industry is now offering products which are undoubtedly less harmful to the environment than those previously available and provided that any claims are accurate and clearly presented we do not object to their environmental advertising platform. We all know that cars cause air pollution but cars running on unleaded fuel will cause less. It was on this basis that we did not object to an advertisement for unleaded fuel which featured an illustration of rolling countryside; the advertised product was unarguably more "green" than normal fuel. We appreciated the complainants' point that pollution from cars can damage the countryside but the message of the advertisement was clear: a car which runs on unleaded fuel does less damage to the environment than one which does not.

When obvious inaccuracies are pointed out to advertisers corrective measures are generally swift. One car advertiser claimed that his unleaded petrol was "good for the environment". We took the view that this was too absolute a claim: unleaded petrol is certainly better for the environment, but claiming that it is "good" is an exaggeration. Within days the advertiser agreed to make the necessary changes.

A leaflet advertising a new soap powder claimed that the product concerned was "greener"; complainants maintained that any washing powder causes some harm to the environment and objected to the claim on this basis. The advertisement did not however claim that the product was green, only greener, and we felt this was reasonable.

We were not so sympathetic to claims by other advertisers that their products did no harm at all to the environment. If advertisers make this type of absolute claim they must be prepared to provide us with detailed substantiation in their support.

It should be noted that we have received several complaints about a recent series of "green" advertisements placed by the nuclear power industry. As we have said many times before such advertisements are clearly putting forward arguments about a matter of public controversy/policy and the ASA would be straying beyond its terms of reference if it sought to censure debate on such matters. This may disappoint many an environmental pressure group but this is the position we must take (and it's also the position we take towards their advertising on the same subject).

Our Monitoring department has specifically targeted green advertisements since May 1989. While we have acted to stop unjustified use of the "environmentally friendly" banner the majority of the advertisements sampled have been unobjectionable. With such a complex subject and such a diversity of claims it is necessary to undertake individual assessments of most advertisements. A claim for environmental "friendliness" may be acceptable in an advertisement for a biodegradeable adhesive tape product but it is most certainly not justified when linked to products still containing many elements which may be potentially harmful to the environment. The removal of one noxious substance alone is not sufficient to make an absolute "green" claim.

Shortly after our first foray into the environmental arena, the Incorporated Society of British Advertisers discussed the development of "green" claims in advertisements and shared our concern that some advertisers were showing a definite lack of restraint in their pursuit of the "green" consumer. ISBA have now published a guidance booklet for their members on making environmental claims and this will usefully support the ASA's efforts to assist the business in this fast-moving area.

The upsurge in requests from advertisers for advice on the content of their "green" advertising is encouraging and demonstrates the responsible attitude many have taken. Several major advertisers made significant amendments to their proposed advertising when possible problems under the Code were pointed out. It can be argued that with the complexity of environmental issues involved and the rate of increase of public awareness even the most careful advertisers can rapidly find themselves up against the thin line of acceptability.

As well as getting their facts *right* advertisers must ensure that facts are presented clearly. There is still a tendency amongst some advertisers to cloak claims that their products are beneficial to the environment in extravagant language. While this may present the claim as forcefully as possible it will most probably have the effect of confusing (and possibly misleading). Shaking consumers' confidence in advertising and provoking cynicism is not the way forward.

In the long term no advertising will be successful unless it is believable and proven to be true. Green advertising is no exception to this rule and generally advertisers appear to have realised that they will do themselves (and their customers) a disservice if they are not as scrupulous about the accuracy of "green" claims as they would be about any other. The trend is unquestionably in the right direction. We intend to make sure it stays that way.'

39. Typical ASA Case Reports

The following are taken from *ASA Case Report 182* (June 1990) and *ASA Case Report 183* (July 1990) two from each respectively:

'BRITISH RAILWAYS BOARD, Central Advertising Services, PO Box 100, Euston House, Eversholt Street, London NW1 1DZ.
Agency: Saatchi & Saatchi
(Previous complaints upheld during last 12 months: 3)

Complaint from: Huntingdon, Cambridgeshire.

Complaint: Objection to a national press advertisement offering free seat reservations to customers travelling in Standard accommodation on all InterCity trains between 18th December and 5th January (with the exception of the Gatwick Express). The complainant was subsequently refused a seat reservation and was informed that he travelled on a non-reservable InterCity train. (B.5.1)

Conclusion: Complaint upheld. The advertisers confirmed that the InterCity service used by the complainant was non-reservable and regretted this unfortunate oversight. The advertisers were requested to ensure that similar advertisements in future mention services to which the offer does not apply.'

'GRUNDIG INTERNATIONAL LTD, Mill Road, Rugby, Warwickshire CV21 1PR.

Complaint from: Higham Ferrers, Northants.

Complaint: Objection to a brochure for Grundig video equipment which featured a VS550 Multi Audio System. The description of the system stated that teletext programming was available and the complainant understood from the introductory section of the brochure that eleven different languages could be used. However, the complainant found that it was capable of programming only in English and he objected that this limitation was not made clear. (B.5.1)

Conclusion: Complaint upheld. The advertisers stated that the technical specification of the products contained in the introductory section of the brochure described the features available across their range of products. Thus, while multi-language programming had been available on one of the models within the range, the VS550 Multi Audio System had never offered such a facility. The Authority was concerned to note that the brochure entry for the VS550 Multi Audio System was open to misconstruction and considered that the advertisers were at fault for failing to clarify the extent of features it possessed. The advertisers were requested to ensure clarity of layout and copy when preparing future brochures.'

'EMI RECORDS (UK), 20 Manchester Square, London W1A 1ES.
Agency: Allen Brady & Marsh Ltd
Complaint from: Henlow, Bedfordshire.

Complaint: Objection to a specialist magazine advertisement for a complete set of Iron Maiden's singles in 12" and compact disc format, which was claimed to be a limited edition. Upon making further enquiries, the complainant failed to elicit an explanation from the advertisers as to the extent of the limitation and he thus objected to the claim. (C.IX.4)

Conclusion: Complaint upheld. The advertisers stated that the collection was limited to 100,000 units. The Authority reminded the advertisers that the Code requires that when an edition is limited by number, the maximum number of articles to be produced must be clearly stated in all advertising material containing any claim that the edition is limited. The advertisers were requested to take greater care over the advertising of future limited editions.'

'KLM ROYAL DUTCH AIRLINES, KLM Building, 8 Hanover Street, London W1R 9H.
Agency: HJSW Ltd
Complaints from: London, NW2; Manningtree, Essex.

Complaint: Objections to an advertisement for KLM headed "Only one airline flies Business Class to Amsterdam". In the main text was a description of the offered service which included the statements, "though others have since introduced similarly named services, none has surpassed Business Class", and that KLM was "The airline that originated it". The complainants objected on the grounds that:

a) the claim, "Only one airline flies Business Class . . ." was completely untrue;
b) the qualifications that " . . . others have since introduced similarly named services . . ." etc were misleading as the title "Business Class" was used by many airlines, as were "economy class" and "first class", and was not an exclusive service, either in name or materially, to KLM.
(B.5.1)

Conclusion: Complaints upheld. The advertisers pointed out that Business Class was not a generic term and asserted that they were the only airline with a Business Class branded product flying from London to Amsterdam. On that basis, the advertisers believed they were entitled to make the claim in their advertisement, although they acknowledged that other airlines had their own branded services. The Authority, however, considered that the claim "Only one airline flies Business Class to Amsterdam" was misleading, given that a number of airlines offered a similar service to business travellers. It considered the advertisers to be at fault for attempting to lay exclusive claim to the use of the term "Business Class" and that the advertisement should have been phrased more clearly. The advertisers were requested to amend future advertisements accordingly.'

40. Avoidance of complaints

The recommendations of the Code are open to interpretation, but it is surprising how many famous names appear in the monthly *ASA Case Reports.* Since the investigations are published it is poor public relations for the companies concerned, whether or not complaints are upheld. It is therefore wise for advertisers or their agents to discuss proposed copy with the ASA before publication and so avoid possible complaints. Usually, the media will be vigilant about this and will reject unethical advertisements. Moreover, it is part of the recognition awarded to agents by the media owners' organisations for commission purposes that they uphold the Code, and they are liable to lose this recognition if they commit offences.

41. Public advertisement

The following are extracts from an ASA advertisement which appeared in journals such as *The Economist:*

'DO SOME ADVERTISERS GIVE YOU TOO MANY FACTS AND TOO LITTLE INFORMATION?

It is not difficult to find yourself blinded by science.

Some advertisers are so wrapped up in their own jargon they fail to realise that to most people it's nothing more than mumbo-jumbo.

But how can you be sure the facts and figures you read are

accurate? And how can you tell if an over-abundance of them is not just a whitewash to conceal the truth.

. . . Financial advertising is a good example. In essence the rules state advertisements must take into account that the complexities of finance may well be beyond the people to whom the offer appeals.

An investment ad inviting direct response has to include a great deal of explanatory wording.

For instance, past growth of 500 per cent in five years would have to be qualified by the exact five years to which it referred.

And all investment ads have to carry wording to the effect that the value of investments and the income from them, if quoted, can go down as well as up.

. . . We once received a complaint that a car with a 1,442 cc engine had been advertised as a "1.5".

People "in the know" apparently accept this as normal. But our complainant pointed out that his employer's mileage allowance for a "1.5" was for engines over 1,451 cc.

What meant little to the car trade meant a lot to him, and we were pleased that the advertiser amended the ad to include the exact engine size in the text.

It's not enough for a building society to promise "worth 13.93 per cent to basic rate income tax payers" when the actual interest rate can fluctuate. This must be made clear.

A hi-fi manufacturer should not merely advertise that his equipment develops a certain number of watts.

Since there are several different ways of measuring sound output, he should state which method he used and give the reader a fair basis for comparison.

And as for computers it is not on to advertise what a piece of equipment will do and simply assume that the reader will know he needs several other items in order to operate it.'

42. British Code of Sales Promotion Practice

This Code is also administered by the ASA, the fifth edition being published in August 1990. It aims 'at regulating in the interests of the consumer, the nature and administration of those marketing techniques which are used, usually on a temporary basis, to make goods and services more attractive to the consumer by providing some additional benefit whether in cash or kind. (The benefit may not be enjoyed by the consumer directly but by some good cause which the consumer supports.)'

The Code covers, among others, premium offers of all kinds; reduced price and free offers; the distribution of vouchers, coupons and samples; personality promotions; charity-linked promotions; editorial promotions; and prize promotions of all types.

The Code also covers sales and trade incentive promotions and some aspects of sponsorship.

The general guidelines, Section 5, deal with such topics as protection of privacy, children and young people, safety, quality, suitability of promotional products, exaggeration, participation, and availability of promotional products. Then in Section 6 the code proceeds to describe how the guidelines apply in particular cases and quotes free offers, promotions with prizes, charity-linked promotions, and promotions and the trade. Then follows a list of relevant legal controls.

In recent years, there has been a prevalence of free draws as distinct from prize competitions requiring an element of skill, and the Code refers to legal requirements. Although not mentioned specifically, the revised Code aims to protect the consumer from some of the dubious free gift offers used to promote time share schemes.

43. Direct Mail Services Standards Board

This Board was set up in 1983 with Post Office support to promote improvements in the ethical and professional standards of the direct mail advertising industry. It introduces a self-regulatory control system for direct mail advertising. Complaints are directed to the Advertising Standards Authority and, if upheld, are referred to the Board if a recognised agency is involved. The Board operates a recognition system for direct mail agencies. Evidence of the Board's desire to maintain ethical direct mail advertising is seen in Post Offices where posters are displayed, naming both the Board and the ASA, and inviting complaints from the public about advertising received through the post which they think is not legal, decent, honest or truthful.

44. European Code of Conduct

Promoted by the European Federation of Sales Promotion, it

lays down guidelines for an industry liable to or threatened by EC regulation. It aims to supplement the law not replace it, and is supportive of sales promotion which, in a single European market, could have restrictions applied to it, e.g. regarding 'free' gifts, which did not formerly apply in Britain.

45. British Transport Advertising Ltd, Code of Acceptance of Advertisements

The following Code applies to advertisements on all bus and rail sites and is adopted by other British transport advertising contractors including London Transport for advertisements on the Underground:

'Advertisements and advertising material will not be accepted for, or retained on, display on British Transport Advertising sites if they:

(1)　depict murder, scenes of terror or acts of violence;

(2)　are calculated to demoralise, extenuate crime, break the law or incite anyone so to do;

(3)　depict or refer to indecency, obscenity, nudity or strip-tease;

(4)　are likely, through wording, design or possible defacement, to offend the general travelling public;

(5)　advertise firms which have been refused a permit for public exhibition;

(6)　might wound racial susceptibilities or those of coloured or foreign people or members of groups who may not otherwise be protected by the terms of this Code;

(7)　refer to religious, sacred or other politically, morally or socially sensitive subjects in a manner which might give offence, or seek to use BTA sites as a medium for controversy arising from such subjects;

(8)　attack a member or the policies of any government;

(9)　are of a political nature, whether produced by a political party or not, other than those which simply announce social activities or meetings together with the names of the speakers and the subject to be discussed; the wording used in announcing the subject must not be politically controversial or call for support for a particular viewpoint, policy or action;

(10)　might foment social unrest;

(11) advertise contraceptives;
(12) conflict with the British Code of Advertising Practice which incorporates the British Code of Standards in relation to the advertising of medicines and treatments;
(13) contain illustrations or copy which are distorted or exaggerated in such a way as to convey false impressions; are calculated to deceive the public, or contain statements of a 'knocking' or extravagant nature;
(14) might adversely affect in any way the Undertaking or Undertakings on whose sites a display is required (e.g. by advertising competitive services; by the use of designs or texts which might lead to confusion or by offers of employment in competition with the requirements of the Undertaking(s) concerned).'

46. IPR and PRCA Codes

The public relations profession is also subject to Codes, the IPR Code of Professional Conduct which is a condition of individual membership of the Institute of Public Relations, and the PRCA Professional Charter which incorporated members of the Public Relations Consultants Associations are required to uphold.

The IPR Code of Professional Conduct contains the following 17 clauses.

1. *Standards of professional conduct.* A member shall have a positive duty to observe the highest standards in the practice of public relations. Furthermore a member has the personal responsibility at all times to deal fairly and honestly with his client, employer and employees, past or present, with fellow members, with the media of communication and above all else with the public.

2. *Media of communication.* A member shall not engage in any practice which tends to corrupt the integrity of the media of communication.

3. *Undisclosed interests.* A member shall have the duty to ensure that the actual interest of any organisation with which he may be professionally concerned is adequately declared.

4. *Rewards to holders of public office.* A member shall not, with intent to further his interests (or those of his client or employer), offer or give any reward to a person holding public office if such action is inconsistent with the public interest.

5. *Dissemination of information.* A member shall have a positive duty at all times to respect the truth and in this regard not to disseminate false or misleading information knowingly or recklessly and to use proper care to avoid doing so inadvertently.

6. *Confidential information.* A member shall not disclose (except upon the order of a court of competent jurisdiction) or make use of information given or obtained in confidence from his employer, or client, past or present, for personal gain or otherwise.

7. *Conflict of interests.* A member shall not represent conflicting interests but may represent competing interests with the express consent of the parties concerned.

8. *Disclosure of beneficial financial interests.* A member with a beneficial financial interest in or from an organisation shall not recommend the use of that organisation, nor make use of its service on behalf of his client or employer, without declaring his interest.

9. *Payment contingent upon achievements.* A member shall not agree terms with an employer or client which guarantee results beyond the member's direct control to achieve.

10. *Employment of holders of public office.* A member who employs or is responsible for employing or recruiting a member of either House of Parliament, a member of the European Parliament or a person elected to public office, whether in a consultative or executive capacity, shall disclose this fact also the object and nature of the employment to the Executive Director of the Institute who shall enter it in a register kept for the purpose. A member of the Institute who himself falls into any of these categories shall be directly responsible for disclosing or causing to be disclosed to the Executive Director the same information as may relate to himself. (The register referred to in this clause shall be open to public inspection at the offices of the Institute during office hours.)

11. *Injury to other members.* A member shall not maliciously injure the professional reputation of another member.

12. *Reputation of the profession.* A member shall not conduct himself in a manner which is or is likely to be detrimental to the reputation of the Institute or the profession of public relations.

13. *Upholding the Code.* A member shall uphold the Code, shall co-operate with fellow members in so doing and in enforcing

decisions on any matter arising from its application. If a member has reason to believe that another member has been engaged in practices which may be in breach of this Code, it shall be his duty first to inform the member concerned and then to inform the Institute if these practices do not cease. It is the duty of all members to assist the Institute to implement this Code, and the Institute will support any member so doing.

14. *Other professions.* A member shall when working in association with other professionals, respect the codes of other professions and shall not knowingly be party to any breach of such codes.

15. *Professional updating.* A member shall be expected to be aware of, understand and observe this Code, any amendments to it and any other codes which shall be incorporated into this Code and to remain up-to-date with the content and recommendations of any guidance or practice papers as may be issued by the Institute and shall have a duty to take all reasonable steps to conform to good practice as expressed in such guidance or practice papers.

16. *Instruction of others.* A member shall not knowingly cause or permit another person or organisation to act in a manner inconsistent with this Code or be a party to such action.

17. *Interpreting the Code.* In the interpretation of this Code, the Law of England shall apply.

Clause 9 was amended at the IPR's AGM in April 1990, and virtually reverses the old ban on 'payment by results' so that the IPR could comply with modern practices, e.g. when there was payment by results, or bonuses were paid, in the case of public relations work associated with new share issues or take-over bids. Even so, the words 'beyond the member's direct control' continues to control the malpractice of guaranteeing media coverage which is beyond a public relations practitioner's direct control.

Progress test 16

1. Distinguish between abuses *of* and abuses *by* advertising. (1)
2. What are the main advantages and disadvantages of both legal and voluntary controls of advertising? (2–4)
3. How are voluntary controls self-regulatory? (4)

4. How does the British Code of Advertising Practice differ from the ITC Code of Practice? **(4)**

5. Distinguish between 'knocking copy' and comparative advertising. **(4)**

6. What are the three essentials of a valid contract? **(6)**

7. Explain the difference between slander and libel. **(11)**

8. Explain the terms 'slander of goods', 'passing off', and 'get-up'. **(12, 13)**

9. Who owns the copyright of artwork produced by an advertising agency to illustrate a client's advertisement? **(19)**

10. How did the Office of Fair Trading rule on the question of the traditional advertising agency recognition and commission system? **(21)**

11. Why have certain advertisements, which appear to be lotteries, escaped the requirements of lottery legislation? **(22)**

12. What are the three main offences which may be committed under the Trade Descriptions Acts, unless the advertiser is very careful about the claims he makes in advertisements? **(25)**

13. Name the characteristics of which at least one must apply to a trade mark if it is to be registrable. **(29)**

14. What legal control exists concerning pirate radio? **(32)**

15. What is the basis of the British Code of Advertising Practice, and what media does it cover? **(36)**

16. Describe the procedure by which the Advertising Standards Authority invites, receives, investigates and reports on complaints about advertisements which appear to offend against the British Code of Advertising Practice. **(38–41)**

17. Describe some of the main requirements of the British Transport Advertising Code of Acceptance of Advertisements. **(45)**

18. What are the main provisions of the IPR Code of Professional Conduct? **(46)**

17

Planning and executing an advertising campaign

Introduction

1. Variations in procedures

Advertising agencies vary in size and structure. They may operate a plans board system (*see* 3:**49**), or have creative groups, or simply have discussions between departmental heads as required. Nevertheless, the general flow and control of work will be similar, with the account executive maintaining liaison between the client and the agency, and the production manager or traffic controller acting as progress chaser to see that each stage of the campaign is completed on time so that advertisements reach the media by the deadlines or copy dates. A number of different campaigns will be progressing through the agency at the same time.

In this chapter the plans board method will be used to discuss the total procedure from the initial briefing to the final assessment of results.

Preliminary discussions

2. Initial briefing

Before anything can be planned an account executive from the agency must obtain from the client the fullest possible information about the product or service to be advertised. It may be a regular client for whom the next campaign is to be prepared, or a potential client for whom a competitive proposition has to be assembled. In the latter case information will be required regarding the client about whom little may be known at this point.

Generally speaking, the sort of data required by the account executive, so that colleagues inside the agency can be properly instructed, is likely to be as follows.

(a) *The budget.* Usually, the advertiser will have decided how much to spend on advertising, and this will be part of an overall marketing budget. It may be divided into above-the-line and below-the-line media, and the agency may be responsible for some or all of this media. Thus, the agency will have to plan the campaign within pre-set financial limits. There can also be occasions when the agency will be asked what it will cost to undertake a campaign for a certain purpose, but it is more likely that the client knows what to spend and the agency will have to do its sums, depending on whether it operates under the commission or the fee system.

(b) *The product or service.* It is essential that the account executive gleans every possible detail, and this may include obtaining first-hand experience depending on the nature of the product or service. The product has to be sampled or studied until the account executive becomes utterly familiar with it, taking nothing for granted. If it is a product that can easily be taken back to the office, so much the better, but it might be something like a tower crane, a new holiday camp or a dish-washing machine. It could also be something institutional like a charity or comparatively intellectual like an election campaign. The account executive has to understand the product or service inside out. Moreover, to produce a sincere campaign, it has to be believed in, and even though he or she may never stay at a holiday camp its value to those who do or might has to be understood. Provided the product or service is not bad or devious, it will usually have its particular market, whether it be a cheap ball-point or a gold-plated gift pen.

(c) *Market.* So what is the market, or the market segment? At whom is the product or service aimed, who is likely to buy it? Was it created to satisfy a particular market? Does the client require marketing advice? Are buying motives known? Is the agency expected to conduct marketing research?

(d) *Distribution.* How will it reach the consumer? What is the distribution channel—wholesalers, retailers, brokers, agents, direct response?

(e) *What is the name?* Has this been decided, or is the agency to find a name, possibly researching a number of names? New product agencies get in at the birth of products whereas full service agencies may have ready-made new products thrust upon them. Ideally, an advertising agency of any kind should be consulted as early as possible.

(f) *Price.* Has this been decided or again, is research necessary to arrive at the best selling price? What is the pricing policy? Is it a psychological, market, bargain or competitive price? Or is the product pitched at a certain price bracket, allied to (c) above?

(g) *Packaging.* Has this been decided or does it have to be designed? Is research necessary? This may concern the actual container, its type or material, the labelling, and any other form of container as when a bottle is packed in a cardboard box.

(h) *Competition.* Is the product unique, or does it compete within an established product group? Or, if it is expensive, what sort of discretionary income expenditure does it compete with? In respect of the latter, a person might sacrifice a holiday in order to buy double glazing. Very cleverly, the price of the Hyundai Stella motor-car was promoted as low enough to allow for a holiday as well.

3. Marketing aspects

The above may seem an untidy list, and it may even seem extraordinary that some of these questions have to be asked at all. In this age of modern marketing it might be assumed that a manufacturer would have prepared a marketing mix, done all the research, and appointed an advertising agency to conduct the advertising campaign required as part of the marketing mix.

The fact is that business management is seldom as marketing-oriented as it should be although it is aware that advertising is necessary. Very often marketing is introduced by the advertising agency, and as already mentioned there are specialist product development agencies which start at the beginning. It is even possible for such an agency to recommend what sort of new product should be developed. Moreover, it is a good idea to bring in the agency at the earliest possible time so that the agency can advise throughout all the stages of the marketing mix, beginning with the new product which may be only at the prototype stage.

4. 'Four Ps' marketing myth

In marketing circles the McCarthy/Kotler 'Four Ps' concept is often adopted as the basis of the marketing mix, but if it is taken too literally it can imply that Promotion (advertising, sales promotion, publicity (presumably meaning public relations!) and selling) is an isolated activity, whereas promotional activities should be introduced alongside the other considerations of naming, pricing, packaging, market segment, distribution and after-sales.

Public relations personnel (whether in-house or consultancy) should be brought in right at the start, and overall marketing communications are essential. They are not limited to promotional activities. Naming a product has great public relations relevance.

Public relations is to do with creating knowledge and understanding whereas Kotler (and marketing people in general) tend to see public relations as a fringe activity concerned only with favourable images and favourable publicity, even with so-called 'free advertising', as product publicity is falsely termed.

The advertiser should seek or be entitled to all the specialist advice he can get. So without trying to promote any fetishes about advertising and public relations it is practical to have marketing, advertising and public relations working as a team as early in the marketing strategy as possible, simply to get the maximum benefit from all three. They are quite different disciplines, as different yet associated as medicine, dentistry and pharmacy.

5. Account executive reports to agency head

Having obtained all the information needed or obtainable, the account executive returns to the agency and reports to a superior who may be the managing director or, in a large agency, the account director in charge of a group of accounts and account executives. This meeting is essential for policy reasons. The senior director needs to know the progress of work, the take-up of agency services and possibly the need for additional staff, plus the financial implications of the new account or renewal business.

In addition to normal business considerations, however, it is necessary for the managing director or account director to examine the *suitability* of the new business. Is it ethically acceptable? It might be for a foreign government which was unpopular. Should the agency handle South African paper-clips or Russian sardines or an Iraqui airline? Apart from the considerations of personal conscience, would there be a risk of offending existing clients? Or is there likely to be a conflict of trading interests between the new and an old account? Sometimes the areas of conflict may be difficult to define. The account executive, eager to accept new business, may not see the possible conflict as keenly as the agency head. The problem will have to be resolved, perhaps by a top level agency decision, or by diplomatic talks with the two clients. It may be, in the case of conflicting interests, that one of these clients will fear lack of confidentiality, but on the other hand both may be delighted to use the same agency which either promises good service or is experienced in their industry.

6. Report to departmental heads

Assuming, however, that the account executive has the go-ahead to accept the account and to prepare a proposal for presentation to the client, a detailed report is now submitted to the departmental chiefs who comprise the plans board. Agencies are structured in various ways, but here it will be assumed that the team will consist of the agency's marketing manager, art director, copy chief and media planner. The production manager (or traffic controller) is not usually required at this stage. If the agency has a public relations manager, or there is a public relations subsidiary company, or the client employs an independent public relations consultant, a public relations representative may also be included. Each will study the account executive's reports, and there may be discussions among them.

Development of copy platform

7. First plans board meeting

Under the chairmanship of the account executive, the departmental heads will attend the first plans board meeting. There will be a detailed discussion during which members will frankly express their views and ideas. Some may like the product, others will not, some will see one way of advertising it and others will have different ideas. Eventually, the account executive will call a halt to the discussion, and each member will go away to work up a scheme to present to the next meeting. The marketing manager may have to consider any necessary research, the copy chief and art director will create a copy platform and its visual presentation, and the media planner will select media and prepare a media schedule. There may also be television and radio commercials to think about. The agency may have a specialist TV producer who will prepare a script and rough storyboard.

8. Second plans board meeting

At this meeting the department heads, who have been consulting with each other in the meantime, will present their ideas for the campaign. A theme or copy platform will have been devised, and copy drafts and rough visuals will have been prepared together with a media schedule. If TV is to be used there will be cartoon-like storyboards showing the sequence of scenes for the proposed commercials. The marketing manager will have studied the market and will make his recommendations. As a result of copy-testing, various ads may have been discarded in favour of the one now adopted.

If relationships are good it can be sensible to invite the client's advertising manager or product manager to attend this meeting. This is a preliminary stage in the planning of the campaign, and it can be helpful to ask the advertising manager to express opinions on the way the campaign is shaping. The agency may have adopted a wrong approach which the client is unlikely to accept, or it may be a novel approach which has to be tried out on the advertising manager before a more complete and costly presentation is made to the company's chief executive and managers.

Preparing the campaign

9. Preparing for the presentation

Once the ideas have been agreed, the campaign can be assembled for presentation to the client. Visuals will be worked up into near-finished layouts even though at this stage professional and commercial artists may not have been engaged for artwork, and the copy will be represented on the layouts and not actually set. This can be done in one of two ways—by ruled lines, or by meaningless 'Greek' wording to resemble typesetting. The media schedules will be plotted carefully, and it will be necessary to make tentative bookings in certain magazines like weekend colour supplements which have lead times of two or three months.

10. Presentation to client

This is the big day when the campaign has to be 'sold' to the client. In making the presentation the account executive must be able to justify the copy platform, the artistic treatment, the choice of media and the dates, sizes and positions recommended. The client has to be convinced that the scheme will achieve the desired result, or at least contribute effectively to the sales target which may depend on other factors (e.g. good product, good public relations, good field salesmen, good trade terms, good distribution, good point-of-sale display, and perhaps a good sales promotion scheme) as well as advertising.

A common problem at client presentations is that approval may be required of a number of company directors and executives representing the board, marketing, sales, advertising and public relations. Some of these people will propose alternative ideas which are usually ones considered and rejected in the agency during the early planning stages. If the advertising manager has worked closely with the agency he or she at least is an ally on the client side who can argue in favour of the agency proposals. With large companies and big accounts the presentation could take all day, especially if it is a complicated campaign covering perhaps more than one product and making use of a variety of media. It can be an occasion of great argument. Everyone thinks they know all about advertising.

11. Putting the scheme into operation

Once the client has given approval (which will involve a contract of service) the creative work and media buying can go ahead. The campaign is not the only one being handled by the agency, and it is necessary to plan the work allocated to each department so that the advertisements are produced, delivered and inserted correctly. This is where the production manager or traffic controller takes charge, preparing time schedules showing when each stage of the work must be completed, i.e. the writing of copy, production of finished layouts, completion of artwork and typesetting, submission to client, return by clients, amendments made and final copy in the desired form being despatched to the media. A daily check will be made to see that all the work is being produced on time. Similarly, with the production of TV commercials, a routine has to be followed which will include appointment of director and film unit, casting, shooting, editing, approval by client, submission to the ITC and ITVA for copy approval, and distribution of videos to the television companies.

12. Liaison work of account executive

The account executive will work closely with agency departments to oversee the preparation and production of the campaign, and will act as the liaison between the agency and the client to present work in progress such as copy, artwork and proofs to obtain approval. The client has to be kept to the time schedule, but there may be amendments which have to be incorporated, and sometimes clients do not know what they really want until creative work has reached an advanced stage. Alternatives can create problems and pressures such as extra costs or extra work when time is running out. Often, the situation calls for the diplomatic skills of the account executive when dealing with both the client and agency staff. The client may be important, but is not the only important client whose work is being handled simultaneously by the agency. A typical client complaint is the size of production costs, but budgets may be exceeded solely because the client insists on last-minute expensive changes.

13. Approved advertisements to the media

When everything has been completed and approved the advertisements are despatched to the media. Even now a hitch can occur if advertisement managers of newspapers and magazines, or the television copy clearance officials, are worried that the advertisement may offend the BCAP or the television code. Amendments may have to be negotiated. This does not mean that the advertiser or the agency has deliberately offended but that a statement or claim may have been made too zealously, or that something unethical can be read into the advertisement which was not intended. Occasionally, in a highly competitive business, a hard-selling advertisement, perhaps containing knocking copy, may have been created deliberately and there may be a dispute over its acceptability. This has occurred a number of times in the motor-car industry. However, as the monthly reports of the Advertising Standards Authority show, offences against the BCAP do slip through or complainants think they have done so. British advertising is subject to both official and private watchdogs!

The campaign and afterwards

14. Appearance of campaign

Both the agency's account executive and the client's advertising manager will study the actual appearance of the advertising. Has it reproduced well? Has it appeared in the right position on the right day? What are the audience ratings (TVRs) for the programmes when the commercial appeared on television? Fresh problems can arise. Insertions may have been made wrongly. Printing quality may have been poor. Perhaps the advertisements did not appear at all because of strikes! The campaign has to be monitored to make sure that the media schedules have been met. This is critical if a new product is being launched in the shops and its success depends upon coincidental advertising. The cost-effectiveness of the campaign could be in peril if something has gone wrong.

15. Recall research

There is still time to improve a campaign and next-day recall research can be conducted to test whether people saw, remembered and maybe responded to the advertising. A TABS tracking study (*see* 15:**25–32**) may be commissioned. Later, dealer audit research will record what effect the advertising had in moving stocks and also the effect it had on brand share and position in the product group.

16. Charging out

It is likely that since production of the campaign may have occupied weeks or months certain expenditures incurred by the agency will have been invoiced already. Agency cash flow demands this, and with technical accounts producing little commission the client may have to pay the agency an advance fund. Media expect prompt payment, and agencies have to invoice clients promptly too. An agency could not survive if it did not render accounts until the completion of a campaign which might run over a considerable period. Strict business accounting is therefore vital, and within the agency this requires the use of job numbers, clearly identified orders and suppliers' accounts, and time-sheets where service is charged on an hourly or daily fee basis.

It will be remembered that a condition of agency recognition is its creditworthiness. This can be maintained only if the agency is strict about charging out what is due to it from clients, and making sure that cash flow is maintained through prompt payment by clients. Long-standing credit cannot be sustained. In this the account executive may in a sense have to play the role of credit manager, certainly insofar as the client may query any bills. The client's advertising manager is responsible for checking and approving agency accounts.

17. Assessment of results

Have the objectives of the campaign been achieved? This may be less easy to assess if the marketing mix contains a number of influences upon sales. However, a new FMCG will either sell or it won't, and it is amazing sometimes how, say, a new chocolate bar will produce a tremendous response following television advertising, and this is quickly assessable in the shops. Long-term advertising, such as that of Brooke Bond PG Tips chimps TV commercials, has created and maintained the product's premier selling position. Some advertising can be measured by the response to offers as when Nescafé print a money-off offer in the press. Direct response marketers can easily measure the number of enquiries or orders received.

The pulling power of individual media can be calculated by keying coupons or addresses for replies, a different key (e.g. DMI on a coupon in the first ad placed in the *Daily Mail*) being used for each advertisement. Thus it is possible to record the response to each advertisement, and by dividing the cost of the space by the number of replies a cost-per-reply figure can be worked out. This will show which media are the most economical. Similarly, cost-per-order or cost-per-conversion-into-sales can also be calculated. This important information will guide the future choice of media.

It may be desired to reach a certain volume of viewers, and weekly audience ratings (TVRs) can be totalled until the required number has been obtained. Then the commercial can be rested, which both avoids boring viewers, and is more economical than saturation advertising.

18. Agency/client relations

It will be realised from the foregoing description of the conception and birth of an advertising campaign that to maintain a good relationship between an agency and a client it is necessary for both sides to work together harmoniously. This is not easy. The pressures are great. Creative and executive people on both sides can be temperamental. A good relationship leads to good advertising, and this calls for both a skilled advertising manager representing the client and a skilled account executive representing the agency, and they need to operate as partners. Otherwise the relationship becomes soured, and the client starts looking for a new agency. It may take months of patient endeavour for agency staff to understand a client and his problems, and it can be very wasteful to change agencies too frequently.

Progress test 17

1. Describe how the account executive is briefed regarding a proposed advertising campaign. What does he need to know in order to report back to his agency? (**2**)
2. Why should the planning of an advertising campaign start as early as possible in the planning of a client's marketing strategy? (**4**)
3. For what reasons might the agency head consider a proposed new account to be undesirable? (**5**)
4. What is the function of the plans board? (**6, 7, 8**)
5. Describe how a proposed campaign is prepared for presentation to the client. (**9**)
6. How can co-operation with the client's advertising manager help to resolve problems during the presentation to client? (**10**)
7. Describe the external and internal liaison duties of the account executive. (**12**)

8. How can budgetary control be applied so that accounts can be rendered and collected efficiently and the agency's cash flow maintained? **(16)**

9. How can the results of an advertising campaign be assessed? **(17)**

10. Why are good agency/client relations essential, and what are the essentials of a good relationship? **(18)**

Appendix 1

Addresses of societies and educational organisations

Advertising Association, Abford House, 15 Wilton Road, London SW1V 1NJ. Tel: 071-828 2771. Federation of advertising organisations.

Advertising Standards Association, Brook House, 2–16 Torrington Place, London WC1E 7HN. Tel: 071-580 5555.

British Association of Industrial Editors, 3 Locks Yard, High Street, Sevenoaks, Kent TN13 1LT. Tel: 0732-459331. Membership: editors of house journals. Entry by examination.

Communication, Advertising and Marketing Education Foundation (CAM), Abford House, 15 Wilton Road, London SW1V 1NJ. Tel: 071-828 7506. Certificate in Communication Studies and Diploma examinations in Advertising, Public Relations and Sales Promotion. Certificate exams in June and November, Diploma exams in June.

Chartered Institute of Marketing, Moor Hall, Cookham, Berkshire SL6 9QH. Tel: Bourne End (06285) 24922. Entry by examination or election. College of Marketing. Publishes *Marketing Business*.

Institute of Practitioners in Advertising, 44 Belgrave Square, London SW1X 8QS. Tel: 071-235 7020. Professional body of service advertising agencies.

Institute of Public Relations, 4th Floor, The Old Trading House, 15 Northburgh Street, London EC1V 0PR. Tel: 071-253 5151. Members elected to grades by age and experience but CAM

Diploma also required in 1992. Lunch-time meetings, annual conference, seminars, regional branches. Publishes *Public Relations.* Code of Practice.

Institute of Sales Promotion, Arena House, 66–68 Pentonville Road, Islington, London N1 9HS. Tel: 071-833 1121. Recognised professional body of that branch of marketing known as sales promotion. Services include standard rules for competitions and annual ISP awards. Works actively with ASA to prepare and monitor British Code of Sales Promotion Practice. Publishes *Speak.*

London Chamber of Commerce and Industry, Examinations Board, Marlowe House, Station Road, Sidcup, Kent DA15 7BJ. Tel: 081-302 0261/4. Third Level Certificate examinations in Advertising, Marketing, Public Relations, Selling and Sales Management (with Group Diploma for passes in three or four subjects taken at same time). The Group Diploma serves as an entry requirement for the CAM Certificate. CAM grants exemptions for LCCI distinctions in Advertising, Marketing, Public Relations. Exams held world-wide in April/May and November/December.

Market Research Society. The Old Trading House, 15 Northburgh Street, London EC1V 0PR. Tel: 071-490 4911. The professional body for those using survey techniques for market, social and economic research.

Appendix 2
Further reading

Advertising Budget, The, Simon Broadbent (NTC, Henley, 1989).

Advertising Made Simple (fifth edition), Frank Jefkins (Heinemann Made Simple Books, Oxford, 1990).

British Code of Advertising Practice (eighth edition) (The Advertising Standards Authority, London, December 1989).

British Code of Sales Promotion Practice (fifth edition) (The Advertising Standards Authority, London, July 1990).

Business to Business Marketing and Promotion, Martyn P. Davis (Hutchinson Business Books, London, 1989).

Case Studies in Marketing, Advertising and Public Relations, Ed. Colin McIver (Heinemann, London, 1984).

Cost Effective Direct Marketing, Christian Brann (Collectors' Books, Cirencester, 1984).

Craft of Copywriting, The, Alastair Crompton (Business Books, London, 1979).

Dictionary of Advertising, Frank Jefkins (Pitman, London, 1990).

Effective Publicity Writing, Frank Jefkins (Frank Jefkins School of Public Relations, Croydon, 1982).

Effective Use of Advertising Media, Martyn P. Davis (Hutchinson Business Books, London, 1981).

Exhibitions and Conferences from A to Z, Sam Black (Modino Press, 1989).

Fundamentals and Practice of Marketing, The (second edition), John Wilmshurst (Heinemann, Oxford, 1985).

Fundamentals of Advertising, The, John Wilmshurst (Heinemann, Oxford, 1985).

Introduction to Marketing, Advertising and Public Relations (third edition), Frank Jefkins (Macmillan, London, 1989).

Modern Marketing Communications, Frank Jefkins (Blackie, 1990).

Printing Reproduction Pocket Pal (fourteenth edition) (Creative Services Association, London, 1989).

Public Relations (third edition), Frank Jefkins (Pitman, London, 1988).

Secrets of Successful Direct Response Marketing, Frank Jefkins (Heinemann, 1988).

Appendix 3

Syllabi for the LCCI Third Level and CAM Certificate in Communications examinations in Advertising

ADVERTISING Third Level (3002) Series 2 and 4

The aim of the examination is to test the candidate's knowledge and understanding of the practice of advertising within the marketing concept, and its economic and social justification.

Syllabus

1 **The Nature of Advertising**

   (a) **Definition of Advertising**
       The three sides of advertising: advertiser, advertising agency and media owner, and their relationships with each other. Identifying and understanding the target audience(s).

   (b) **Types of Advertising**
       Consumer, industrial, trade, retail, financial, corporate, recruitment, co-operative, generic and direct response.

2 **The Advertiser**

   (a) **The Advertising or Product/Brand Manager**
       Managing the advertising department. Working with the advertising agency and other suppliers of services. Division of work/responsibilities between the advertising department and the advertising agency. How and why some companies operate an in-house advertising

department exclusive of an advertising agency. Setting objectives and evaluation of results. Cost-per-reply, cost-per-conversion.

(b) **The Advertising Appropriation**
Different methods of deciding the appropriation (budget). Allocations for various purposes.

3 The Advertising Agency

(a) **Kinds of Agency**
Full service, media independents, specialist and à la carte agencies.
Recognition or accreditation by media owners' associations. Commission and fee systems of remuneration. Effect of Restrictive Trade Practices Act 1976 and Office of Fair Trading ruling on recognition now given by NPA, NS, PPA, ITVA, AIRC. Legal status of advertising agent who 'acts as principal'. Agency–client relations, contracts of service, ownership and assignment of copyright materials.

(b) **Agency Functions and Personnel**
Range of services provided by full service agencies and specialist services of other kinds of advertising agencies. Agency departments and their personnel. Plans board, review board and creative groups. Use of freelance services and buying of services.

4 The Media Owner

(a) **Types of Media**
Primary and secondary. Comparative costs and value. Above-the-line and below-the-line media.

(b) **Methods of Selling Media**
Organisation of the Advertisement or Sales Department, and roles of managers and representatives. How media are sold to advertisers and advertising agencies. Use of statistics, e.g. circulation, readership and audience statistics. Cost-per-thousand sales/readers. OTS figures.

5 Creative Advertising

(a) **Layout**

The design of advertisements and the basic elements of design—balance, proportion and contrast. Use of display and text type, illustrations and logos. The design of coupons.

(b) **Copywriting**

The writing of copy for advertisements, including headlines, slogans, sub-headings, text and the wording of coupons.

(c) **Production processes**

The effect of different production processes upon creative work.

6 Other Related Activities

(a) **Sponsorship**

The use of sponsorship for advertising, PR and marketing purposes.

(b) **Sales Promotion**

Techniques to stimulate sales at the point-of-sale.

Note

Candidates should be aware of current trends in this syllabus area.

(c) **Public Relations**

How advertising and public relations differ. Consultancies and internal departments. How public relations can contribute to success of advertising. Press relations. External house journals. Documentary films and video-tapes.

(d) **Marketing Research**

Organisations providing circulation, readership and audience statistics.

Research particularly applicable to advertising: motivational, discussion groups, copy testing, recall, impact, reading and noting tests and tracking tests, opinion polls, image studies, consumer panels and dealer audits.

(e) **Law and Voluntary Codes**
Statutes, regulations and common law relating to Advertising. Voluntary codes and self-regulatory procedures. The inter-relationship between legal and voluntary controls.

Examination Requirements
A 3-hour examination. One question is compulsory; four other questions are to be answered from a choice of nine.

CAM Certificate in Communications

Advertising

Aim
Successful completion of the module should provide candidates with understanding of two aspects of advertising. First, the role of advertising in society: its function as a method of marketing and social communication, and how advertising is controlled to avoid exploitation of the consuming public.

Secondly, the practice of advertising: the ways in which advertising is effectively planned and produced to achieve the objective outlined in the overall marketing or business plan, i.e. to economically deliver specifically defined product messages to clearly identified consumer targets.

Objectives
On completion of this module candidates will have:

— a broad knowledge of the historical development of the structure of advertising; and a good understanding of the methods by which the industry is controlled to maintain a responsible service to society
— a knowledge of the respective roles of advertisers/agencies/ media owners
— an understanding of the important contribution of advertising to 'branding' and 'image'
— an understanding of the creative and production procedures involved

— a good description of media availability and characteristics
— an understanding of campaign development and its measurement
— relevant examples of good advertising practice

SECTION 1: Organisation of the Advertising Industry. General function and organisation.

— Origins and development of the advertising industry
— Uses and users of advertising
— Types of advertising, commercial and non-commercial
— Professional bodies and associations

1. The Advertiser
— Work of an advertising department and advertising managers
— Relations with the advertising agency, media owners and other suppliers

2. The Advertising Agency
— Range of services
— Recognition and remuneration. Legal status
— How an agency is organised. Main departments
— How an agency is selected
— Media independents

3. The Media Owner
— Services rendered to advertising, including direct mail
— Selling organisation
— The advertisement manager, role and activities

SECTION II: Planning Advertising Campaigns

1. Campaign Development
— The mix of activities available
— Relationship between above and below-the-line activities
— Setting campaign objectives
— Steps taken in developing a campaign

2. The Advertising Appropriation
— Ways of calculating a budget

— Allocation
— Budgetary controls

SECTION III: Creating and Producing Advertisements

1. The Creative Function
— Deciding what is to be communicated
— Creative values of the different media
— Establishing creative strategies
— How advertisements communicate

2. The Creative Process
— Steps in creative planning, development and execution
— The Creative Brief
— Advertising themes and concepts
— Assessing creative work, in terms of objectives and execution

3. The Creative Team
— The creative department of an agency
— Function of different creative specialists
— How the team works together

4. Basics of TV, cinema and radio production
— TV and film production development
— Scriptwriting approaches
— Filming techniques
— Radio production
— Budgetary considerations

5. Basics of Press Production
— Steps in developing a press advertisement
— Work of copywriter and art director
— Basics of copy, and press design
— Press production, black and white and colour
— Budgetary considerations

6. Printing
— Types of process, letterpress, litho, gravure, screen printing
— General choice and use

SECTION IV: The Advertising Control System

1. Legal Control
— The main areas of legal control and the principal statutes

2. Self-regulatory Control
— The ASA and the British Code of Advertising Practice
— Controls from trade associations, e.g. PAGB, alcohol and tobacco

3. Media Controls
— ITC, ITVA, press controls, DMSSB

Appendix 4

Specimen papers

**London Chamber of Commerce and Industry:
Third Level**

SERIES 2 EXAMINATION 1990

WEDNESDAY 25 APRIL—1800 to 2100

ADVERTISING
(CODE No: 3002)

INSTRUCTIONS TO CANDIDATES

(a) *Answer **five** questions—the **compulsory** question (Question 1) and four others.*

(b) *Candidates **must** attempt the compulsory question or they will not be eligible for the award of a Pass.*

(c) *All questions carry equal marks.*

(d) *All answers must be clearly and correctly numbered but need not be in numerical order.*

(e) *Write legibly on both sides of the page. Rough work (if any) must be crossed through after use.*

(f) *If supplementary sheets are used, the candidate's number must be clearly shown and the sheets securely inserted inside the answer book. The question(s) to which they refer must be clearly numbered.*

COMPULSORY QUESTION

1   (i) Write the complete copy for a black and white advertisement, offering a free booklet about a new

banking service. You may choose any kind of service. The copy should include everything which is to be printed, including the wording of the coupon. This copy should be written as if it is to be typewritten and supplied to the printer with the layout.

(10 marks)

(ii) Draw the layout of the above black and white advertisement to show the printer how and where the copy and the coupon are to be typeset.

(10 marks)
(Total 20 marks)

2 What are the advantages and disadvantages to an advertiser of (a) placing all his media buying and creative advertising with a full service advertising agency, or (b) dividing his advertising between a media independent and an à la carte advertising agency?

(20 marks)

3 (i) Before the media organisations grant "recognition" to advertising agencies, what **two** requirements have to be satisfied?
(ii) Why does a media buying advertising agency require "recognition"?
(iii) Why is "recognition" not required by an à la carte agency?
(iv) What is meant by the expression *"the agency acts as principal"*?

(20 marks)

4 (i) Which advertising media in your country are the most effective? Give your reasons.

(10 marks)

(ii) Which advertising media in your country are the least effective? Give your reasons.

(10 marks)
(Total 20 marks)

5 Describe the responsibilities of the product or brand manager in charge of the promotion of a popular consumer product.

(20 marks)

6 (i) How is circulation certified?
   (ii) How is readership measured?
   (iii) What is a controlled circulation magazine?
   (iv) What is the cover price?
   (v) What is a free newspaper?

(20 marks)

7 Sports sponsorship is the most popular form of sponsorship, and almost every sport has its commercial sponsors. Choose your own product, and choose the sport you consider most appropriate to sponsor on its behalf.

State what marketing, advertising and public relations benefits you expect to gain from this sponsorship.

(Do not confuse this practice with sponsoring a sports event on television, as occurs in some overseas countries.)

(20 marks)

8 Write short paragraphs about **four** of the following forms of advertising research:
   (i) Recall test
   (ii) Folder technique
   (iii) Reading and noting test
   (iv) In-theatre test
   (v) Split run test
   (vi) Tracking study

(20 marks)

9 (i) What is knocking copy?
   (ii) What is comparative copy?
   (iii) What controls exist concerning knocking and comparative copy?
   (iv) Give a real or imaginary example of each of the above.

(20 marks)

10 Advertising and public relations are both forms of marketing communications. Explain how they differ.

(20 marks)

Communication Advertising and Marketing Education Foundation Limited

CERTIFICATE IN COMMUNICATION STUDIES

Examination in

ADVERTISING

JUNE 1990

———

Time allowed: THREE HOURS.

All candidates are required to answer QUESTION ONE and THREE OTHER QUESTIONS (one each from Sections B, C and D).

All questions carry equal marks.

Rough work should be included in the answer book(s) and ruled through, but it will **not** be accepted as part of the candidates' answers.

Whenever possible, candidates should include examples from real life situations.

———

SECTION A

Question One (Mandatory)

Assume a national network of fully equipped fitness and leisure centres is to open on a 24 hours a day basis. Called "Super-Stretch", with programmes for slimming, cardio-vascular exercise and regular fitness—there will be gymnasiums, swimming pools, saunas, aerobics and exercise groups, all for an annual membership of £250. Making any necessary further assumptions:

(a) Write a 60 second T.V. commercial to launch this project.
(b) Explain what approvals are necessary concerning T.V. commercials.
(c) How is T.V. time evaluated and purchased, and how does this differ from press and magazine advertising?
(d) Can a sequence from this T.V. commercial be enlarged for a separate poster display? Will this pose technical problems, if so what are they and how can they be overcome? How would you recommend these posters are printed assuming, 200 sites 6 months display?

SECTION B

Answer ONE question only.

Question Two

Imagine you have gained your CAM qualifications and established a reputation in the advertising business. Congratulations! Now you are planning to open a full service advertising agency.

(a) What agency recognitions are you likely to need and what are the main qualifying criteria?
(b) What options for agency remuneration are you likely to propose to your potential clients?
(c) What will be the legal status of the agency in respect of payment for media bookings and the commissioning of special creative services?
(d) Assuming satisfactory levels of business, what departmental structure would you choose for your agency?
(e) How would you expect to attract and win potential new business?

Question Three

You are to address a commercial delegation from an Eastern European Country who are keen to adopt Western business standards. How would you explain the evolution and various uses and users of advertising, and modern trends in advertising creativity and media use?

SECTION C

Answer ONE question only.

Question Four

V.90 is as yet an unnamed garden weed killer to be launched with advertising in gardening magazines, the weekend press and television. Because V.90 becomes attached to the soil particles it works rapidly, even without rain, and safely provides weed free lawns, flower and vegetable beds. Assuming adequate budgets and any other necessary information write a full brief to your creative department for this campaign.

Question Five

A new brand of perfume is to be launched. The packaging, aroma and name will be dramatically exciting. An image of the highest quality is required. From a creative viewpoint what are the advantages and disadvantages of:-

(a) Posters   (d) Television
(b) Press   (e) Radio
(c) Magazines

Assume a magazine advertisement is to be designed and produced. Explain the roles of the Copywriter and Designer from establishing the creative strategy to completion of the production.

SECTION D

Answer ONE question only.

Question Six

Explain which legal or voluntary controls of advertising are relevant in the context of the following examples, and explain why:-

(a) Mail order press advertisement for army surplus clothing.
(b) Magazine advertisement for natural homeopathic remedies.
(c) Campaign featuring a consumer competition.

(d) T.V. advertising featuring a toy for 6/8 year-olds.

(e) Poster campaign featuring an unpleasant illustration in connection with a charity appeal.

Question Seven

What do each of the following mean, how do they differ, and when and why do you think each would be used?

(a) Line and wash illustration and air brush illustration.

(b) Plantin and Helvetica.

(c) Thermographic and offset printing.

(d) Double head and answerprint.

(e) Satin finish cartridge paper and white art paper.

Question Eight

Explain fully the role of the typographer. Why do you think the typographers' contribution is important, and how does he or she interact with the conceptual and studio functions?

Appendix 5
Examination technique

1. Preliminaries

(a) *Preparation.* Ample preparation, followed by thorough revision to consolidate the knowledge already gained, is necessary for any examination. Without it, a list of examination hints is virtually useless. Nevertheless, even a well-prepared candidate can fail through faulty presentation of his work, waste of valuable time and irrelevancy; it is for such a candidate that these hints have been compiled.

(b) *In the examination room.* Even before he comes to grips with the actual questions on the examination paper, the candidate can improve upon, or mar, his chances; therefore at this stage the following points ought to be borne in mind.

(i) *Read carefully* the instructions on the outside cover of the answer book.

(ii) *Supply the information required* on the outside cover, e.g. date, subject, candidate's letter and number. (At the end of the examination enter the number of questions answered in the space provided.)

(iii) *Follow carefully the other instructions* as and when they become applicable; e.g. note the style of answer required such as 'explain briefly', 'discuss' or 'prepare a report'.

(iv) *Write answers legibly* on both sides of the paper provided, but commence each answer on a fresh sheet. An instruction to this effect is usually given on the outside cover. If you cross out mistakes in your answers do so neatly with one line.

(v) *Number the answers.* Be careful to number the answers so as to indicate the questions to which they refer and, where applicable, continue the numbering on to any additional sheet or sheets. Also, remember to number each page.

(vi) *Use the paper provided.* Usually the examining body provides headed paper, with spaces left for subject, and candidate's identification letter and number. This paper only must be used, and the spaces properly completed.

(c) *Planning the approach.* Having followed and/or memorised the procedural instructions, the candidate may now turn to the examination paper itself. *This is the crucial stage of the examination,* and the following suggestions for a planned approach are not to be regarded as wasteful of time; just the reverse, in fact, as an answer which has been planned (and is therefore logically arranged) saves time in the writing of it and, moreover, avoids much repetition. Another important advantage is that the finished answer will be less haphazard and easier to mark; therefore the examiner is less likely to miss the points you have attempted to make, and may even be sufficiently appreciative to award bonus marks for a well-planned answer.

(i) *Read carefully through the examination paper.* This enables the candidate to get a general impression of the nature and apparent difficulty (or relative simplicity) of the questions, from which he can plan his approach.

(ii) *Read the instructions.* Return to the beginning of the paper and read (or re-read) the instructions, e.g. number of questions to be attempted overall and (where applicable) from each section of the paper; compulsory questions, if any; number of marks allotted to each question, where some questions carry higher marks than others, and any other special instructions.

(iii) *Allot the available time* according to the number of questions to be answered, taking into account those cases where some questions earn higher marks than others. An allowance of, say, five to ten minutes ought to be made for the final reading through of the answers.

(iv) *Choose the first question* to be attempted. Obviously, it is not necessary to answer the questions in the same order as they appear in the paper, but the candidate must decide at this point whether to deal first with a compulsory question (where applicable), one of the questions earning higher marks, or one of the simpler (or shorter) questions earning lower marks. So long as the compulsory questions are not overlooked, the choice is not vitally important, although it is usually advisable to deal first with a question that the candidate feels is well within his ability to handle. A good start engenders confidence, and may well boost his morale.

(v) *Plan the answer* to the first question. Having read the question again in order to understand clearly what is required, it will probably be found that it consists of two, three or more distinct parts. Underline the key word of each part and then make a note of the various key words on a separate rough working sheet. Alongside, or underneath, each key word jot down your ideas at random, leaving space for any after-thoughts. Rearrange the various points you have made and commit them to your examination script in a logical sequence. In this way the candidate will ensure that each part of the question is dealt with; moreover, he is less likely to omit important points which the examiner is looking for in the answer.

Plan the answers to the remaining questions in the same way.

(d) *Rough notes on working papers.* If the candidate uses a separate sheet (or sheets) for his rough notes, it should be securely attached to his examination script, but he must be careful to cancel the sheet or mark it clearly as 'rough notes'. Failure to do this might cause some confusion for the examiner—and prove disastrous for the candidate.

2. Answering the questions

The foregoing hints might well be applied to practically any written examination, but it is now necessary to deal specifically with those examinations in preparation for which this HANDBOOK is primarily intended.

(a) Questions requiring brief explanations of a list of terms should be answered with one sentence explanations. These explanations should be explicit. If asked to explain 'Newsprint' it would be inadequate to write 'A kind of paper': it would be necessary to write that it is a kind of low quality paper used for printing newspapers.

(b) Questions with two, four or five parts usually require each part to be answered in equal detail, as equal marks are usually awarded for each part.

(c) Discussion questions require detailed answers of from one and a half to two pages, and marks are awarded for quality of answer. Answers may be arranged neatly with section headings, but they should not be decorated with coloured pens. Many questions are not capable of precise answering, nor is there one correct answer: marks are given for intelligent application of knowledge.

(d) While it is a good plan to practice answering previous questions during study, it can be fatal to memorise such answers and to try to repeat them in the examination room: examination questions are never the same from year to year.

Index

à la carte agency, 43, 46, 47
Abbey National Building Society, 137
above-the-line, 5–6, 25, 63–101, 116, 142, 156, 290
account,
    competing, 52, 293
    director, 52, 292–3
    executive, 52, 53, 55, 60, 289, 293–4, 295, 296
    planner, 61
ACORN, 150–1, 153
ad hoc surveys, 243
adbags, 110
adequate distribution, 28, 29, 54
Advertisements (Hire Purchase) Act 1967, 266
Advertisers Annual, 73
advertising,
    above-the-line, 5–6, 25, 116, 142, 156, 290
    advocacy, 230, 232–3
    aerial, 108–9
    agencies, 2, 18, 19, 25, 26, 38–62, 238, 289–99
    arena, 25, 31, 51, 133
    below-the-line, 6, 25, 102–14, 156, 290
    burst, 255
    cinema, 92–5
    classified, 21
    consumer, 21–5
    co-operative, 28, 32

defined, 4, 13, 18, 22
direct response, 21, 31, 142, 155–64
drip, 255
ethics of, 257, 258–61
European, 18–19
expenditure on, 5–6, 18, 43–4, 158
financial, 21, 33–5, 158, 235–6
free, 27, 211, 295
history of, 1–2, 38–9, 44, 53, 65, 69, 75, 89, 95, 168, 244, 258, 273–4
industrial, 21, 25–7
institutional, 10
issue, 230, 232–3
Japanese, 19
law of, 257–8, 261–73
manager, 51, 53
off-the-page, 29
press, 6, 17, 56, 64–75
prestige, 230–2
radio, 75–9, 79–80
recruitment, 21, 35–7, 38, 43
research, 9, 10, 238–56
retail, 21, 29–32
sponsorship, objectives of, 133–5
television, 5–6, 12, 17–18, 22–3, 24, 26, 28, 31, 34, 36, 45–6, 55–8, 63–114
trade, 10, 21, 27–9
transportation, 31, 98–106

voluntary control of, 257,
258–61
advertising agencies,
à la carte, 43, 46, 47
direct response, 48
full service, 43, 152
industrial, 44
media independents, 44–7, 79
medium size, 44
new product development, 21,
48, 54, 291
personnel, 51, 57–60
sales promotion, 49–50, 116,
117
sponsorship, 50–1, 132
Advertising Association, The, 42,
142, 259, 274, 301
Advertising Standards Authority,
14, 258–60, 267, 275, 297, 301
Advertising Statistics Yearbook, 142,
252
advertorials, 123
advocacy advertising, 230, 232–3
aerial advertising, 108–9
affluent worker, 24
after-market, 1, 9
after-sales service, 12
AGB/TCA, 30
AGB Sportswatch/BARB survey,
131–2
agency–client relationship, 299
agent acts as principal, 41
AIDCA, 184, 189–91
AIDS, 14
airships, 108, 109, 135
airtime buying, 79
alliteration, 179, 180
alternative television, 45, 84–92,
156
American Express, 16, 34, 117
animation, 201
apathy, 220, 221
arena advertising, 25, 31, 51, 133
armchair selling, 16, 156

art director, 58, 60
ASA Case Reports, 276–82
ashcanning, 261
ashtrays, 107
Association of Free Newspapers,
70
Association of Independent Radio
Contractors, 42, 78, 248
Association of Mail Order
Publishers, 153
Association of Media
Independents, 44
Astra, 251
Attitudes to Television in 1989, 80
Audience Delivery Plan, 95
audience figures, 56, 82, 89, 238,
240
poster, 247
radio, 248–9
ratings, 250, 297
transportation, 248
audio cassettes, 110, 111
Audit Bureau of Circulations, 56,
68, 244–5
audit net sales, 244
Audits of Great Britain, 140, 250
Automobile Association, 160

back-selling, 185
badges, 114
balloons, 109
banded packs, 122
Bank of Scotland Press Awards,
137
Barclays Bank, 130, 131, 138
bazaar, 12
BBC, 76, 79, 80, 140, 249
below-the-line, 6, 25, 102–14, 156,
290
Bemrose, 109
Benn's Media Directory, 63
Bernstein, David, 13
billboards, 97
billings, 44, 61, 156

birth control, 13, 14
Bisto, 16
Black, Sam, 174
Black Cat cigarettes, 13
black market, 12
Blue Circle Awards, 137
body media, 110
bolt-on promotion, 124
Bonusprint, 113, 155
book advertising, 113
bookmatches, 112
Boot, Jesse, 30
Botswana, 87, 185
brand,
    awareness, 253
    health, 252
    image, 253
    loyalty, 117
    manager, 51, 53
    passing off, 265
    share, 243
    switching, 117
branding, 1, 7, 9, 54
    familiarisation of, 136
breakfast TV, 46, 84, 255
British Airways, 16, 117, 232
British Association of Industrial
    Editors, 301
British Code of Advertising
    Practice, 42, 165, 187, 224,
    259, 265, 264, 267, 275–82,
    296, 297
British Code of Sales Promotion
    Practice, 115, 274, 282–3
British Code of Standards in
    Relation to the Advertising of
    Medicines and Treatments,
    274
British Diabetic Association, 92
British Direct Marketing
    Association, 142
British Market Research Bureau,
    248, 249
British Railways Board, 278–9

British Rate and Data, 173, 245
British Satellite Broadcasting, 251
British Telecom, 19, 81, 91, 158,
    161, 172
    Gold, 164
British Transport Advertising
    Code of Acceptance, 284
Broadcasters' Audience Research
    Board, 56, 82, 89, 249–51,
    252
Broadcasting Act 1990, 18, 46, 79,
    88, 260
*Broadcasting in the 90s: Competition,
    Choice and Quality*, 79
broadsheet, 28, 103, 143
Brooke Bond PG Tips, 82, 255
BSkyB, 89, 251
budget, 290, 296
Bulk Verification Service, 246
bulletin board, 98
Burke's Peerage, 113
burst tactic, 255

Cable and Wireless Easylink, 164
Cable Authority, 79, 88
cable television, 88–9, 249
    How does cable get to your
        home?, 90
CACI Market Analysis Division,
    150
Cadbury's, 3, 12, 126, 131
calendars, 109–10
    printers of, 109
CAM examinations, v, 53, 80, 301
    past examination paper, 315
    syllabus, 308
camera-ready copy, 32, 59, 60, 198
Campaign, 36, 125
Canon (UK) Ltd, 130, 131, 133,
    138, 223
Carrick James Market Research, 94
carrier bags, 110
Carta Mundi, 112

cash,
    dividends, 119
    flow, agency, 297–8
    premium vouchers, 120
catalogue selling, 29, 31, 48, 160
CAVIAR, 94
Ceefax, 91, 161
Channel 4, 46, 82, 254
Channel Three, 79
charity promotions, 50, 117, 122
Chartered Institute of Marketing,
    v, 301
Checkout, 153
cherry picker, 117
China, 96
Churchill, Winston, 13
CIM examinations, v
cinema,
    admissions, 93
    advantages of, 93
    advertising, 92–5
    Audience Delivery Plan, 95
    Forces, 94
    -going frequency, 94
    in-flight, 94
    mobile, 94
    shipboard, 93–4
Cinema Advertising Association,
    93, 94, 95
cinemas, 87, 93
circulation, 10, 17, 24, 26, 35, 56,
    67, 68, 71, 244–5
classified, 21, 74, 161
clichés, 147
clocks, 106
club catalogues, 29, 160
coasters, 107
Coca-Cola, 12, 107, 136, 137
colloquialisms, 180
colour, 195–6
Colt Car Co. Ltd, The, 130
commercial break, 84
commission system, 25, 42–3, 45,
    46, 216, 268, 297

common law, 261–5
comparative advertisement,
    260–1, 265
competitions, prize, 50, 118
computerised photo-typesetting,
    69, 198–9
consumer,
    durables, 21, 22
    goods, 21, 22
    panel, 243
    protection, 164–6, 266, 271
    rights, 269
    services, 21, 22
    trade practices, 268
Consumer Credit Act 1974, 266
Consumer Protection Act 1987,
    266, 271
Consumers' Charter, 268
contact report, 53
continuous research, 243, 252
contract,
    in advertising, 263
    law of, 262–4
    packer, 124
    right to cancel, 266
    unfair, 275
Control of Misleading
    Advertisements Regulations
    1988, 266
controlled circulation journals,
    24, 73, 246
Cook, Thomas, 222
cooling-off period, 266
co-operative advertising, 28, 32
copy, 16, 35, 44, 59, 96, 192, 260
    camera-ready, 32, 59, 60
    chief, 58, 60, 294
    devices, 177–81
    different meanings, 61
    knocking, 260–1, 297
    platform, 58, 189, 240–1, 293,
        294, 295
    seven elements of, 182–8
copy-testing, 10, 238, 240, 241–3

Copyright, Designs and Patents
  Act 1988, 267
copywriter, 58–9, 176, 180, 189,
  271
copywriting, 38, 176–88, 231
  action words, 178
  clichés, 177
  special literary style, 176–7
Coral racing, 131, 133
Cornhill Insurance, 130, 136
Coronation Street, 250
corporate,
  advertising, 230–6
  identity, 111, 136, 140, 198
  image, 139, 140, 223, 234
cost-per-conversion, 10, 145, 242,
  298
cost-per-reply, 10, 66, 145, 242,
  298
cost-per-thousand, 56, 70, 245
Council of Outdoor Specialists,
  247
coupon, wording of, 186–7
cover price, 67
Cranfield School of Management,
  212
creative group, 289
creativity, 17, 18, 47, 238
credibility, 210, 211
credit accounts, cards, 31, 48,
  104, 155, 191
creditworthiness, agency, 43
crisis situations, 210–11, 215,
  234–5
cross branding, 120
  couponing offers, 120
cross-couponing, 50
Crown Berger, 122
Crown Solo paint, 120–22
crowners, 107
Croydon Post, 246
CSS Promotions, 132
Cyprus sherry, 271

Daihatsu, 134
Daily Express, 23, 240
Daily Mail, 23, 67, 68, 207, 240
Daily Mirror, 23, 68, 240
Daily Star, 23, 67, 68, 240
Daily Telegraph, 23, 36, 68, 162
Daily Times, 67
Dallas, 80
Data Protection Act 1986, 267–8
  Register, 268
databases, 150, 267
Datsun, 4, 260
dealer audit, 139, 243
decay of impact, 255
de-duplication, 143
defamation, 264–5
definitions,
  above-the-line, 64
  advertising, 4, 13, 18, 22, 176,
    238
  below-the-line, 64, 102
  copy, 61
  direct mail, 143
  mail order, 143
  marketing, 4
  outdoor advertising, 96
  primary media, 64
  public relations, 211
  secondary media, 64
  sponsorship, 129
  trade description, 270
  transportation advertising, 96
demassification, 84–7
denigration, 260, 265
Dentsu, 19, 132
Department of Trade and
  Industry, 169, 270
Derby, The 130, 226–9
derogatory statements, 265
design, law of, 192–7
Dichter, Dr Ernst, 241
direct mail, 6, 10, 14, 26, 28, 29,
  31, 32, 35, 64, 142–54, 161,
  267

characteristics of, 143–5
enclosures, 147
envelopes, 147–9
ethical, 283
expenditure on, 142
house, 149
mailing lists, 143, 149–52
postage, 148
sales letter writing, 145–7
Direct Mail Services Standards
    Board, 164, 286
Direct Marketing Awards, 143
Direct Response, 73, 156
direct response,
    agency, 48, 156, 158
    marketing, 29, 31, 35, 142,
        155–64, 267, 298
director, television, 59
discussion group, 241
dispenser boxes, cards, packs, 106
display material, 31, 106, 281
    outers, 107
    stands, 106
distribution, 1, 7, 10, 54, 55, 290
    adequate, 28, 29, 54
diversification, 233
door-to-door distribution, 31,
    128, 154
doorstopper milk bottles, 113
double crown, 96, 97
draw, free prize, 118
drip,
    mats, 107
    tactic, 255
Dunlop, 138
Dynasty, 80

EastEnders, 250
Economist, The, 33, 57
electronic mail, post, 154, 164
EMI Records (UK), 280
emphatic full point, 181
enclosures, direct mail, 147
envelopes, 148

printed, 147–8
environmentally friendly, 276
ethical pharmaceuticals, 22
European advertising, 18–9
European Communities Act 1972,
    266
European Community, 266, 284
European Federation of Sales
    Promotion, 115, 286
Eurotunnel, 171, 221–2
Ever Ready, 226–9
Eversheds, 109
examinations, v, 53, 80, 192, 301,
    302, 308, 315
Exhibition Bulletin, 173
Exhibition Industry Federation, 168
exhibitions, 6, 10, 26, 28, 168–74
    build-up, 174
    centres, 168, 169
    certified attendances, 245
    characteristics of, 172
    checklist for potential
        exhibitions, 173
    history of, 168
    knock down, 174
    public relations/exhibition
        press officer, 174
    types of, 169–71
*Exhibitions and Conferences from A to
    Z*, 174

Fair Trading Act 1973, 268
Fair Trading, Directory-General
    of, 266, 268
family, 198
Family Law Reform Act 1969, 264
favourable, 213, 292
fees, 43, 212, 216
Fidelity International, 111
finance houses, 81, 158
Financial Times, 23, 33, 34, 137,
    158, 196, 234, 236, 247
*Financial Times Industrial Companies
    Year Book*, 147

flags, 111–12
flash packs, 50, 123
flatbed, 203, 204
flexography, 60, 67, 74, 197, 207
flutter signs, 95
FMCGs, 22, 24, 80, 81, 96, 125,
    222, 240, 253
Football League, The, 130, 138,
    223
Ford, 13, 19, 32, 43
    Cortina, 260–1
fount, 197–8
Four Ps, 7, 54–5, 211, 292
free, 177, 275
    gifts, 119
    magazines, 73, 245
    newspapers, 24, 31, 36, 45, 69,
        70, 73, 245–6
        circulation figures, 245–6
        mail drops with, 154
    prize draws, 118
Freefone, 74, 113, 163, 177
Freepost, 74, 146, 177
Friends of the Earth, 14
fulfilment house, 49, 124, 125
full service agency, 43–4

Gallup Poll, 95
games, promotional, 50, 123
get-up, 265
gift coupons, 119
gifts, free, 119, 169
gimmicks, 116
giveaways, 112
glancers, 16, 183
goodwill, 116, 135, 136
Goodyear airships, 108, 135
Graf Zeppelin, 222
Grand National, The, 130, 138
Great Universal, 162
green,
    campaign, 14
    issues, 276–8
Greenpeace, 14, 233

Grundig International Ltd, 279
guarantee cards, 104
    exclusion clauses, 272
    unfair, 209
Guardian, 23, 35, 36
Guinness, 12, 13, 110, 131
Guinness Book of Records, 82

halftone, 67, 74, 203, 205
Hanson Trust, 226–7
hard-dot photogravure, 207
headline, 182–3, 196–7
Heinz, 12, 215
high street redemption schemes,
    50, 120
hoardings, 95, 97
*Hollis Press and Public Relations
    Annual*, 132
Homelink, 162, 163
Hong Kong, 11, 23–4, 65, 96, 99,
    136
    Mass Transit Railway, 99
Hood, Peter, 126
hospitality, 136
hostility, 219–20, 221
House of Commons, 215
house journals,
    external, 26
    internal, 212
Hyundai Stella, 162, 260–1

ignorance, 220, 221
illuminated displays, 106
image,
    brand, 253
    company, 122
    corporate, 139, 140, 223, 232
    favourable, 213, 292
    printing, 204
    product, 7, 9
impulse buying, 116, 123
Incorporated Society of British
    Advertisers, 244, 246, 247,
    248, 277

Independent, 23, 35, 36, 67, 68, 69
   On Sunday, 67, 68
Independent Broadcasting Act
   1973, 260
Independent Broadcasting
   Authority, 75, 79, 80, 88
Independent Television
   Association, 42, 44, 244, 296
Independent Television
   Authority, 75
Independent Television
   Commission, 42, 79, 88
   Code of Practice, 260, 273
India, 11
Indonesia, 12, 136, 257
industrial agencies, 26, 44
inertia selling, 272
inflatables, 109
inserts,
   in mailings, 116
   in publications, 158, 160
Institute of Practitioners in
   Advertising, 4, 22, 40, 42, 80,
   176, 238, 244, 247, 248, 301
Institute of Public Relations, 211,
   212, 273, 301
   Code of Professional Conduct,
   274, 285
Institute of Sales Promotion, 115,
   302
in-house public relations, 212, 213
in-store,
   advertising, 108
   demonstrations, 123
   displays, 31
   exhibitions, 170
intaglio printing, 207
Investors Chronicle, 33
invitation to treat, 263
Islamic sensibilities, 259
issue advertising, 230, 232–3
ITV, 79, 80, 84, 95, 249
   areas, 85, 95

Japan, Japanese, 4, 10, 12, 19,
   130, 131, 132, 133, 134, 136,
   138–9
jingle, 16, 47, 183
job numbers, 298
Johnnie Walker, 106
Joint Industry Committee for
   Cable Audience Research,
   249
Joint Industry Committee for
   National Readership Surveys,
   56, 246–7
Joint Industry Committee for
   Poster Audience Research,
   247–8
Joint Industry Committee for
   Radio Audience Resarch, 56,
   248–9
journalists, 136–7, 174
journey cycle, 54
jumbo packs, 122
junk mail, 152, 161

Kays, 162
Kellogg Company of Great
   Britain, 19
Kelloggs Bran Flakes, 120–2
Kenya, 239
keys, 66, 242, 298
Klischograph photogravure, 207
KLM Royal Dutch Airlines, 280
Knight Advertising, Austin, 35
knocking copy, 260–1, 297
Kotler, Philip, 7, 292

Lane, Alan, 113
laser printing, 144
layout, 44, 59, 192, 294
   artist, 58, 59, 191
LCCI examinations, v, 15, 80,
   192, 302
   past paper, 312
   syllabus, 305

legislation,
Advertisements (Hire
Purchase) Act 1967, 266
Broadcasting Act 1990, 18, 46,
79, 88, 260
Consumer Credit Act 1974, 266
Consumer Protection Act
1987, 266, 271
Control of Misleading
Advertisements
Regulations 1988, 266
Copyright, Designs and Patents
Act 1988, 267
Data Protection Act 1986,
267–8
European Communities Act
1972, 266
Fair Trading Act 1973, 268
Family Law Reform Act 1969,
264
Independent Broadcasting Act
1973, 260
Lotteries and Amusements Act
1976, 269
Marine Broadcasting Offences
Act 1967, 75
Restrictive Trade Practices Act
1976, 42, 63, 268–9
Sale of Goods Act 1893, 269
Sound Broadcasting Act 1972,
75
Supply of Goods (Implied
Terms) Act 1973, 269, 272
Trade Descriptions Act, 1968,
123
Unfair Contract Terms Act
1977, 272
Unsolicited Goods and Services
Acts 1971 and 1975, 272
Wireless Telegraphy Act 1984,
273
Legoland, 171
letterpress, 67
Lever Brothers, 19

libel, 259, 264
lifestyles, 150
lighted aircraft, airships, 108
Linguaphone Institute, 158, 159
Linotronic, 198
list-brokers, 149
literacy, 65
litho stone, 204
lithography, 204–5
Lloyd's Bank, 80, 140
Lockwood, K & J, 109
logotype, 32, 37, 108, 113, 136,
181, 196
London marathon, 130
London Transport Advertising, 248
London Underground, 56, 64,
98, 99, 100, 244, 248
Lonrho, 92
lottery, 118, 269
Lotteries and Amusements Act
1976, 269

Madonna, 137
mail,
drops, 154–5
order, 16, 29, 31–2, 48, 123,
142, 156, 275
shot, 143, 144, 145, 153
mail-in, 119
mailing list, 143, 149–52, 267
computerised, 152
culling of, 152
sources of, 149–50
Mailing Preference Service, The,
152–3
Mailsort, Royal Mail, 142, 148
Malawi, 87, 92, 239
Malaysia, 10, 136
malredemption, 124
Marine Broadcasting Offences Act
1967, 75
market,
black, 112
education, 7, 10, 15

penetration, 246
research, 139
segment, 7, 9, 54, 137, 139,
150–1, 290
Market Research Society, 302
marketing, 1, 4, 55
communications, 11
defined, 4
direct response, 29
international, 138
manager, 51, 54, 55, 60, 294
mix, 6–9, 54, 55, 292
research, 7, 9, 12, 15, 238–56
sponsorship, objectives of,
137–9
theory, 12
Marketing, 50, 126, 251, 260
Marketing Week, 68, 70, 72, 73, 81,
131
Marks & Spencer, 31
Marlboro cigarettes, 133
married print, 201
Mars, 113, 130, 180, 215
matching halves, 117, 120, 269
McCarthy, Jerome E., 7, 292
McDougalls flour, 123
MEAL, 68, 69, 70–1, 72, 81, 251–2
MEAL Quarterly Digest, 251
Mechanised Copyright Protection
Society, 273
media, 5–6, 12, 17–18, 22–3, 24,
26, 28, 31, 34, 36, 45–6, 55–8,
63–114
advertising, 102, 115, 140, 155
banned, 133
body, 110
buyer, 57–8, 60
consumption, 254–5
created PR, 212
de-massification of, 84–7
independents, 44–7, 63
mix, 6, 56
owners, 42
planner, 55–7, 66, 294

primary, 25, 56, 64, 144
research, 243–52
sales representatives, 57–8
schedule, 57, 294
secondary, 56, 64
menu cards, 108
merchandising, 49, 115
Metroliner offset-litho press, 69,
206
Mexican Statement, The, 211
Michelin Man, 106
Micronet 800, 161
milk bottle advertising, 113–14
Mintel 'Sponsorship 1988', 129
misleading,
advertisements, 266–7, 275
prices, 266
testimonials, 275
trade descriptions, 269–70
misredemption, 124, 126, 127
Mitsubishi, 131, 191
models, scale, 106
working, 106
money-off offers, 50
Monica, 150
monitoring media coverage, 139
MOSAIC, 150
motivational research, 240
motives, 241
motor racing, 51, 129, 132, 133
multiple packs, 122
multiplex cinemas, 93
Murdoch, Rupert, 89
Murray, Bill, 172

naming and branding, 1, 7, 9, 54,
55
familiarisation of, 136, 140
National Vigilance Committee,
258, 273
Neighbours, 250
Nestlé, 12, 19, 298
networking, 82

new product development
    agencies, 21, 48, 54, 291
New Smoking Mixture, 222
New York Times, 65
newly industrialised countries, 11
news,
    and advertising compared, 224
    release, 224, 225
News Centre, Portsmouth, 69, 206
News International plc, 89
Newspaper Publishers
    Association, 42, 44
Newspaper Society, 42
Nielsen Clearing House, 127–8
Nigeria, 11, 15, 17, 65, 239, 265
Nikon, 131, 137

off-air programmes, 89
off-the-page, 29, 32, 35, 48, 142,
    158–60, 166
Office of Fair Trading, 42, 63,
    266, 271
offset-litho, 32, 60, 66, 67, 68, 74,
    197, 204, 208
Oliver, Brian, 126
Olympic Games, 122
on-pack direct marketing, 123
on-the-run colour, 68
one-piece mailers, 147
opinion poll, 139, 239
opportunities to see, 253
Oracle, 91, 161
OSCAR, 247
OTC, 22
outdoor advertising, 95–8, 247–8
    audience research, 247–8
    characteristics of, 96–7
    importance of, 96
    weaknesses of, 97
Outdoor Advertising Association,
    244, 247
own label, 30

pack recognition, 82

packaging, 1, 7, 9, 12, 16, 54, 55,
    291
paper clips, 112
paperless newsroom, 69
Pascoe Associates, Alan, 132
passing off, 265
Pearl and Dean, 95
pedestrian housewife poster, 97
perimeter boards, 133
Periodical Publishers Association,
    42, 44
persuasion, 14, 29, 31
petrol company promotions, 117,
    269
photogravure, 60, 66, 67, 205, 206
picture cards, 119
pirate radio stations, 75, 273
Pirelli calendars, 109
planographic printing, 204
plans board, 60–1, 289
plastic records, 110
Player, John, 26
    John Player Special, 133, 134
Players Please, 13, 180
playing cards, 112
point-of-sale, 10, 49, 96, 114
    display material, 104–8
Poor Man's Art Gallery, 95
population figures, 12, 240
    triangle, 11
positioning,
    company, 233
    product, 137
Post Office, 143, 152, 164, 213, 283
    Consumer Location System,
        150, 153–4
    electronic post, 154
    maildrop service, 154
    videoservice, 113
postage, 148
post-production, 201
posters, 95, 96
    sizes of, 96–8
Powergen, 80

PR Week, 36, 73
prejudice, 220, 221
premium,
    houses, 48–9
    offers, vouchers, 117, 124, 127,
        154
pre-printed colour, 68
presentation,
    advertisement, 61
    client, 61, 295
press, 6, 17, 56, 64–75
    advantages of, 74
    American, 65
    characteristics of, 66–7
    consumer, 24
    controlled circulation, 24
    disadvantages of, 74–5
    distribution of, 73
    national, 67–8
    Nigerian, 65
    overseas, 65
    professional, 72
    regional, 31, 36, 68–9
    relations, 40, 210, 224–5
    special interest, 72
    Sunday, 67, 74
    technical, 26, 36, 72
    trade, 10, 26, 27, 36, 72
    women's, 24
Press Research Council, 244, 246
Prestel, 91, 161
prestige advertising, 230–2
pre-testing,
    copy, 240
    direct mail, 145
price, 185–6, 291
    legislation on, 266
pricing, 1, 7, 9, 12
printing processes, five, 203–18
privatisation, 80, 81, 158, 215,
        232, 236
Procter & Gamble, 12, 19, 43, 128
producer, television, 59, 294
product, 7, 290

life cycle, 7–9
    manager, 51, 53
production manager, agency, 60,
        289
Production 2000 Ltd, 142
programme listings, deregulation
        of, 70
projected advertisements, 109
promotion, 43, 210, 268
promotional games, 123
propaganda, 232
public,
    interest, 15
    relations, 15, 26, 27, 40–1, 102,
        109, 122, 125, 210–29, 292
        and advertising, 219–22
        consultancies, 212, 214–16
        corporate, 7, 10
        crisis, 210–11, 215, 234–5
        difference between
            advertising and, 210–13
        exhibitions, 174
        financial, 7, 10
        in-house, 212, 213, 216–19
        personnel, 212
        positioning of in-house PR
            department, 217
        post-advertising, 222–3
        pre-advertising, 221–2
        transfer process, 219–20
Public Relations Consultants
        Association, 214, 273
publics, 212, 213–14
publisher's statement, 244
puffery, 211, 225
pull-push strategy, 29
push-pull strategy, 29

quad crown, 97, 99
quotations, printing, 208
radio, 75–9, 79–80, 273
    African, 239
    audience research, 248–9
    BBC, 76

characteristics of British, 77
continental, 75
independent local, 75, 77–9
overseas, 76
split frequency, 76
Radio Authority, 42, 75, 80, 249,
    273
Radio Jackie, 273
Radio Luxembourg, 75, 78
Radio Times, 70, 160, 223
Rank Screen Advertising, 95
reader service, 123
Reader's Digest, 110, 148, 247
readership, 10, 17, 35, 36, 56, 57,
    238, 239, 244, 246–7, 254
    quality of, 57
reading and noting test, 242
recall, next day, 10, 242, 252, 297
Reckitt-Colman, 12
recognition, agency, 42–3, 63, 268
redemption, 120, 124, 127, 128
relief printing, 203
reminder advertising, 96
Rentokil, 171
repetition, 82
reputation, 140, 181
Restrictive Trade Practices Act
    1976, 42, 63, 268, 269
results, assessment of, 298
retailers,
    and misredemption, 126–8
    and sales promotion, 116, 126
    support for, 137
retailing without shops, 29, 48,
    142
RETAL service, 127
review board, 61
Rockware, 113
Rolex, 231
roof cards, 98, 100
rotary press, 203, 204, 207
roughs, 59
Royal Mail Mailsort, 142, 148
    marketing, 154

Royal Mint, 160
Royal Society for the Protection of
    Birds, 92
Royal Wedding, 89, 108
RSMB Television Research, 250–1

Saatchi & Saatchi, 18, 39, 43, 47,
    278
safety, 266
sale prices, false, 270–1
Sales and Marketing Management,
    172, 173
sales,
    force, representatives, 7, 10,
        54, 126, 246
    letters, 145–7
        example of, 146–7
        four-point formula for, 146
    literature, 103
    promotion, 6, 9, 10, 49–50,
        115–40, 243
        agencies/consultancies,
            49–50, 116, 117
        problems and risks, 124–7
        reasons for growth, 115–17
        terminology, 124
        types of scheme, 117–23
Sales Promotion, 50, 115
salutation, 144
samples, free, 107, 123, 154
Sandeman figure, 106
Satellite Television plc, 89
satellite TV channels, 88–9, 251
saturation advertising,
    maildrop, 155
    TV, 82
scamps, 59, 191
Scanachrome poster, 98
scratch-card, 124, 269
screen advertising, 92–5
scriptwriter, 58
Seagram, 130, 132
secondary suppliers, 25
See You in Barking, 248

self-liquidating premium offer, 50
self-regulatory controls, 259
Selfridge, Gordon, 30
selling-in, selling-out, 28, 29
serif, 198
share registers, 35
shelf edgings, 107
shopping without shops, 29, 48, 142
signature slogan, 187–8
signs, 96
silk screen, 207–8
Singapore, 11, 76, 136
    underground railway, 99
Single European Market, 18, 284
sky,
    banners, 108
    shouting, 108
    writing, 108
Sky,
    Movies, 80, 88, 251
    satellite television, 79, 80, 88, 137
        channel, 89, 137, 251
slander, 264
    of goods, 264–5
sleeve, 205
slogans, 13, 16, 17, 108, 187–8
Smith Foods, 125
Smith's screensport, W.H., 251
soap operas, 80, 250
social grades, 21, 22, 23, 24, 35, 57, 240
    and the national press, 22–3, 246
socio-economic groups, 22, 240
Sony, 222
Sound Broadcasting Act 1972, 75
South African sherry, 272
South China Morning Post, 24
South Korea, 11, 12
Soviet Union, 96
space broker, 39, 41, 53
split frequency, 76

sponsorship, 25, 50–1, 120–40, 222–3
    agency, 50–1, 132
    arts, 129, 130, 131, 135
    cost-effectiveness of, 139–40
    Ever Ready Derby, 226–9
    examples of, 131
    objectives of, 132–9
    relaxation of broadcasting rules, 80
    sports, 129, 130, 131, 132, 133, 135, 136
    what can be sponsored, 130
statute law, 261, 265–73
Sterling Health's Baby Wet Ones, 125
stickers, 107, 114
stockists' lists, 32
store traffic, 30
Stork margarine, 13, 113
storyboard, television 59, 200–1, 294
strapline, 187
Strutz decorating machine, 113
stuffers, 103–4
subheadings, 183, 192
Sun, 23, 57, 137, 138, 240
Sunday Times, 36, 162
Super Profiles, 150
supersite, 98
Supply of Goods (Implied Terms) Act 1973, 269, 272
Swan Vestas matches, 123
swing tabs, 104

tabloid, 36
TABS Ltd, 252–6, 297
Taiwan, 11
take-over bid, 233–4
target group index, 153, 248, 252
targeting, 152, 153, 158, 230
Tate & Lyle sugar, 123, 234
taxi cab advertising, 99
technical press, 26, 36

Teledata, 45, 162, 260
telemarketing, 161
tele-ordering, 162
telephone selling, 74, 161
tele-shopping, 161, 162
television,
   advertising, 28, 39, 55, 59, 64,
     79–84
     advantages of, 82–3
     commercials, 19, 59 74
     maps, 85–6
     prime-time, 240
     regional companies, 84
     weaknesses of, 83–4
     what is advertised, 81
   alternative, 45, 84–92, 152
     director, 59, 201
     producer, 59, 201, 294
Tellydisc, 160
test marketing, 7, 10, 54
Texaco, 13
text, 183–5
Thailand, 13, 136
That's Life, 153
Third Wave, The, 84
Thomas Cook, 222
Thompson, J. Walter, 39, 40
tickets, 107
time-sheets, 298
Times, 23, 34, 67, 68, 158, 180,
   234, 236
TNT, 143
Today, 23, 67, 240
Toffler, Alvin, 84
Tomorrow's World, 221–2
tonal pictures, 203
top British advertisers, 19
top ten,
   direct mail agencies, 156, 158
   sports programmes, 132
   TV programmes, 250
   users of magazines, 72
   users of newspapers, 68
   users of television, 81

Top twenty,
   advertising agencies, 39
   media independents, 45
tracking studies, 10, 248, 252–6,
   297
trade,
   description, 270
   figures, 106
   press, 10, 26, 27, 36, 72
   typesetting houses, 198
Trade Descriptions Act 1968, 123,
   269–71
trading stamps, 50
traffic controller, 60, 289
transfers, 106, 114
transportation advertising, 31, 96,
   98–100
   characteristics of, 99
   importance of, 98
   indoor sites, 96
   sites, 98–9
   weaknesses of, 100
Truman, 139
t-shirts, 51, 110
Tube Research Audience
   Circulation, 248
TV-am, 84
TVRs, 250, 297
TV Times, 70, 83, 160
twenty-eight day clause, 270–1
typefaces, 59, 176, 198, 199
typographer, 58, 59, 176
typography, 197–8

UK Press Gazette, 131, 137
ultravision sites, 95
underground railways, 98–9
understanding, 135, 136, 211,
   213, 219
Unfair Contract Terms Act 1977,
   272
UniBus, 99
Unilever, 12, 18

Unsolicited Goods and Services
    Acts 1971 and 1975, 272
USA, 18, 40, 65, 80, 108, 161, 207,
    232, 241, 261
USA Today, 65

vandal-proof vinyl, 97
Verified Free Distribution, 245–6
video,
    cassette-recorder, 87, 89, 91,
        110
    cassettes, tapes, 110, 130, 201,
        212
    documentaries, 26, 92
    games, 91
    media, 112–13
Viewdata, 46, 91, 161
Viewtel Club 403, 162
VIPS formula, 13
visualiser, 58–9, 176, 189
visuals, 191, 193, 294
voice, share of, 253
Vortex cleaner, 128
voucher,
    clerk, 62
    copy, 61

Waddington, 112
Wall Street Journal, 65, 234
web, 203, 204

web-offset-litho, 68, 74, 207
weekend magazines, 70–1, 245,
    254
Western Union Priority Mail, 164
Westfield, 112
Which Exhibition, 174
White Horse, 13, 32
white space, 196
Whitehead & Sons (Malawi) Ltd,
    David, 92, 239
White's advertising agency, 38
women's magazines, 24, 68, 70–2
    clones of French/German, 70,
        71
Woolwich Equitable Building
    Society, 16, 137, 200
Woolworth, 32, 81, 117
Wunderman, Lester, 161
Wyatt, Woodrow, 69

Yamaha,
    keyboards, 133
    motor-cycles, 133, 138
Yellow Pages, 73, 81
Young Musician of the Year, 80, 140

Zambia, 11, 239
zapping, 83
Zenith, 45
Zimbabwe, 108
zoning, 82, 93, 97, 99